Understanding
THOMAS
JEFFERSON

OTHER BOOKS BY E. M. HALLIDAY

John Berryman and the Thirties: A Memoir
The Ignorant Armies

Understanding
THOMAS
JEFFERSON

—— •◆• ——

E. M. Halliday

HarperCollins*Publishers*

HarperCollins books may be purchased for educational, business, or sales promotional use. For information please write: Special Markets Department, HarperCollins Publishers Inc., 10 East 53rd Street, New York, NY 10022.

FIRST EDITION
Designed by Joseph Rutt

Library of Congress Cataloging-in-Publication Data
Halliday, E. M. (Ernest Milton), 1913–
    Understanding Thomas Jefferson / E. M. Halliday.—1st ed.
        p. cm.
Includes index.
ISBN 0-06-019793-5
1. Jefferson, Thomas, 1743–1826. 2. Presidents—United States—Biography. I. Title

E332 .H183 2001
973.4'6'6092—dc21
[B]   00-061419

01 02 03 04 05 ❖/RRD 10 9 8 7 6 5 4 3 2

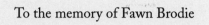

To the memory of Fawn Brodie

CONTENTS

———•◆•———

Contents

Contents

Introduction

————— ◆ —————

The prevailing tendency in Jefferson biography in recent years has been to regard him as a man of such contradiction and paradox as to be, in the end, essentially a puzzle, an enigma. The subtitle of *The Inner Jefferson,* by Andrew Burstein (1995), was *Portrait of a Grieving Optimist,* which itself proclaims a paradox; and in 1997 the National Book Award for nonfiction went to a biography by Joseph J. Ellis called *American Sphinx: The Character of Thomas Jefferson.* As everyone knows, a sphinx symbolizes an unsolvable—or at least extremely difficult—riddle.

Jefferson was unarguably a complicated man, and there are indeed many puzzling aspects to his character. How could a man who became world famous as a champion of human freedom, the author of the Declaration of Independence and its timeless "all men are created equal," have been a lifelong and large-scale slave master, possessing hundreds of slaves almost none of whom he ever freed? How could a man who repeatedly asserted his disgust for sexual mixing of the races have taken as his concubine one of his own slaves, the beautiful and very young Sally Hemings? Yet in the autumn of 1998 careful DNA tests revealed a high scientific probability that Jefferson had indeed fathered the last one of

Sally's children, which along with circumstantial evidence strongly suggested that he fathered them all. (Joseph J. Ellis, although he thereupon hastily reversed his view on the paternity question, declared that the new evidence "only deepens and darkens" Jefferson's image, and that he is now "more a sphinx than ever before.")

That remains to be seen. In any case, there are lots of other "puzzles" to be looked into. For example, since Jefferson was forever telling his daughters and his friends how much he hated politics and longed to retire to the pastoral pleasures of Monticello, how did it happen that he spent half his life in government service of one kind or another, and in the process founded one of the most powerful and successful political parties the United States has ever known? Why was it that, although he professed a firm belief in God, he was all his life fiercely antagonistic to organized religion? Why, although he often expressed great admiration and respect for cultivated and attractive women, was he in fact what almost any feminist today would denounce as a male chauvinist?

Enough examples. The view taken in this book is that the "sphinx" approach to Thomas Jefferson tends to mystify rather than enlighten, and can lead to badly skewed misinterpretations. I believe that his contradictions and paradoxes are reasonably understandable when observed in the light of his personal and social circumstances, and considered in the light of common human experience. Unquestionably, he was a man whose character was far from perfect; but who among us can claim to be otherwise?

He fell short of living up to his own ideals; but the ideals he stood for and championed were very high and very American. Although he was by nature and breeding an aristocrat, he ardently believed in government of the people, by the people, and for the people, made possible by complete freedom of thought and expression. These things, I think, are what largely explain the hold he continues to have on public interest in this country and world-wide.

Beyond this, it is relevant to notice how do-it-yourself-American was the way he *arrived* at his beliefs about religion, morality, sex, race, slavery, government, science, education, and the pursuit of happiness, among other things. For if ever there was a man who disdained conventional wisdom and insisted on working these things out for himself on the basis of his own tireless reading and thinking, Thomas Jefferson was such a man.

The first half of this book aims to be a short yet fairly comprehensive sketch of Jefferson's whole life, with the focus more on the personal and private than the public and political. The second half consists of a series of closely-related essays on crucial topics such as his almost symbolic feud with Alexander Hamilton; his views on slavery and race; the surprising distortions to be found in some of the most distinguished biographies; Jefferson's literary taste, moral philosophy, and religion; his adamant opinions on women; his ideas about democracy, freedom of expression, and education, plus an estimate of his place in American history; and finally, a rumination on history versus historical fiction.

I hope he emerges not as an enigma, but as a Founding Father who, all things considered, clearly deserves his place on Mount Rushmore.

Understanding
THOMAS
JEFFERSON

———◆———

I

"The Vaunted Scene
of Europe"

———•◆•———

In June 1782, a few months after he had proudly played a crucial
role in the defeat of Cornwallis at Yorktown, Virginia, Marie-
Joseph-Paul-Yves-Roch-Gilbert du Motier, the Marquis de
Lafayette, was an honored guest at possibly the most lavish full-
dress ball that Marie-Antoinette, Queen of France, had ever given
at Versailles. Still only twenty-four, Lafayette was already a general in both the American and the French armies, and lionized in
both countries. A startling amalgam of ultra upper-class French
snobbery and passionate dedication to *liberté* and the rights of
man, he had gone to help the American cause entirely on his own,
even purchasing outright (from an exceedingly large fortune) the
vessel that took him there. Now, back in his native land, he dances
a quadrille "flawlessly" (according to an observer) with the young
queen in the Gallery of Mirrors, which scintillates with the
reflected light of five thousand candles. The king has gone to bed,
but his twenty-seven-year-old blue-eyed consort and diamond-
bedecked entourage of courtiers dance, sip, and sup the night
away, finally wandering off to one bed or another as the sun is ris-

ing and the peasants of the metropolis are trudging sullenly to their ill-paid travail—if they are so lucky as to have jobs at all.

The sexual mores of this haut monde, on the fringe of which widower Thomas Jefferson, the newly appointed American minister to France, soon was to find himself, are rather touchingly hinted at by the story of Lafayette's marriage. It had been arranged by his noble family and the more or less equally noble family of his bride, Adrienne de Noailles, and took place when she was fourteen and he sixteen. Quite to the surprise of both families and probably of the adolescent couple themselves, they promptly fell in love, and stayed much that way until her death, thirty-three years later. Yet when they entered Parisian society soon after the wedding, young Lafayette almost immediately realized that he lacked one thing essential to being perceived as à la mode: a mistress. This was quickly remedied, and Adrienne, although she adored Gilbert, did not complain—either then or as the succeeding years brought a train of other mistresses.

This bust of Lafayette by the famous sculptor Jean-Antoine Houdon, made in 1786, gives a good view of the hero's formidable expanse of forehead.

Such a combination of true conjugal affection and extramarital gallantry, however, was unusual. About the time of the queen's great ball in 1782, there appeared a book that became an instant bestseller. *Les Liaisons dangereuses*, published almost but not altogether anonymously under the initials C[hoderlos] de L[aclos], depicts the sexual adventures of two wickedly attractive nobles, the fictitious Vicomte de Valmont and the Marquise de Merteuil, who, having become jaded with their own love affair, have now entered into a ferocious contest to see which one of them can more viciously ruin the happiness of other human beings by luring them into deep erotic intrigues and then betraying them. Their sadistic pleasure is derived not through inflicting physical pain, but by deliberately breaking hearts and arousing suicidal despair. "There is nothing more diverting," says Mme. de Merteuil, "than the misery of the lovelorn," and Valmont wolfishly agrees. The book, though not quite pornographic, was found to be enormously exciting by literate Parisians, and the first edition sold out rapidly, to be followed by many others, some of them pirated. Marie-Antoinette, aware that her courtiers were feverishly reading it, acquired a copy that she had specially bound with no title on the binding, perhaps to avoid the notice of her royal husband.

Les Liaisons dangereuses was a well-written novel, but its chief attraction was that in it the society swirling around the court of Louis XVI saw their own behavior etched with cutting precision. Allowing a little room for artistic hyperbole, they had no difficulty in making the identification; in fact a lively parlor game of the season was guessing who among their acquaintance most perfectly fit the roles of Valmont, Merteuil, and their various victims.

Although the sexual roundelay of the fashionable nobles was not quite matched by the behavior of the Parisian public, the general atmosphere was subtly erotic. It was epitomized, during the years of Jefferson's sojourn in Paris, by the entertainment offered at the Palais-Royal, an enormously popular amusement arcade near the Jardin des Tuileries that resembled the midway of an unusually permissive world's fair. There were cafés, puppet shows, mimes, jugglers, improvisational theaters, freak shows, magic-lantern shows, wine and beer stalls, hawkers of sweets and hawkers of bawdy songs, strolling musicians and strolling *filles de joie*, all bathed, as it were, in an anything-goes aura that most citizens seemed to find delightfully titillating.

While theoretically there were restrictions on pornography, the Paris book stalls and shops abounded with obscene items, many of them illustrated and many with a political slant. An especially favored subject—a straw in the wind of the revolution that was coming—was the alleged sexual depravity of Marie-Antoinette. A purported confessional autobiography that depicted her as an insatiable nymphomaniac, masturbator, and lesbian was a big success and frequently reprinted. Another work, more specifically political, featured among its illustrations an engraving showing Lafayette kneeling in adulation before the queen (whose dress and petticoats she has pulled up above her navel) with his hand on her pudendum; the caption reads, *"Ma Constitution."* A particular irony was that in reality, according to the best available evidence, Marie-Antoinette, though certainly frivolous and flirtatious, was much less inclined toward debauchery than most of her courtiers. A more general irony was that along with the popularity of such scurrilous stuff as this, there was in the last years of the Old Regime a widespread fad for the sentimental pieties of Jean-Jacques Rousseau, including his idealization of sexual innocence and purity. It was thus possible to advocate these virtues as expressive of the true spirit of la belle France, while at the same time getting a patriotic but prurient kick out of explicitly citing and denouncing the depravity of the nobility.

It was this paradoxical but essentially licentious social climate

An illustration for Rousseau's novel La nouvelle
Héloïse *by Moreau le Jeune depicts a virtuous young
man who has managed to tear himself away from the
bosomy temptation of extreme décolletage.*

that Thomas Jefferson encountered when he got himself and his
daughter Patsy settled in Paris in the fall of 1784. Whether he read
Les Liaisons dangereuses or looked at the "biography" of Marie-
Antoinette is not known, but he was a bookish man if there ever
was one, and these books were very available and much talked
about. In any case, he was inevitably thrown in with the court
crowd to a considerable extent, and he was not blind. Comparing
what he saw around him with his nostalgic memories of his life
with his wife, Martha, he summed up his reaction in a letter to an
American friend after about a year had gone by: "The domestic
bonds here are absolutely done away. And where can their com-

pensation be found? Perhaps they [the French] may catch some moments of transport above the level of the ordinary tranquil joy we experience, but [these] are separated by long intervals during which all the passions are at sea without rudder or compass." (This suggests that if he had heard the widespread rumors that Lafayette, with whom he was developing a close friendship, had recently been bedding down one of the most beautiful young ladies of the court, he was unaware that Adrienne Lafayette loved her wayward husband as devoutly as Martha Jefferson had loved her faithful one.) About the same time, offering advice to a Virginia youth who was visiting France, Jefferson cautions that in Paris a young man is likely to be "led by the strongest of all the human passions into a spirit for female intrigue destructive of his own and others [*sic*] happiness, or a passion for whores destructive of his health, and in both cases learns to consider fidelity to the

An example of the "voluptuary dress" Jefferson took note of at fashionable venues like the theater.

marriage bed as an ungentlemanly practice and inconsistent with happiness: he recollects the voluptuary dress and arts of the European woman and pities and despises the chaste affections of those of his own country."

Censure, especially in sexual matters, often implies an element of conscious or unconscious envy, and it is not difficult to believe that the Parisian social scene was putting Jefferson under a good deal of stress. He was in his early forties, and it had now been about three years since he had enjoyed the intimate company of an attractive woman. He was meeting many, of course, introduced not only into the choicest of the intellectual salons such as that of Benjamin Franklin's favorite, Madame Helvétius, but invited frequently to fashionable dinners, and regularly exercising his privilege as a diplomat to attend the court levee held weekly by Louis XVI, where elegant females in "voluptuary dress" abounded. Then too, as a lover of music and the theater he went often to concerts and plays, where there was more of the same to be seen. The couturiers of the period seemed to be in a competition over who could design the most outrageously low-cut décolletage, and the display of bosoms was outstanding, to say the least, not seldom affording a glimpse of a vagabond nipple or two. It was enough to make a vigorous but lonely American gentleman feel quite desperate.

In Jefferson's case there were, to be sure, dampening factors. One of them was Abigail Adams, who was in Paris with her husband, John, and their two teenaged children, and whose American-style dinners Jefferson gratefully enjoyed. Abigail, though one of the more intelligent and witty women he had ever met, was something of a bluenose, Puritan Massachusetts having left its stamp: she looked askance not only at the uninhibited yet undeniably attractive prostitutes who paraded the avenues, but at the undeniably brilliant and eloquent French ladies of the salons who (she observed with a delicious orthographic mutation)

7

"wrapturously" threw their arms around gentlemen of their acquaintance by way of greeting. Her reactions to contemporary French manners, which she expressed in letters sent back to America, make wonderful reading, inventive spelling and all—for instance, this description, sent to her sister Mary, of the Parisian ballet: "I felt my delicacy wounded, and I was ashamed to be seen to look at them, girls cloathed in the thinest silk and gauze ... springing two feet from the floor poising themselves in the air, with their feet flying, and as perfectly shewing their Garters and draws, as tho no petticoat had been worn."

Abigail took fondly to Thomas Jefferson, and did her best to make his bachelor existence less lonely and homesick—and indeed, his visits with her family in their Paris suburb of Auteuil must have resounded with rich conversation, which he always found to be one of the most delightful of human diversions. There were, after all, three future presidents of the United States at table, as well as a future first lady brainier than most who would play that part until Eleanor Roosevelt and Hillary Rodham Clinton came along. (Her son, John Quincy Adams, was only seventeen at the time, but his informal education, which had even included a long stay in Russia, was so extraordinary that his subsequent years at Harvard must have seemed a considerable anticlimax.)

It could be said, however, that Abigail's solicitude for Jefferson was perhaps overly maternal. She must have felt that he needed female companionship, but she seems to have been wary for fear some glamorous European siren might capture his vulnerable heart and trap him into an unsuitable relationship. Certainly she did nothing to encourage him to find a lady friend among French high society, and if he felt inclined to do so during this period, the thought of Mrs. Adams's sure disapproval may have cooled him a bit.

Actually, in spite of the provocative Parisian ambiance, he probably was not yet in a disposition for romance. In January 1785

Lafayette returned from a trip to America bringing Jefferson a painful message. Little Lucy Elizabeth, whose birth had precipitated Martha Jefferson's final illness in 1782, had lost a battle with whooping cough and had died in October 1784; Lafayette had made the Atlantic crossing much faster than the letter from the Jefferson family doctor confirming the appalling news. The social and artistic pleasures of Paris, which had begun to lighten Jefferson's outlook, now faded swiftly into an overcast of anguish: the endearing little girl who had seemed in some measure to palliate the horror of his wife's early death had all too soon followed her mother into the realm of "eternal separation."

It did not help matters that in the spring of 1785 the Adams family packed off to London, where John was to commence his duties as American minister to England. ("I shall really regret to leave Mr. Jefferson," Abigail wrote her sister. "He is one of the choice ones of the earth.") On top of this, Patsy Jefferson was now installed in one of the best boarding schools in Paris (run by the nuns of a prominent convent), so that her father hardly saw her except on weekends.

A sad man, he tried with some success to lose himself in his work. He had recently succeeded Dr. Franklin—not "replaced" him, which Jefferson always insisted was an impossibility—as America's chief diplomat in France, so he kept fairly busy. Among his more interesting assignments was dealing with the famed French sculptor Jean-Antoine Houdon, who on his recommendation had been commissioned by the state of Virginia to make an appropriately heroic statue of George Washington. Houdon, who had achieved a huge reputation for creating amazingly lifelike images of his subjects, took this job very seriously, insisting that he must journey to the United States to study the general's physiognomy, take precise measurements, and so on. His bust of Franklin, done a few years earlier, looks so real today that a viewer almost expects the splendid old gentleman to say something—something wise and witty, of course. Jefferson later ordered a bust of himself from Houdon, and beyond a doubt the striking result tells us what Jefferson looked like in his mid-forties better than any portrait painted of him during that period.

There were other absorbing distractions. He had brought to France the manuscript of his book *Notes on the State of Virginia*, and had tinkered with it and expanded it from time to time. Although diffident about it, he was pleased that several friends had urged him to publish it. A French printer who had done good work for Franklin set the type and ran off two hundred copies in the spring of 1785—not exactly "publication," but enough so that Jefferson could send copies to friends and a few other "estimable characters," as he put it. Almost inevitably a Paris bookseller got hold of a copy, had it translated into French, and was ready to publish when the distinguished author heard about the piracy. He took one look at the translation and found it bad. A friendly member of the French Academy made some improvements in it, but Jefferson was still not much pleased with the French version—which nonetheless soon came out under the title *Observations sur la Virginie*. The possibility then struck him that this book might sometime be translated back into English and be more inaccurate than ever. To fend this off, he thereupon arranged for a carefully supervised and proofread English edition to be published in London. It was his single venture in the fascinating but sometimes perplexing world of book publishing.

One of Jefferson's fondest intentions, in compiling *Notes on Virginia*, had been to refute the contention of the famous French naturalist Georges Buffon that animals of the Americas as well as indigenous human beings were inferior in size, strength, and vigor to those of Europe—due, according to the Frenchman's theory, to adverse climate. Jefferson challenged these alleged facts with

Thomas Jefferson as sculpted by Houdon in 1789.

statistics on sizes and weights of various animals, and actually brought from America a huge panther skin, which he presented to Buffon; later he sent the old scientist the horns and skeleton of a seven-foot moose from New Hampshire's White Mountains. As for human beings, he cited his own extensive knowledge of American Indians, and with polite scorn dismissed Buffon's claim that they were degenerate or inadequate in strength, sexual ardor, genital dimensions, or moral qualities. Thus his devotion to scientific knowledge supported his devotion to his native country.

A visit to England in the spring of 1786, in response to an urgent suggestion from John Adams, was still another effort to beguile his discontent, but—aside from some pleasant hours spent with the Adams family seeing the sights that London and its environs had to offer—it did little to alleviate Jefferson's essential loneliness. His deeply rooted prejudice against the British was moreover confirmed by his firsthand observations, and he returned to Paris convinced that his earlier impression of them as a race "of rich, proud, hectoring, swearing, squibbling, carnivorous animals" was not far off the mark.

So much for a quick sketch of Thomas Jefferson's first experiences with what he called "the vaunted scene of Europe." It was yet to be the scene of one of the most significant events of his career—one that, though it amazingly involved no famous person or great lady, but only a fifteen-year-old slave girl who would unexpectedly appear, was to shape the contours of his private life for all the years ahead. But where did this most American of Americans come from, and how did he happen to find himself in this exotic environment at the midpoint of his biography?

2

Surges of Youth

————•◆•————

In 1757, when Thomas Jefferson was fourteen years old, his father unexpectedly died. Peter Jefferson had been an impressive man, and certainly a powerful role model for his son. Well over six feet tall and locally famous for his physical strength, he was a kind of aristocratic pioneer—a man of a leading upper-class Virginia family, and master of a substantial plantation and several score of slaves, but choosing to live on the near-frontier, just east of the Blue Ridge. A talented surveyor, he was co-maker of the best map of Virginia produced during the Colonial period, yet he saw to it that his son's early education should be broadly liberal, and he himself gathered a library that included such authors as Shakespeare, Swift, and Addison, as well as works on surveying and mathematics.

Beyond the fact that Tom Jefferson's early adolescence was traumatized by his father's premature death, not much is known of it—except that it was exceedingly studious. He was scholarly by nature, and between the ages of fourteen and sixteen he was under the tutelage of the Reverend James Maury, an ultra-conservative Anglican clergyman who demanded many hours a day spent on Greek and Latin. But Jefferson loved languages and worked hard at his books, and even Maury's abrasive emphasis on religion, traditional morality, and reactionary politics may have germinated good fruit by inclining the future author of the Declaration of Independence in a contrary direction. In addition, the young scholar had the solace of congenial companionship, since there were several other boys of his age under Maury's scowling pedagogy, among them Dabney Carr, who became his best friend and a few years later married his sister Martha.

Then there were the weekends. His little boarding school was near Fredericksville, only a few miles from Shadwell, the family plantation, and in those familiar fields and woods he could hunt or fish, while in the big, comfortable house his mother, six sisters, and a baby brother enveloped him in more than enough family ambiance. Meanwhile, the sap of puberty was inevitably flowing, and it can easily be imagined that certain events ordinary to any large farm—a stallion mounting a frisky mare, roosters chasing hens across a barnyard, a couple of lusty hunting dogs pursuing happiness out by the corncrib—had acquired for the teenager a new and absorbing gloss. Whatever the strictures of the Reverend Maury's curriculum, we can be quite sure that young Thomas Jefferson had no need of basic sex education.

Yet he grew up shy, when it came to his own introduction into the world of sexual adventure. Although there was lots of mixed company at Shadwell, especially during holiday seasons, with two of his sisters already of a marriageable age (that is, in their late teens), Tom had no father to encourage him, nor an older brother either. At seventeen he went off to the College of William and Mary, in Williamsburg, well possessed of such mandatory social graces as dancing, singing, and cardplaying, but there is no evidence that at this stage he had experienced the joys and worries of having what today we would call a girlfriend. He was still notoriously studious, imposing on himself a fierce schedule of scholarly

An eighteenth-century engraving showing the College of William and Mary more or less as it looked when Jefferson enrolled there in 1760.

labor. By his own account, he got out of bed at dawn, even when the days were long, and put in an hour of voracious reading before breakfast—and he usually continued at that pace, attacking everything from physics and mathematics to philosophy, history, and literature in carefully planned segments, until he blew out his candles late in the night to get some sleep.

Still, Williamsburg was the social as well as the political capital of Virginia, and young Jefferson was by no means immune to its lures. His principal college instructor, a Scotsman named Dr. William Small, was a brilliant polymath whose passion for knowledge overflowed the classroom: he was avid for enlightened conversation, and in this he found an enthusiastic disciple in the young man from Shadwell. Luckily for Tom, Small was a close friend of the British governor of Virginia, Francis Fauquier, whose elegant dinners and soirées at the Colonial palace invariably offered not only good food and wine, but also scintillating talk and delightful amateur music. By the time Jefferson was nineteen he was regularly included in the governor's inner circle, for young as he was he had the curiosity, the manners, and the conversational eloquence that suited these occasions. Besides, as a result of assiduous practice for several years, he had become a very competent violinist, so that he was a doubly desirable guest.

There were also less elevated but no doubt equally attractive pleasures available in Williamsburg—horse races, gambling on a harmless level, card games, theatrical productions, and dances at the pleasantly appointed Raleigh Tavern, where a bevy of pretty girls could be counted on to show up as partners. It was probably at one of these dances that Tom was introduced to sixteen-year-old Rebecca Burwell, who evidently sent a shaft of keen desire to his heart on first sight.

In discussing Jefferson's infatuation with Rebecca, it is well to remember that he was still a teenager at the time, and by all indications a very inexperienced one at that. The first romantic forays of a boy who has been unusually slow to start are likely to be clumsy, tentative, and foolish. But the circles Jefferson moved in fostered early marriage, and many of his contemporaries had already picked out girls they thought of and talked about as future wives. Peer pressure was thus strong, and the generalized lust that besieges a normal nineteen-year-old was always lurking, making it easy to confuse sheer desire with love.

In this connection the social mores of eighteenth-century Virginia did their part to make matters more difficult. It was unthinkable that a nubile daughter of a distinguished family would be anything but a virgin on her wedding night, and if a young man was to experience sexual intercourse before that occasion it was likely to be with prostitutes or—quite commonly, it seems—with slave girls on the plantation. Though we know not much about Tom Jefferson's youthful character, we know enough to doubt that he took either of these avenues to sexual knowledge. As his scrapbooks and notebooks of this period show, he had already, under the banner of Dr. Small, become an acolyte of Nature and Nature's laws as the best indicator of God's will and of correct moral conduct. The idea of paying a professional money to perform the natural act of love probably seemed as reprehensible to him at nineteen as it did in his mature years, when he specifically censured it. As for the Southern plantation version of the feudal *droit du seigneur*, though he may well have discussed it with his aristocratic college friends, it is hard to imagine the fierce denouncer of the tyranny of slavery actually exercising this "right," even under the pressure of adolescent lust.

In any case, Tom Jefferson decided, in 1762, that he was in love with beautiful and (it is to be presumed) sexy Rebecca Burwell, and proceeded to conduct a most desultory and bungling campaign—supposedly to win her heart. It was the sort of bagatelle that most of us go through at such an age and later remember with bemused nostalgia if at all, but it has been dealt with at some length by Jefferson biographers because there is so little else to go on from this period of his life.

The documentation they have to work with consists almost entirely of a series of intimate letters written by Jefferson not to Rebecca, but to his pal and fellow student John Page. Page was the scion of one of Virginia's wealthiest and most eminent families, a handsome and accomplished young gentleman whose sense of noblesse oblige was strongly developed, so that he took his studies seriously enough to win Dr. Small's respect and special attention along with Jefferson, and who shared with his less patrician friend the delights not only of Governor Fauquier's entertainments but also the flirtatious excitements of the Raleigh Tavern.

These two young blades were almost exactly the same age, and it is not surprising that when they were away from Williamsburg, each at his plantation home, they would write to each other about their doings and their interests. Biographer Dumas Malone, judiciously considering Jefferson's adolescent letters to Page, found them "not without charm and cleverness," but so callow and undignified that they probably would have "horrified" Jefferson at a more mature age: "Worst of all, they are full of references to girls." This indeed they were—inevitably, it might be thought, for two healthy nineteen-year-olds exposed to the stimulating charms of young Virginia beauties in the first bloom of womanhood.

Caught up in these torrents of spring, Tom Jefferson did what so many young men have done: he focused his abundant and general sexual yearnings on one person, in this case Rebecca Burwell. The fact that she was far away from him nearly all the time of his infatuation with her, that in all truth he barely knew her and almost certainly had never kissed her, that she showed very meager interest in his advances—all this projected just the aura of unreality into the scenario to make it intensely romantic. He could gentrify his tormenting lust by convincing himself that it really was a passionate love for Rebecca, and that he ought to offer her his hand in marriage. He discussed various approaches with Page, who urged him to hurry to Williamsburg to make a frontal assault before some rival made off with "Belinda" (as they called her among other "code" names). But Jefferson remained self-rusticated at Shadwell for many months, morosely studying his law books and dreaming of a voyage to Europe with Page in a homemade boat he said he was actually building, and which would be named, of course, *Rebecca*. In this, two romantic fantasies somewhat collided, as Tom himself seemed to recognize when he wrote Page, "This, to be sure, would take us two or three years and if we should not both be cured of love in that time I think the devil would be in it."

But in the end reality prevailed over fantasy, as usual. A profile silhouette that Rebecca had given him soon after they met, which Jefferson had enclosed in the back of his pocket watch, suffered the unromantic fate of getting rain-soaked from a leak in his bedroom roof, and when he tried to get it out he managed to tear it beyond repair. As if this were an omen of the outcome of the fragile affair itself, when he at last got himself back to Williamsburg in the autumn of 1763, his attempt to express his love to the young lady as they danced at the Raleigh Tavern turned into disaster; as he recounted it to John Page: "I had dressed up in my own mind such thoughts as occurred to me, in as moving language as I knew how, and expected to have performed them in a tolerably creditable manner. But, good God! When I had an opportunity of venting them a few broken sentences, uttered in great disorder, and interrupted with pauses of uncommon length, were the too visible marks of my strange confusion!" Rebecca, who was now a ripe seventeen and not inclined to wait upon the dubious intentions of such a stumbling suitor, turned a fonder eye on Jacquelin Ambler, another of Jefferson's fellow students at William and Mary, and shortly thereafter became his bride.

Biographers have speculated variously about the psychological effect on Jefferson of this early defeat in love, but it seems likely that relief, which could easily be disguised as melancholy resignation, was a prominent factor in his reaction. He had many intellectual projects that he was eager to pursue in addition to his serious and assiduous study of law under the aegis of George Wythe, one of the most brilliant legal scholars of the day, and he must have been acutely aware that the role of paterfamilias was not very congenial to these interests. In the world of the Colonial Virginia plantation, children in large numbers were as much the expected result of marriage as plentiful ears of corn were the result of spring planting. Jefferson was to observe his friend Page, who before long

The younger set dancing a quadrille in the eighteenth century, as Jefferson did with Rebecca Burwell at the Raleigh Tavern.

took to wife one of Rebecca Burwell's cousins, eventually become the father of twenty offspring.

In any case, though it appears that Tom Jefferson was not inclined to repair his feelings by immediately wooing some other eligible young lady, there were alternate consolations available. He wrote to William Fleming, another college friend: "Well, the lord bless her [Rebecca] I say! . . . Many and great are the comforts of a single state, and neither of the reasons you urge [to marry] can have any influence with the inhabitant, and a young inhabitant too, of Williamsburg. For St. Paul only says that it is better to be married than to burn. Now I presume that if that apostle had known that providence would at an after day be so kind to any particular set of people as to furnish them with other means of extinguishing their fire than those of matrimony, he would have earnestly recommended them to their practice."

This passage has always been a puzzle. What were the "other means of extinguishing their fire than those of matrimony"? St. Paul doubtless had been referring to burning in hellfire, but Jefferson, true to his adolescence, took the biblical phrase as an allusion to the fire of sexual desire. Fleming's letter has not survived, so we don't know what the two "reasons" he offered were, but whatever they were, Jefferson said they did not apply to a "young inhabitant" of Williamsburg. Was he talking about the availability of prostitutes? Williamsburg very probably had some, but there is no hint of evidence that young Jefferson was given to whoring. And as observed earlier, it is unlikely that any of the upper-class girls he knew were ready to compromise their marriage prospects by giving up their virginity just for fun. Well, he was twenty years old—a time of life when what were in that era politely called (if mentioned at all) "nocturnal emissions" tend to be very frequent. And, surely since prehistoric times, millions of young males, aware that "wet dreams" provide a considerable relief from sexual tension, have discovered that wet daydreams, assisted by a certain amount of physical stimulation, are hardly less natural and can be extremely pleasurable. This was certainly a subject that interested Jefferson, as indicated by his later acquisition of a French work entitled *Onanisme*. (Onan, as the biblically inclined will recall, was the poor fellow in Genesis who was slain by the Lord because rather than impregnate his dead brother's widow he "spilled" his semen "on the ground" [Genesis 38:9]). Perhaps the fire extinguisher Jefferson had found in Williamsburg was mutual masturbation, or perhaps fellatio—which, after all, was not invented in 1996.

At any rate, the general tenor of his life for the next few years was far from gloomy. He spent long hours with his law books, attending court in Williamsburg to observe the law in action, and discussing intricate cases with George Wythe, but there was plenty of diversion, what with the entertainments of the Raleigh Tavern, just a few steps away from his lodging, the very active theater nearby, vacation weeks at Shadwell, and visits to Rosewell, the lavishly comfortable home of John Page, where there was always lively and delightful company, including the very pretty Mrs. Page, whom Jefferson seems to have been fond of. A brief but poignant interruption of his routine did occur in 1765, when his beloved elder sister Jane suddenly died at the age of twenty-five. She had been a close friend, and he planned a "small Gothic temple of antique appearance"—never in fact built—for her grave site, with this epitaph:

Ah, Joanna, puellarum optima!
Ah, aevi virentis flore praerepta!
Sit tibi terra laevis!
Longe, longeque valeto!

• • •

(Ah Jane, best of maidens!
Ah, snatched away in the bloom of youth!
May the earth rest lightly upon you!
Long and long-lasting farewell!)

He was not long deflected from his work, however. In 1766, having in the informed opinion of Mr. Wythe adequately finished his preparation to practice law himself, he celebrated by making his first trip outside Virginia, traveling by one-horse carriage up through Maryland, Delaware, and Pennsylvania to New York— after a layer in Philadelphia to take the risky step of having himself inoculated against smallpox. The only social visit of any duration that he made along the way, it seems, was a three-night stop at the home of one Sukey Potter, a Virginia maiden remembered fondly from student days in Williamsburg. Her allure must have been quite arresting. As for New York, it failed to impress him favorably: "New York," he was to write later, ". . . like London seems to be a cloacina of all the depravities of human nature."

Tom Jefferson took up the practice of law with well-founded confidence, and was soon, at the age of twenty-four, a busy attorney with clients across the Virginia countryside as well as in Williamsburg, where his cases were tried. While most of his business had to do with such dry matters as property disputes and wills, occasionally something more earthy came along. In 1767, for example, he initiated a suit for slander against a man named James Burnside, who had accused an acquaintance, David Frame, of committing adultery. Jefferson's notes on the case are remarkably free of eighteenth-century circumlocution: "Burnside said he caught Frame (who is a married man) in bed with Eliza Burkin, put his [hand] on Frame's ——— as he lay in bed with the girl and felt it wet, and then put his hand on her ———, and felt it wet also." Jefferson indicates that the case was dismissed at Frame's request without going to trial. Perhaps, in view of the graphic details that Burnside was prepared to aver in court, Jefferson had advised his client to let it go.

The young lawyer's own life at this period was not without erotic episodes. He had remained a good friend of John Walker, who had been with him at both the Reverend Mr. Maury's little school and at William and Mary, and who now, not long married, had established himself and his young wife, Betsey, at an estate called Belvoir, just a few miles from Jefferson's place at Shadwell. Although not a man of intellectual bent, Walker felt close to his more cultured classmate. His father, Dr. Thomas Walker, had been one of Jefferson's guardians after Peter Jefferson's death. Jefferson himself had been a "member" of Jack Walker's wedding to Betsey; two of her brothers were William and Mary alumni and her father, Colonel Bernard Moore, exchanged agricultural tips with Jefferson when he was not too busy with his law practice. It all seemed very warm and convivial, and Jack Walker had good reason to feel that in Jefferson he had a wonderful neighbor and trusty old friend.

But the obligations of friendship sometimes waver when Eros intervenes. In July 1768, when Jefferson was twenty-five, John Walker was appointed secretary to the Virginia delegation for an important treaty with the Iroquois Indians at Fort Stanwix, near what is today Rome, New York—in Colonial times, many days' journey away from Virginia. It seems like an odd assignment for a young man to have accepted when his marriage was still fresh and his attractive spouse was caring for an infant daughter: there was the expectation that he would be gone for a long time, and it would have been impractical to think of their going with him. He was not incognizant of this, and decided to make his will before departing. Not only did he name Tom Jefferson as his principal executor, but asked "the friend of my heart" (as he put it later) to pay special attention to Betsey while he was away, visiting Belvoir often and making sure she and the baby were well.

This Jefferson did and then some. Exactly what happened will probably never be known, but it is certain that an amorous interlude occurred at Belvoir between Betsey and Jefferson during the four months of Jack Walker's absence. Some sixteen years later, having been strangely silent on the subject until then, Betsey presented to her husband a rambling account of repeated attempts on her virtue by Jefferson, all of them (according to her) indignantly rejected. Walker later reported that he had written complaining letters to Jefferson about this, but he was vague as to when they were written, and none has been found. Yet by some process that has never been ascertained, the story leaked into the whirlpool of national political gossip and circulated in variously embellished versions until ultimately, during Jefferson's first term as president (1801–1805), it was published in the Federalist press as one of many efforts to smirch his reputation.

The journalist chiefly responsible was James Callender, the same acrimonious scribe who would first publish the claim that Jefferson kept a slave mistress (Sally Hemings) at his plantation home. In this case he got most of his information from John Walker himself, but his telling of what came to be called "the Walker affair," printed in the *Richmond Recorder* in the fall of 1802, was so ambiguous that Walker felt his honor and that of his wife had been impugned. What to do? Perhaps the proper thing was to challenge the president to a duel? He discussed it with his wife's nephew by marriage, Henry (Light-Horse Harry) Lee, a political enemy of Jefferson's (and the man who not long after was to do the U.S.A. the doubtful favor of fathering Robert E. Lee). He maliciously said yes, and agreed to convey the challenge to the White House.

It was an age when a challenge to a duel could not be taken

lightly—as Alexander Hamilton and Aaron Burr demonstrated convincingly two years later on the heights of Weehawken. Jefferson, who regarded this means of settling a dispute as barbaric, was appalled at the very idea of it, quite apart from the uproarious public reaction that could be expected if any such confrontation were to take place. As for Walker, he may have had second thoughts upon reflecting that just the challenge alone might well be interpreted by many as confirming him as a cuckold—the very thing he was trying to avoid. At any rate, a meeting without benefit of pistols was hastily arranged between the two old friends—both of them now teetering on the edge of sixty—at the home of James Madison, long since one of Jefferson's closest political advisers, where it was agreed that both parties would do everything they could to quiet down the gossip in the newspapers they had connections with, in order (as Jefferson put it to Walker in a conciliatory letter written at the time) "to consign this unfortunate matter to all the oblivion of which it is susceptible."

But stories about the sexual peccadilloes of famous men die hard, and sure enough, two years later in Puritan Massachusetts (which seemed to have a particular appetite for such tales) the "Walker affair" came up again in the anti-Jefferson press, to Jack Walker's consternation. This time the trouble was settled, more or less to his satisfaction, by having Jefferson send letters to his attorney general, Levi Lincoln, and to Secretary of the Navy Robert Smith, with the understanding that the two would convey their essence to other important gentlemen in government and social circles. These letters have since unfortunately disappeared, probably destroyed by someone even more intent on oblivion than Jefferson was—but their gist survived in a covering note, in the president's hand, that he sent along to Smith: "You will perceive that I plead guilty . . . that when young and single I offered love to a handsome lady. I acknolege [sic] its incorrectness."

It's a good bet that Jefferson pondered carefully before settling on the phrase "I offered love." It surely is a euphemism for whatever actually happened, and it leaves unanswered the intriguing question of whether the "offer" was refused or accepted. His object, nevertheless, was to allay Jack Walker's anxiety about a public perception that he had been horned as well as duped, so in all probability the mea culpa letters, however politely couched in the rhetoric of the period, gave the impression that while Jefferson had transgressed, Betsey Walker had not. ("As a gentleman," remarks Dumas Malone in a flurry of vicarious Southern gallantry, "he could do no less.") But when the circumstances of that long-ago summer of 1768 are recalled, it is hard to believe that only Jefferson's youthful libido was involved. He may well have been stirred by Betsey's sexual allure for years, and lubriciously excited at the surprising opportunity—by the obligation, almost—of spending lots of time alone with her. Yet there is reason to think that he was still quite inexperienced in love, and the certainty, from all that is known about him, that aggressive sexual advances upon a woman who had given no signal of invitation were contrary to his nature and his code of conduct. Betsey, having learned the pleasures of the marriage bed, and quite possibly caught up in a confusion of frustrated desire and resentment at her husband for having disappeared into the wilderness for such an unconscionable stretch of time, could easily have made the first move.

Infidelity by a woman with one of her husband's good friends (and, no doubt, with the genders reversed) has a very long history, its fictional manifestations extending at least from Homer and Arthurian romance to countless novels and films featuring the "Dear John" letters of World War II. As for the moral calculus involved, the timeless observation of Leonardo in one of his notebooks that "the penis has a mind of its own" is relevant. But beyond that, there would seem to be some special attraction between a close friend's spouse and the interloper, as if an unconscious rivalry were being exercised, or even as if the adulterous act achieved a unique kind of three-way intimacy. The sexy Virginia summertime was in full flower when Jefferson started his promised visits to Betsey that July, and it is very conceivable that the lines of magnetic force between these two handsome young people were charged with an irresistible erotic energy. Still, the episode remains something of a puzzle. If in truth Betsey indignantly spurned Jefferson's amorous moves, as her husband later said she did, why would she have waited sixteen years to tell him about it? Walker said that according to Betsey, she kept the secret "from fear of its consequence which might have been fatal to me"—apparently implying that in her judgment a revelation would probably have led to a duel. This has some plausibility but, ironically enough, more so if it is assumed that Jefferson and Betsey actually went to bed together than if the scene was one of virtuous resistance on her part. And it leaves hanging the question of why in 1784 she finally decided that it was time to take the pig out of the poke. She knew, of course, that even at that late date the story would discomfit her proud and jealous husband, and it is hard to avoid the conclusion that she wanted to do exactly that— for whatever motives, sprung from the infinite array of available marital disjunctions, struck her at the moment.

Betsey Walker's version of what happened between her and Jefferson, sieved through a sixteen-year-old memory and later rather incoherently relayed by her husband in a letter to Henry Lee, was the sine qua non of the whole business: if she had remained mum it all would have faded into the vast silence of unrecorded history. Her disclosure assured her a niche in Jefferson's biography, and enables us to glimpse him as a virile young man whose lusty appreciation of a curvaceous female body overwhelmed, at least temporarily, his shyness and his sense of propriety.

He was, in fact, at this point in his life, very nearly an exemplification of the "truth universally acknowledged" with which Jane Austen wryly begins *Pride and Prejudice*—he was a single young man in possession of a large fortune, and he was in search of a wife.

And unbeknownst to him she was awaiting him, that very summer that he "offered love" to Betsey Walker—a lovely young woman whose husband, another of Jefferson's college mates at William and Mary, had tragically just died, leaving her a widow at the age of nineteen.

3

"Unchequered Happiness"

———— •◆• ————

It might be supposed that when a president of the United States describes the only marriage he ever had as a period of "unchequered happiness," a great deal of historical information must exist to document and illustrate the particulars of the blissful partnership. That was the descriptive phrase Jefferson used in his autobiography, written when he was seventy-seven years old, and his only other reference to the marriage in that abbreviated account of his life is this laconic statement: "On the 1st of January, 1772, I was married to Martha Skelton, widow of Bathurst Skelton, and daughter of John Wayles, then twenty-three years old."

That was nearly all that posterity was ever to get from Jefferson himself about his relationship with "the cherished companion of my life," as he called Martha. The irony is that his silence on the subject is largely attributable to the intensity of his love. The shock of her death, after only ten years of married life together, was so devastating that when he partially recovered from it several months later, he apparently found it almost unbearable even to speak her name. Moreover, either then or at some later time, he systematically destroyed every letter that had ever passed between them.

This, plus the odd fact that not one portrait of Martha Wayles Jefferson has survived, though it would seem likely that there must have been one or two, has sadly dimmed the reality of her personality. Yet there is a fair amount of indirect evidence suggesting that she was extremely beautiful and vivacious, bright and accomplished—as indeed would be expected by anyone familiar with Jefferson's tastes.

It is not known exactly when or where they met. Her young and ill-fated first husband, Bathurst Skelton, had been part of the college social set Jefferson moved in at Williamsburg during the early 1760s, but evidently Martha Wayles—who was five or six years younger than the members of that group in any case—was not on the scene. She must have matured quite early, however: she had just turned eighteen when she and Skelton were married in the fall of 1766. While still nineteen she gave birth to a son, and before the boy was a year old his father was dead, ambushed by one of the marauding diseases that caught so many young people of the period unawares. The teenaged widow, no doubt considerably stunned, took her baby and herself back to her father's plantation, The Forest, to the west of Williamsburg, where she knew she would find warm and sympathetic shelter.

John Wayles was an unusual man. An immigrant from England, he was by his thirties solidly established in Virginia as a combination planter, slave trader, and lawyer. He was not profoundly steeped in legal studies, but he had, wrote Jefferson, "great industry, punctuality, and practical readiness," and his business grew rapidly. At the same time, he was a man of large gusto, a generous host and convivial entertainer—"a most agreeable companion," in Jefferson's opinion, "full of pleasantry and good humor, and welcomed in every society."

One pleasure that clearly was important to Mr. Wayles was that of the connubial bed. His first wife, Martha's mother, died a few short weeks after the little girl was born in 1748. He soon married a second wife; this one survived long enough to bear him four more daughters. After her death, he made one more trip to the altar, this time with the widow of Reuben Skelton, Bathurst's older brother—but she lasted less than a year. (Just to keep track: by this time Martha Wayles was thirteen.)

Possibly discouraged with the fragility of Virginia upper-class ladies, Wayles then persuaded a good-looking slave of his, Betty Hemings—who had proved her endurance by having already, though only in her twenties, borne four black children—to become his concubine. She proceeded, in rather rapid succession, to produce six more offspring, all fathered by Wayles. The youngest of these, a girl named Sally, was born in 1773. They were all quite "light," since Betty herself was a mulatto, but more significantly they were, of course, half-siblings of Martha Wayles. This genetic fact would be important in determining their destiny, and in Sally's case it would even turn out to be of historical importance—as will be seen later.

But this puts us a bit ahead of the story. Martha settled in at The Forest in 1769, taking care of her child, acting as hostess for her father's dinner parties, overseeing domestic logistics—and, it seems, dealing as she saw fit with numerous suitors, for her personal attractions were lent an extra glow by her father's ample fortune.

Prominent among the suitors was Tom Jefferson. It was an extraordinarily busy time for him even before he began to woo her. His old family home at Shadwell burned to the ground early in 1770, the flames consuming not only the house but nearly all of his books and papers as well. Painful as this certainly was for him, it was somewhat relieved by the fact that his plans for a permanent mansion not far distant were by now well under way. The top of a small mountain had been decapitated to make a level space for a large dwelling and grounds, quantities of lumber were being assembled, and thousands of bricks were being made. The Shadwell conflagration brought a special push of activity to the mountaintop, for Jefferson needed a roof over his head. A brick outbuilding that he called "the south pavilion" was constructed in the spring and summer of 1770, and in November he moved into its one living area, eighteen feet square, which served him "for parlour for kitchen and hall. I may add, for bedchamber and study too," he wrote to a friend. It was, relatively speaking, camping out; but it was the first realization of what was to become for him a lifelong obsession: Monticello.

This view of the south terrace of Monticello has two points of particular interest: it shows (at the far end) the "south pavilion," where Jefferson first lived on the mountain and where he and his bride spent most of their honeymoon; and it shows a row of the "dependencies" beneath the big mansion, which among other functions housed a few favored slaves—including (according to Jefferson's grandson, Thomas Jefferson Randolph) Sally Hemings.

There he could breathe the fresh mountain air, delight in the blazing autumn foliage, gaze off to the majesty of the Blue Ridge on his western horizon—and dream about Martha Wayles. She had been encouraging, and as he sketched his plans for the big house it was surely as a home for her and for him and their children that he envisaged it. He was in love with her from the start, and his behavior showed it. Knowing he had rivals, he set out to dazzle her, spending more than he was used to on clothes, inquiring about getting a family coat of arms (even if he had to buy it), ordering a custom-made solid mahogany pianoforte as a present, and making increasingly frequent trips to The Forest to see her. They had discovered a mutual fondness for music, and according to family tradition the courtship was conducted to a considerable extent by duet—Jefferson's violin with Martha's harpsichord, or their two voices raised together in romantic harmony. One story told fondly by their descendants was that two other suitors, who happened to arrive at The Forest simultaneously, were stopped in the hall outside the drawing room by the melodious sound of the lovers' duet. After listening disconsolately for a minute or two, they both put on their hats and departed without further ado. By the summer of 1771, although no formal announcement had been made, Tom Jefferson and Martha Wayles Skelton had apparently agreed to get married. Probably the prospective bridegroom hoped that construction at Monticello would go fast enough so that before very long he would have something more suitable than his one-room pavilion to take her to. But then as now, home-building projects seemed to consist of one delay after another. The momentum of a passionate love affair, by contrast, often seems to accelerate as time goes by.

And there is good reason to believe that this affair was passionate. That centuries-old inhibitor, sanctified virginity, was not on the scene: Martha had nothing to lose by giving in to—or, indeed, by encouraging—Jefferson's urgent desires, and he, for his part, had shown by the Betsey Walker episode that in his view extramarital love was not necessarily a heinous thing. They were going to get married, and premarital love probably struck him as quite in accord with the laws of nature that he had chosen as his guide.

It is interesting that in the end the actual marriage took place rather hastily. The dead of winter is not a popular season for weddings, even in a southern region like Virginia, where freezing temperatures, though rare, are far from unknown. But on December 30, 1771, in Williamsburg, Thomas Jefferson paid for a license to marry Martha Wayles Skelton. He then rode on to The Forest, and on New Year's Day, 1772, the customary holiday festivity provided by Squire John Wayles was joyously crowned by the nuptials of his delightful eldest daughter.

Twelfth-night came and went, and the happy pair were still at the big mansion, enjoying the paternal hospitality. It was obvious that the cornucopian comforts of The Forest offered a more propitious ambiance for their honeymoon than the spartan facilities of Monticello in its then embryonic state.

So it was past the middle of January when they finally made it on horseback—their phaeton having been abandoned—up the steep and primitive road to the little mountain's summit, arriving very late at night and with (according to Jefferson) "the deepest snow we have ever seen" covering the ground. Their first child, Patsy, was to tell the story in later years with ladylike comments about "the horrible dreariness" of their first homecoming. But any young couple who have (for instance) struggled through a storm to reach a vacation hideout, got there at last, lighted a fire, and snuggled down under a blanket with a good bottle of wine would know that for Tom and Martha it probably became one of their most delightful memories. Incidentally, Patsy Jefferson (christened Martha, after her mother) was born on September 27, 1772, a few days less than nine months after the wedding. Given the normal fluctuation of the length of pregnancy, this leaves room for the speculation that she may have been conceived either somewhat before that event, or during the honeymoon fortnight at The Forest. If it was before, and Martha Wayles Skelton was aware of it or suspected it, we have an explanation for the abruptness of the marriage. Either way, it suggests no lack of lively sexual activity by her mother and father, who were to continue for a decade to provide evidence of a loving relationship in which the erotic component played a very important part.

So began the Jeffersons' ten years of "unchequered happiness." Without questioning the sincerity of that evaluation, it may strike some modern readers as surprisingly sanguine in view of the fact that during the same ten years three children born to them died in their infancy. The first to go was Jane, born in April 1774; she lived less than eighteen months. Even before that, Martha's little boy Jack Skelton died of some childhood plague, never having had a real chance to know his stepfather. Such early deaths undoubtedly caused sorrow but, in those pre-antibiotic days, hardly horror or even great surprise. In the typical large family it was actually a rare thing for all the children to reach adulthood, as whooping cough, measles, mumps, and scarlet fever took their annual toll. Nor were the Jeffersons spared the loss of older relatives and friends during their short marriage. Martha's father, John Wayles, was dead and gone at the age of fifty-eight, just a little beyond a year after their wedding; Jefferson's mother, also not yet sixty at her death, never knew of her son's authorship of the famous Declaration; Dabney Carr, his brother-in-law and the closest friend he ever had, was carried off by an intestinal fever while still in his twenties—and there were others.

Add to all this the political toil and trouble for Jefferson of the years 1772–1782, when he sweated his pints as a leading statesman and revolutionary at both the national level and in Virginia (whose extremely harassed war governor he was from 1779 to 1781), and the phrase "unchequered happiness" seems all the more puzzling. There were plusses on the material side, of course—for example, from the estate of John Wayles there came several plantations, totaling some eleven thousand acres, together with an additional 135 slaves, bringing Jefferson's captive workforce up close to 200. Yet for Jefferson this could not have been without ambiguity, since the more he pondered slavery the more sure he was that this blight on civilization must ultimately be wiped out. Much less uncertain was his pleasure in seeing the great house at Monticello take shape according to the architectural plans that he had made himself— though even this was qualified by the maddening slowness of the building process.

The solution to the puzzle, however, is probably simple enough, and by implication tells much about the character of the relationship between Tom and Martha. That, almost exclusively, was what he must have been thinking about when he chose the unusual expression by which he described his married years, and it meant that regardless of external storms and stresses, no wedge of rancor or ennui had been allowed to intrude upon their love.

This of course was a retrospective view, looking back at a marriage that had ended tragically nearly forty years earlier, and time may have softened the edges of Jefferson's memories. They were both very bright and lively people, and it is not supposable that there was never any difference of opinion or emotional friction between them. But Jefferson had decided—perhaps even as a boy observing his parents—that quarreling between husband and wife was destructive of love and happiness, and that mutual respect, compromise, and quick resolution of arguments were essential to marital contentment. "Nothing can preserve affections uninterrupted but a firm resolution never to differ in will," he advised his daughter Polly not long after her marriage in 1797.

Referring to Jefferson's burning of his correspondence with Martha and his stubborn reluctance to talk about her, Dumas Malone remarks: "Because of this impenetrable silence on his part, probably we shall never know much about Martha Wayles Jefferson and her life with him." Following this assumption, most Jefferson biographers have settled for the usual sketchy descriptions of her as beautiful but slight, a devoted mother, genteel and charming in her behavior, and musically gifted—the sort of thing summed up by a Hessian officer who was entertained at Monticello and was struck by her skill at the harpsichord: ". . . In all respects a very agreeable, sensible & accomplished Lady."

But this image of Martha Jefferson as principally a refined gentlewoman and elegant hostess is by no means the only one available. In an extraordinary and highly original book, *Jefferson and Monticello: The Biography of a Builder* (1988), Jack McLaughlin has shown by diligent research that she was also a most industrious and capable manager of the myriad and demanding domestic requirements of a large and mostly self-sustaining estate. In this role she had come to Monticello with some experience from a brief tenure as mistress of her father's plantation at The Forest, but in her new situation her responsibilities were decidedly more extensive.

The Jeffersons had many slave house servants, and young Mrs. Jefferson was their supervisor, allocating their duties, monitoring their performance, settling their disputes, and seeing to it that they were well fed and clothed. Jefferson, who always knew what he wanted when it came to food and drink, undoubtedly let her know what that was, but making sure that it actually got to table was up to her. This was a complicated business, especially in the early days at Monticello before the estate's own resources such as gardens, orchards, dairies, and smoke rooms had been established, and she had to negotiate with slaves and overseers to supply much of the fruits and vegetables, butter and poultry, and so on. Given her husband's proclivity for extravagantly generous hospitality, even when his mountain home was in its rudimentary stages of construction, it is not surprising that large quantities of food were consumed regularly at Monticello, yet her notation of merely the pork eaten at the master's dwelling in about three weeks of the year 1773 is still rather startling: six hams, four shoulders, and two sides of bacon. Concern for cholesterol, obviously, was a thing utterly unheard of.

Martha's father, John Wayles, had apparently been fond of good beer, since she seems to have brought to Monticello a thorough knowledge of how to make it. Only a little over a month after settling there in January 1772, she recorded in her account book—which her meticulous husband presumably required her to keep—the brewing of a fifteen-gallon cask of "small beer." This was the equivalent of more than twenty-five "six-packs" in today's common measure, yet before the year's end she had brewed ten more casks.

She was soon engaged in overseeing the manufacture of more utilitarian products. Soap, essential for plantation masters and slaves alike, was made by boiling lye (from ashes) with fat (from pork and other sources) together. Martha and her slave assistants made it with a frequency and in amounts that would astound a modern housewife—sometimes hundreds of pounds at once. Candles, the chief means of illumination after dark, were molded with tallow obtained usually from beef fat. They were a good deal bigger than the kind generally used today as decorative lights; three or four were considered adequate for a large dining room, for instance. They burned for only a few hours, however, and Martha made them several dozen at a time. There was always sewing or knitting to be done, as well—dresses or aprons to be made or

A page from Martha Jefferson's household account book for 1772 indicates that one activity helping to make Monticello self-sufficient was the frequent brewing of beer.

mended, linen to be finished into sheets and pillowcases, clothing contrived for the slaves. As for cooking, although she probably did little handling of pots and pans herself, she closely supervised the cooks and undoubtedly planned the menus. Isaac, slave son of Ursula, a house servant who was already a trained pastry chef when Jefferson bought her in 1773, recalled in an oral memoir many years later how Mrs. Jefferson would "come . . . with a cookery book in her hand and read out of it to Isaac's mother how to make cakes, tarts, and so on."

In the midst of all this domestic hustle and bustle, Martha Jefferson was not allowed to forget two of her primary obligations as the wife of an upper-class plantation owner. She had to be a gracious and delightful hostess—the one role for which she is usually applauded in accounts of life at Monticello—and she had to provide her husband with a family.

In terms of her background and experience, Martha was essentially provincial. There is no evidence that she had traveled outside Virginia—nor was she, in her short life, ever to do so—but Jefferson's fascination with European culture ensured that any passing chance to widen Monticello's cultural horizons would be seized upon, to her advantage. In the fall of 1773 an Italian gentleman, Philip Mazzei, who was planning to start a vineyard in Virginia, stopped at Monticello for the night, and by the next day his wine-loving host had persuaded him that the land in the immediate vicinity was the place to do it. Mazzei brought in a corps of Italian workmen for his vineyard and to build him a suitable house, and before long was established, together with his wife and daughter, as a nearby resident. The Jeffersons entertained them frequently, and Martha began to pick up whiffs of a way of life intriguingly different from what she was accustomed to.

When Mazzei departed for Europe in 1779 their house was rented by Major General Friedrich von Riedesel, commander of the Hessian troops who had been captured at Saratoga in 1777 and subsequently marched to Virginia for holding. Although technically a prisoner, the German baron was permitted to live far more comfortably than most Virginians, and in the peculiar manner of eighteenth-century warfare was soon hobnobbing with his distinguished American neighbor. His wife, a large, exuberant woman who sang—very well, by her own testimony—much enjoyed Martha's musical talents, and with their three young daughters, who in age were within congenial range of seven-year-old Patsy, the Riedesels spent many an enjoyable evening with the Jeffersons, the company pleasantly augmented from time to time by other cultivated Hessian officers from the baron's staff. It was all civilized and sophisticated, and gave Martha Jefferson not only a respite from her busy life as Monticello's domestic manager, but an opportunity to polish the social graces that she knew her position called for.

Her other main wifely obligation, producing children, was fulfilled with great ardor but often without good luck. Martha gave birth six times during the decade of her marriage, despite her husband's unavoidable absence from home for long intervals, and there are indications that she also may have miscarried at least once. He hated being away from her. Although he was a rather recently elected member of the Virginia Colonial legislature, he stayed home at Monticello (that is, in the little south pavilion) for over a month after they set up housekeeping there in January 1772, thus missing a whole session of the House of Burgesses. It may have been this conspicuous absence during the honeymoon period that started what later became, it seems, a common gibe among his Revolutionary compatriots: that Tom Jefferson was inordinately fond of his wife's embraces. It was an age when such things, though certainly joked about in private conversation, were put into writing only circumspectly. Yet so annoyed were some of Jefferson's colleagues at even the temporary loss of his enormously useful skills in the difficult proceedings of the Continental Congress that they made saucy remarks in letters to him, trying to get him to come back to work quickly. Phrases like "your retreat to the Delights of domestic life" (John Adams), "your pleasure at home" (Edmund Pendleton), and "your darling Pleasures" (John Page) were thin disguises for what they actually referred to; and Pendleton, having failed to persuade Jefferson to stay longer in Philadelphia in the summer of 1776, put his finger on what he was sure the problem was when he suggested that at least in Virginia, "having the Pleasure of Mrs. Jefferson's Company, I hope you'll get cured of your wish to retire so early in life from the memory of man, and exercise your talents for the nurture of Our new Constitution."

But there was no "cure" for Tom's wish to be with Martha as much as possible. It is true, as the Virginia historians like to emphasize in explaining his homing penchant, that Martha Jefferson was often ill, and that Jefferson, a most solicitous husband, naturally wanted to be beside her at such times. Most of her ailments apparently had to do with pregnancy or childbirth. He remembered, of course, that her mother had never recovered from bearing Martha, so that his anxiety was heightened when she was with child—which was, over the years, just about half the time. Yet there are grounds for suspecting that occasionally Martha's indispositions were exaggerated into illnesses to justify her husband's hasty returns. Moreover, periods of domesticity at Monticello were so often followed by another pregnancy that awareness of a cause-and-effect connection between childbirth and sickness does not seem to have put much if any restraint on their love life: evidently they found each other sexually irresistible.

Whatever the details of their marriage may have been, it is clear that there was a persistent conflict between Jefferson's love for Martha and Monticello, on the one hand, and his love for politics, statesmanship, and his country on the other. He worked energetically and brilliantly when he had a congressional task to perform, but the itch to go home seldom left him. On the great day of the adoption of the Declaration of Independence, when he might have been expected to join John Adams in a congratulatory drink or two, he was off shopping for Martha: his account book for that famous Fourth of July records the purchase of seven pairs of women's gloves.

And before the summer was over he had resigned from the Congress to go back to Virginia and work on a series of reform bills in the state legislature. Luckily, his old mentor George Wythe had offered comfortable lodging in his Williamsburg home, and Martha agreed to join her busy husband there in September of that year. Their reunion, not surprisingly, was celebrated in bed, and nine months later Martha gave birth to the one son they were ever to have. Unhappily, the baby boy was ill from the start and died a fortnight later, still without a name.

This melancholy pattern of events was not yet over for Tom and Martha Jefferson: in the autumn of 1780 another daughter, Lucy Elizabeth, was born to them, and for a while seemed to be doing well—but only four and a half months later she too suddenly died. In the interim, however, there came the only child other than Patsy (then almost six years old) who was to survive into adulthood—Maria Jefferson, nicknamed Polly, born August 1, 1778.

Quite aside from domestic concerns, this was a difficult period for Jefferson. Without having campaigned or maneuvered for the job, he was elected governor of Virginia by the state legislature in 1779, the runner-up being his old college pal John Page. He well knew that it would be a burden, "especially in times like these," as he put it—for the American Revolution was in full blaze, and war was a business in which, unlike George Washington, he had no experience whatsoever. Virginia had not yet been invaded by the British, but for over a year he had to deal with nearly unsolvable problems involving galloping inflation, steep trade deficits because of the war, and needed but unprocurable arms and clothing for the troops the state was contributing to the national struggle.

Then, early in 1781, Virginia and its governor suffered a rude surprise at the hands of the man who, after a star performance as an American general, had become almost an eponym for treason. Benedict Arnold swooped into Chesapeake Bay in command of a British raiding party that moved rapidly up the James River, pillaging and burning as they went. Jefferson was not fiddling, but he was slow to call out the Virginia militia, and Arnold encountered little opposition. Dumas Malone, who seldom said anything negative about Jefferson, remarked that in his explanation of his behavior during this episode the governor was not entirely "candid": "It would have been better if he had admitted the unvarnished truth: Arnold had caught him off his guard."

Worse followed soon after. Several thousand British soldiers under the aggressive command of General Charles Cornwallis joined Arnold's force near Richmond, and most of the members of the Virginia Assembly decided that Charlottesville, a long march westward, would be a better place to hold their next session. At least it was near Monticello, whither Jefferson went, full of apprehension about the enemy's next move. Sure enough, Cornwallis quickly dispatched the famous cavalryman Banastre Tarleton with a company of dragoons to capture as many Virginia legislators as possible—plus, of course, Thomas Jefferson. But the governor was lucky: a Southern counterpart to Paul Revere was on hand. Jack Jouett, hanging out at a roadhouse jauntily named the Cuckoo, about forty miles from Charlottesville, overheard some dragoons, paused for refreshment, discussing their mission. He jumped on his horse and made a crashing night ride to Monticello, arriving about dawn. Jefferson, not one to panic easily, gave him thanks and a quaff of good wine with breakfast. He then set about moving his family out of there and gathering a few things for his own imminent departure, no doubt wondering nervously whether his beloved home might soon be burned to a shell. Tarleton, however, had given strict orders to his men to leave the building undisturbed—either in accord with the polite code of the eighteenth-century gentleman-officer, or because he planned to use the place, with its superb view of the surrounding countryside, as a lookout post. An abrupt change of military plans then took Tarleton's force away from the Charlottesville area, and Monticello remained pristine.

But Thomas Jefferson had hit bottom in his political career, and he knew it. His term as governor was just over, and he had no desire to try it again—in fact, he told his friends that he was through with politics forever. A depressing sense of failure lingered, inevitably: to George Washington he wrote that he felt reduced to a state of "perpetual decrepitude." Since he was not yet thirty-nine, this may have struck the forty-nine-year-old general as a bit excessive.

The brighter side to Jefferson's cloud of gloom was that he now felt ample justification for doing what he had long dreamed of: retiring to Monticello to oversee his plantations, prune his fruit trees, read whatever he chose, think, write, play his violin, ride his favorite horse around his estate, entertain selected guests, make scientific observations, and enjoy Martha's charms with no immediate prospect of separation from her.

This relatively idyllic interlude was not to last long, but while it did it facilitated the writing of the only book Thomas Jefferson ever completed. Happily for him and his country, this singular work—which he modestly entitled *Notes on the State of Virginia*— was of excellent quality, and has been regarded by knowledgeable critics as the most important book of scientific observations, not only on Virginia but on North America generally, that had yet been written. It was occasioned by a request from a French diplomat for information about the state's history, geography, natural resources, economy, demography, flora and fauna, and political institutions, on all of which Jefferson happened to know more, in all probability, than any other one person in the world, and he fell to his task with enthusiasm. Once he got into it, moreover, he found it a wonderful chance to expatiate on his own personal views with regard to such matters as natural rights, democratic government, religion, and slavery. Far more than any other single thing he ever wrote, including his abortive autobiography, *Notes on the State of Virginia* was thus a revelation of the mind of Thomas Jefferson.

So, for a few happy months in late 1781 and early 1782, he lived the life of the country squire, gentleman scholar, and amateur scientist that he believed he was best cut out for. Shortly after he had finished the first draft of his book, he entertained for several days a distinguished French visitor, the Marquis de Chastellux, who, though a general in the French army, was also an intellectual and a man of keen discrimination. In a travel journal that he published later, he gave a sharply etched impression of Jefferson at this time:

> Let me describe to you a man, not yet forty, tall, and with a mild and pleasing countenance, but whose mind and understanding are ample substitutes for every exterior grace. An American, who without ever having quitted his own country, is at once a musician, skilled in drawing, a geometrician,

Opposite: Contents page of the first edition (Paris, 1785) of Jefferson's Notes on the State of Virginia, *of which only two hundred copies were printed. They were not offered for sale but distributed to friends and acquaintances.*

NOTES on the ſtate of VIRGINIA;

written in the year 1781, ſomewhat corrected and enlarged in the winter of 1782,
for the uſe of a Foreigner of diſtinction, in
anſwer to certain queries propoſed by him
reſpecting

Thomas Jefferson

MDCCLXXXII.

[Paris 1785]

an astronomer, a natural philosopher, and statesman . . . before I had been two hours with him we were as intimate as if we had passed our whole lives together . . . above all a conversation always varied and interesting . . . made four days pass away like so many minutes.

Chastellux unfortunately did not leave a comparable sketch of Martha Jefferson, but did report that she was "mild and amiable"—and that she was obviously well along in a pregnancy.

It was to be her last. The baby, who was named Lucy Elizabeth after the one they had lost a little over a year earlier, was born on May 8, 1782, and endured the event well, apparently a strong and healthy child. Martha, however, did not: on May 20 Jefferson wrote to his friend James Monroe, "Mrs. Jefferson has added another daughter to our family. She has ever since and still continues very dangerously ill." The exact nature of her problem is not known, but whatever it was, no cure was available. She lingered on through the spring and summer, her husband in an anguish of fear and dubious hope. He hardly left her bedside, doing what work he could in an adjoining room. She had survived other childbirth illnesses, but this obviously was more severe—and on September 6, 1782, he wrote in his account book, "My dear wife died this day at 11:45 a.m."

Despite the stoic brevity of that entry, there is convincing evidence that Martha's death struck him a formidable blow. Their almost ten-year-old daughter Patsy was an eyewitness to her mother's last moments and to her father's reaction, and although it was many years before she wrote down her impressions, they were naturally vivid—"beyond the power of time to obliterate," as she put it herself. As she recalled it, Jefferson was led from the room into the library by his sister just before the fatal moment, "almost in a state of insensibility," and then fainted dead away. Thereafter,

Detail of Jefferson's account book, recording the death of his wife on September 6, 1782.

she said, he stayed indoors for three weeks, constantly pacing up and down. "When at last he left his room he rode out and from that time he was incessantly on horseback rambling about the mountain in the least frequented roads and just as often through the woods; in those melancholy rambles I was his constant companion, a solitary witness to many a violent burst of grief . . . "

Edmund Bacon, who had been chief overseer at Monticello for many years, gave this hearsay account of the death scene to an interviewer in 1862:

The house servants were Betty Brown, Sally, Critta, and Betty Hemings, Nance, and Ursula . . . They were in the room when Mrs. Jefferson died . . . They have often told my wife, that when Mrs. Jefferson died, they stood around the bed. Mr. Jefferson sat by her, and she gave him directions about a good many things that she wanted done. When she came to the children, she wept, and could not speak for some time. Finally she held up her hand, and spreading out her four fingers, she told him she could not die happy if she thought her four children were ever to have a stepmother brought in over them. Holding her other hand in his, Mr. Jefferson promised her solemnly that he would never marry again. And he never did. He was then quite a young man,

49

and very handsome, and I suppose he could have married well; but he always kept that promise.

Bacon was wrong about the number of surviving Jefferson children—there were only three—but in other respects his story sounds convincing. Martha Jefferson herself had to endure more than one stepmother, and there were other obvious reasons why the thought of being replaced was a painful one—proportionally, no doubt, to the intensity of her love for her husband. In return, it seems quite believable that to Jefferson in those last mortal moments, the idea of another mate was repellent. The ironic fact that Martha's death was inextricably connected to childbirth and thereby to their physical passion for each other could not have been lost on him; he had, in effect, loved her to death. If a sense of guilt for this aggravated his grief, it may have been compounded by the knowledge that the completion of the dream mansion they had planned had been woefully delayed. As Jack McLaughlin put it, "It was by his own admission a house only half finished, and this was the only Monticello she knew."

Among the family relics found after Patsy's death in 1836 there was a folded sheet of paper with a lock of chestnut hair and a notation in her handwriting: "A Lock of my Dear Mama's Hair inclosed in a verse which she wrote." It was not in fact a verse, but a few lines of prose:

> Time wastes too fast: every letter I trace tells me with what rapidity life follows my pen. The days and hours of it are flying over our heads like clouds of a windy day never to return more—everything presses on—

This much was in Martha Jefferson's hand; the rest had been added by Jefferson:

—and every time I kiss thy hand to bid adieu, every absence which follows it, are preludes to that eternal separation which we are shortly to make.

This almost unbearably poignant passage turned out to have been extracted from, of all things, Laurence Sterne's *Tristram Shandy*. It had long been one of Jefferson's favorite books—or series of books, for Sterne's meandering narrative had been published in nine separate volumes between 1759 and 1767. Jefferson bought the whole set from an English bookseller shortly before his marriage, and recommended them strongly to Martha's brother-in-law, Robert Skipwith, as part of a basic collection for establishing a good personal library.

What is fascinating about this, aside from the touching relevance of the quoted passage to the situation at Monticello in the summer of 1782, is the light it throws on Jefferson's taste in fiction. *Tristram Shandy* is no ponderous tale of moral edification, but an amazing collage of narrative sketches, satirical skits, mock essays, and whimsical digressions, composing a very long work that is saturated from start to finish with sexual innuendo—now and then poking through to explicit albeit witty obscenity. The passage that Martha and Tom copied (with slight changes) is a rare interpolation of solemnity and, coming as it does near the end of Sterne's last volume, a reminder that he himself was to be dead of tuberculosis in a very short time. But there is every reason to think that the Jeffersons were equally familiar with many other passages, and in happier days may have read some of the more delightfully suggestive ones to each other with appropriately lascivious chuckles.

It seems likely that if Martha Jefferson had lived a long and healthy life, the United States never would have had her husband as a president. But her early death—she was only thirty-three—demolished his fantasy of undisturbed country retirement, and once he had begun to emerge from what he described, in a letter to his French friend Chastellux, as "that stupor of mind which had rendered me as dead to the world as she was whose loss occasioned it," he began to think of a return to public life as the best possible therapy for his misery.

An appointment by Congress as minister plenipotentiary to join Benjamin Franklin and John Adams in Paris in their work on a peace treaty with England must have seemed to him like a lifesaver, and he quickly grabbed it. The appointment, however, fell through for various official reasons after he had already journeyed to Baltimore to await a sailing, and he went back to Monticello for the summer of 1783. At least there were plenty of distractions: plasterers and carpenters were busily at work on the house and it was alive with children—six of them nieces and nephews, the offspring of his dead friend Dabney Carr and Jefferson's sister, who had come to live there, plus his own two daughters and the baby girl whose arrival had so shortly preceded his wife's death. It was also, he found, a good time to devote attention to his cherished library, and by the fall of the year he had meticulously classified and catalogued 2,640 books—a most impressive number for a private collection, especially considering that it had been started from scratch in 1770, after the burning of Shadwell.

Some men, after the death of a spouse, set out almost immediately to find a substitute, and this may be more likely when the widower is a young man. Jefferson had just turned forty in the spring of 1783, and as Edmund Bacon observed, he was eminently eligible—tall, strong, rich, good-looking, and already quite famous throughout the newly united states. But evidently he was in no mood to seek a replacement for Martha, quite aside from his last vow to her. Clearly, for him, she had been unique among women, and for a long time after she was gone there was no room in his heart for any other. He avoided fashionable dinner parties and contented himself with a vicarious interest in the courtship efforts of close friends like James Madison, who at the age of thirty had been ardently wooing a beautiful fifteen-year-old girl named Catherine Floyd. He was turned down, and Jefferson wrote him a commiserating letter that expressed among other things his own bafflement at the psychosomatic mysteries of the human animal: "Of all machines ours is the most complicated and inexplicable."

In the fall of 1783, having been again elected to Congress, Jefferson took his daughter Patsy to Philadelphia to live in the home of Francis Hopkinson, a fellow signer of the great Declaration of 1776, where he knew she would be well cared for by Hopkinson's mother. Acutely sensitive to the fact, however, that Patsy had lost the guidance of her own mother, Jefferson went to great pains to make sure the adolescent girl would be properly educated, hiring tutors in French, music, and dancing. Her reading, of course, he directed himself, drawing up a formidable schedule to acquaint her thoroughly with "the best poets and prose-writers," and not overlooking "the graver sciences." Not content merely with these arrangements, he followed through, after he had left to join Congress in Annapolis, with a series of admonitory letters demanding frequent reports on her progress, and even implying that his love for her might fluctuate according to how well she did. Patsy, who knew better, remained calm and apparently had a rather good time in Philadelphia.

Jefferson himself, meanwhile, though plagued by melancholy and frequent headaches, plunged almost fiercely into legislative work, believing (as he remarked to Madison) that "unremitting occupations" were the only palliative for loss and grief. Among the many bills he introduced in Congress during a period of a few months was one that, if it had passed, might conceivably have prevented the Civil War, for it required that after 1800 "neither slavery nor involuntary servitude" would be allowed in any new states taken into the Union, and that these states should be forever inseparable from the United States. Nearly all of the Southern delegates voted against the antislavery proposal, some of them no doubt especially outraged that it had come from a man who himself owned about two hundred slaves. Nevertheless, the vote could not have been closer: all the Northern states voted aye, which would have just carried it—but one of New Jersey's two delegates, John Beatty, was sick and absent, so that the state's vote was not counted, and the measure was defeated. Jefferson was well aware of the tragic magnitude of the decision, later writing to a French historian, "The voice of a single individual . . . would have prevented this abominable crime from spreading itself over the new country. Thus we see the fate of millions unborn hanging on the tongue of one man . . . "

A good thing happened to Thomas Jefferson in the spring of 1784, shortly after his forty-first birthday. On May 7 Congress again appointed him to go to France, as a negotiator for European commercial treaties along with Benjamin Franklin and John Adams—and there was no likelihood this time that the arrangement would collapse. Not only was he desperately in need of a vacation from his congressional labors, but he had dreamed of visiting Europe ever since his college days—and particularly France, which he considered the most enlightened of nations for all the arts and sciences in which he was so devoutly interested.

It was an enticing prospect, enough even to lift him somewhat out of the deep depression he had fallen into after Martha's death. He would not see Virginia again for an unknown length of time and would have to leave his two younger daughters there, but Patsy, he decided, was old enough to go with him—and what better place in the world to put a cosmopolitan polish on a young lady's education than Paris? He hurried to Philadelphia to get her, and they spent two weeks in the invigorating task of outfitting themselves for the grand trip. No definite date had yet been set for sailing, but Boston had been chosen as the port of departure. Jefferson wanted to see a little of New England and gather useful information about the region's industry and trade before he left America, so after a few days in New York they coached up to New Haven, where his brilliant conversation so dazzled Yale's distinguished president Ezra Stiles that a year or so later the college honored him in absentia with the degree of doctor of laws. Brief excursions to Providence and to Portsmouth, New Hampshire, augmented Jefferson's introduction to New England, and by mid-June father and daughter were in Boston enjoying a good deal of honorific hospitality while they awaited a proper ship for the voyage. One soon appeared in the form of a recently built beauty called *Ceres*, after the Roman earth goddess associated with fertility rites as well as rites for the dead—a fact that Jefferson, given his extensive classical knowledge, may have found interesting.

And so, as dawn was breaking over Boston's harbor on July 5, 1784, they set sail for what he later called "the vaunted scene of Europe." They were lucky with the weather—sunny skies and smooth seas—and with only six other passengers, life aboard was very comfortable. There was good food and wine, good conversation, a total absence of committee meetings, and plenty of time for books. Jefferson had brought along copies of *Don Quixote* in English as well as Spanish, and by comparative reading taught himself the foreign language (or so he was to boast) in the nineteen days the fast *Ceres* took to span the Atlantic. It was an auspicious start to a chapter in his life that was to unfold many exotic wonders, cultural, political, intellectual, artistic—and erotic.

4

My Head, My Heart, and . . .

———•◆•———

Jefferson's visit to London in 1786 did by chance lead to a surprising change in his personal life. He had met there the young American artist John Trumbull, whose paintings of heroes of the American Revolution were destined to become famous, and who almost immediately began to look on Jefferson as an inspiring mentor. When Trumbull crossed the Channel to France in August, he was invited to join the Jefferson household for the length of his stay, and the two were soon traipsing convivially around Paris together. One afternoon in August, Trumbull persuaded Jefferson to visit the Halle au Bléd, the big grain market that had the architectural distinction of being covered by an enormous wooden dome. While Jefferson was taking note of the interesting construction details, Trumbull interrupted to introduce him to an even more interesting sight—a sight so arresting that he instantly forgot about the Halle au Bléd.

This stirring vision was Maria Cosway, a petite blue-eyed curly-haired blond, who greeted him in dulcet tones with a distinct trace of a bewitching Italian accent. Her elegant dress did not conceal a perfect figure, and her conversation immediately struck him as witty, good-natured, and sophisticated all at once.

Jefferson, writing to Maria Cosway about their first meeting (at the Halle au Bléd in Paris) said that he saw there "the most superb thing on earth"—not the building, but Maria. This engraving of her, by F. Bartolozzi, is after a painting by her husband.

She was with her husband, Richard Cosway, a well-known English portrait painter and also a well-known fop—who had the virtue, however, of seeming less jealous than amused by the obvious gravitation between his wife and the tall American. Describing the meeting later, Jefferson recalled that as dinnertime approached—

meaning, presumably, late afternoon—all four members of the party agreed that they were having far too much fun to keep their previous engagements. "Lying messengers" were therefore dispatched to give contrived excuses, and the quartet drove off to St. Cloud to have dinner together. What with good food, wonderful wine, and the seductive magnetism between Jefferson and Maria, it was essential to prolong the entertainment into the evening. They headed back into Paris, stopped to watch the spectacular fireworks display put on by the famous Ruggiere brothers, and wound up at the home of Johann Krumpholtz, a composer whose wife played the harp beautifully. It probably was there that Jefferson made the exciting discovery that Maria was, to crown her other charms, an accomplished musician: she too was a harpist.

It was all quite overwhelming for the widower who had absented himself from this particular kind of felicity for over four years. The dart of infatuation had pricked his heart, and for the next fortnight Maria was not often out of his thoughts. She was very often in his company as well. Her small husband—he was just about a foot shorter than Jefferson—was now busy executing a miniature for the Duc d'Orléans, and seems to have paid scant attention to their busy flirtation. (These exquisitely detailed little paintings were his specialty, and he had done very well with them in London, notoriously among the young gallants who surrounded the rakish Prince of Wales and who paid good money to own one of Cosway's ivory snuffboxes, decorated with highly explicit pornographic scenes. His work for Orléans was evidently of a more domestic genre.)

Jefferson's outings with Maria were certainly romantic and in all likelihood, within limits that he would have loved to stretch, erotic as well. September in Paris, while less celebrated in love songs than April, can be a wonderfully sexy time of year. The leaves of the chestnuts are starting to turn yellow and red; the sun warms the cool air to a caressing temperature; the outdoor cafés and restaurant terraces invite lingering aperitifs; the greenswards of the Bois de Boulogne command *déjeuners sur l'herbe.* In this sybaritic ambiance the enchanted couple reveled, leisurely visiting most of the tourist attractions of the city and its outskirts, ambulating through art galleries, luxuriating in heavenly music, eating delicious food, sampling vintage wines, and gazing at each other.

Like most people suddenly in love, Jefferson found that everything around him had changed its look. Not long before, he had written to an American friend that despite the amiability of the French, the great majority of them appeared to be "more wretched, more accursed in every circumstance of human existence, than the most conspicuously wretched individual in the whole United States." Now a delightful transformation had taken place, as he told Abigail Adams in a letter written about a week

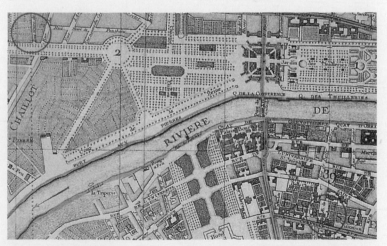

The superimposed circles on this detail from a 1790 map of Paris indicate the location of Jefferson's mansion, the Hôtel de Langeac (upper left corner), *and that of his daughters' school, the Abbaye de Panthémont* (lower right corner).

after he met Maria: "Here we have singing, dancing, laughter, and merriment. No assassinations, no treasons, rebellions nor other dark deeds. When our king goes out, they fall down and kiss the earth where he has trodden; and then they go to kissing one another. And this is the truest wisdom." (Abigail's sniff, upon reading this, can be imagined.)

But there is little doubt that this osculatory wisdom was being practiced in Jefferson's carriage as he and Maria drove about Paris on those languorous September days, and it would be no surprise to learn that parts more private than their lips were often in a state of urgent arousal. Did they actually make love? There is no way to know for sure, but a reasonable conjecture would be that Jefferson was ready, and Maria was not. He was a man, as his life until that time makes clear, who believed that sexual intercourse was the right and natural expression of romantic love. Now, after four years of emotional and sexual drought, he was in love, and every nerve of mind and body must have called for consummation. As for the adulterous aspect of the situation, he had been in Paris long enough to take a more relaxed view than formerly—he hardly had a French friend who was not involved in an extramarital liaison of some kind—and he knew by now that Richard Cosway had been extravagantly unfaithful to Maria.

What about her? Unquestionably, she was flattered and pleased to have this famous and attractive American showering her with attention, and she was not unresponsive. For her, however, there were obstacles. In spite of her husband's nonchalant attitude she knew that he was proud, and capable of great cruelty when he felt ignored or disdained—and he was almost entirely in control of her material welfare. Maria was an enormously successful hostess and social luminary in London, and her musical and artistic talents were widely praised; but her lavish lifestyle depended on Richard Cosway's money. It would be risky to make him angry. Beyond that, she was a devout Catholic—as a teenager in Italy she had yearned to become a nun, until her English Protestant mother whisked her safely off to live in London. Beneath her outwardly flirtatious manner, the impulse toward celibacy apparently lingered, and a forward glance at her later life lessens the likelihood that she did succumb to Jefferson's advances that summer. Although she eventually bore a child to Cosway after a complaining pregnancy, she was a rather negligent mother, and soon deserted the infant to run off on a European tour for several months in 1790. Significantly, her traveling companion was not a lover but a eunuch—a famous castrato named Luigi Marchesi, who had an extraordinarily beautiful soprano voice. After that she tried unsuccessfully to enter a convent, and lived out her life in Italy as the founder of a convent school for girls. All told, her career suggests a somnolent libido that was no match for Jefferson's virility, and perhaps explains to a considerable extent what happened—or, rather, failed to happen—between them. It was quite probably a case of unrequited lust.

Blissfully unaware of these things in the summer of 1786, Jefferson pursued his doomed romance. Although he had been fond of English poetry in his youth, he had paid it little attention since. Now, stimulated by his intensely lyrical feelings for Maria, he took to browsing through a big anthology of British verse, picking out (he said) "the most pregnant passages, those wherein every word teems with latent meaning." Whether he was a bit embarrassed to find himself doing this, or whether a scholarly approach had simply become habitual, he disguised the exercise as "Thoughts on English Prosody"—a subject on which he was by no means an expert. The result was a series of quoted passages that, while certainly pregnant with clues about Jefferson's emotional state, fall notably short as a bouquet of great love poems—for instance:

With her how I stray'd amid fountains and bowers!
Or loiter'd behind, and collected the flowers!
Then breathless with ardor my fair one pursued,
And to think with what kindness my garland she view'd!

This, though pretty awful, at least sounds optimistic, but the next couplet hints at serious misgivings:

But be still, my fond heart! this emotion give o'er;
Fain would'st thou forget thou must love her no more.

And the careless rapture of the amour was indeed to be roughly interrupted shortly after Jefferson finished his poetic survey. Out for a walk along the Seine with Maria on September 18, he was seized by a youthful impulse to jump an adjacent fence. Whether there was some practical reason for this or merely a wish to demonstrate his athleticism to Maria, he miscalculated, caught one foot, and went crashing to the ground on his right wrist. It hurt intensely and quickly began to swell; a French doctor who examined it soon after diagnosed a dislocation, and probably manipulated it to restore the alignment. But this failed to help, as the ensuing days painfully proved, and in retrospect modern medical opinion is that at least one bone had been fractured.

In any event the injury was slow to heal, and though the couple managed to see each other fairly soon, the bliss had been damaged along with the wrist. Richard Cosway, possibly annoyed by the solicitude that his wife exhibited for Jefferson, informed her that they would be leaving for London on October 5, willy-nilly. "Nothing seems redy [sic]," she told Jefferson in a despairing farewell note, "but Mr. Cosway seems more dispos'd than I have seen him all this time." They did not, in fact, leave until October 6, giving Jefferson enough time to pull himself together, ignore his

> Th: Jefferson 'o mrs Cosway
>
> I have passed the night in so much pain that I have not closed my eyes. it is with infinite regret therefore that I must relinquish your charming company for that of the Surgeon whom I have sent for to examine into the cause of this change. I am in hopes it is only the having rattled a little too freely over the pavement yesterday. if you do not go to day. I shall still have the pleasure of seeing you again. if you do, god bless you wherever you go. present me in the most friendly terms to mr Cosway, & let me hear of your safe arrival in England. Addio Addio.
>
> Thursday
>
> let me know if you do not go to day.

It has been presumed that because of the painful injury to his right wrist, Jefferson wrote this note to Maria, on October 5, 1786, with his left hand—though the awkward penmanship might have been an index of how much it hurt to use the right. Either way, he stuck to his stubborn habit of refusing to capitalize the first letter of a sentence unless it was "I"—perhaps in emulation of classical texts.

aching wrist, and see them on their journey as far as the faubourg St. Denis.

A pall of gloom descended on Jefferson as he watched the wheels of their departing carriage begin to turn. What had seemed a glimpse of paradise had vanished, and he was full of doubt as to whether it could ever be recaptured. But at least there was not the sense of absolute dissolution that had stricken him numb when Martha had died. He and Maria could write to each other, and perhaps keep the spark of their love alive until they might meet again.

He felt impelled to seek this consolation as soon as he got back to his fireside, plunging into the longest and most remarkable personal letter he was ever to write in his life. It would run on for nearly five thousand words—and every one of them, presumably, written with his left hand. (It would seem that he must always have been somewhat ambidextrous, for despite his remark at the time that the left hand was learning to perform the functions of the right "awkwardly and slowly," there was nothing clumsy about the very readable script that it produced.)

This lengthy composition—which kept him laboring for a whole week—was as close to belles lettres as Thomas Jefferson ever came. He cast it as a dialogue "between my Head and my Heart," and he obviously hoped to impress Maria with the elegance of his prose. Along with rhapsodic recollections of their wondrous days together and almost fulsome citations of her beauty and charm, it attempted to be the kind of rambling, digressive rumination that Laurence Sterne, his favorite fiction writer, had spun off with such facile and witty eloquence; but it did not flow easily from Jefferson's quill, and the result was a rather stiff and even slightly tedious document.

Nevertheless, "My Head and My Heart," as it has come to be called, is an obviously sincere and poignant expression of his love for Maria Cosway. She was gone, leaving him in a wallow of despair and sexual frustration, and John Trumbull, the young confidant who might best have understood his woe, was no longer in Paris. There was nobody to tell his troubles to except Maria herself—and even with her he had to be circumspect, since there was the chilling possibility that her husband's eyes might scan his impassioned essay. So he mustered up as much control over his turbulent feelings as he could, and did his best to reinforce this with his imagined dialogue.

True to the psychological ambivalence of the author, the Head argues for a rational analysis of every situation, no matter how alluring, and a stoical avoidance of any pleasure that may have painful consequences, while the Heart insists that more often than not the pleasures of human sentiment and sympathy and love are well worth their attendant pains.

"Let the gloomy Monk," declaims the Heart, "sequestered from the world, seek unsocial pleasures in the bottom of his cell! Let the sublimated philosopher grasp visionary happiness while pursuing phantoms dressed in the garb of truth! . . . they mistake for happiness the mere absence of pain. Had they ever felt the solid pleasure of one generous spasm of the heart, they would exchange for it all the frigid speculations of their lives."

In particular, the Heart continues—speaking well for the ethical philosophy of Thomas Jefferson—the realm of morals belongs to taste and feeling rather than to calculation and logic:

When nature assigned us the same habitation, she gave us over it a divided empire. To you [the Head] she allotted the field of science, to me that of morals . . . Morals were too essential to the happiness of man to be risked on the incertain combinations of the head. She laid their foundation therefore in sentiment, not in science.

Applying this triumphant defeat of the Head to Thomas Jefferson's relationship with Maria, the Heart (which is given the entire last four pages of the debate) declares that in spite of gnawing doubt about the likelihood of her return to France, "when I look back on the pleasures of which it is the consequence, I am conscious they were worth the price I am paying." And the dialogue closes on a hopeful note: the lady had said, after all, that she would come back in the spring, "and I should love her forever, were it only for that!"

There is little doubt that Jefferson awaited Maria's reply with exquisite emotional suspense. He probably hoped that his rhetorical subtleties would convey not only his passion for her, but his longing to find in her the kind of mental compatibility that he had so fondly shared with his wife. Unfortunately, intense sexual desire can sometimes make a rhapsody out of a jingle: an intellectual but fervent lover can construe as a marriage of true minds what turns out to be a hopeless mismatch.

And sure enough, Maria's answer to "My Head and My Heart" was as limp as a collapsed balloon. It was suddenly clear that she was not capable of being won by philosophical discourse, however imbued with emotion: she had been mostly just baffled by the great dialogue. The first one-third of her reply was in stumbling and nearly incoherent English. "Your letter," she wrote in the most lucid passage, "could employ me for some time, an hour to Consider every word, to every sentence I could write a volume . . . Why do you say so many kind things? Why present so many opportunities for my feeling undeserving of them? Why not leave me a free consolation in admiring a friend, without temptation to my Vanity?" She does realize she's doing badly: she abruptly shifts into Italian for the rest of her letter, explaining rather winningly, *"non sapevo cosa facevo"*—"I didn't know what I was doing." But even in Italian she shows no sign of having really understood

Jefferson's artful love missive, going on instead about the melancholy mood induced in her by the dismal London weather; she has almost nothing to say about missing him or about nostalgia for their intimate hours together in Paris, and finishes with a conventional flourish that Jefferson could have done without: *"Mio Marito gli fa Mille Complimente"*—"My husband sends you a thousand compliments."

Even allowing for the now obvious problem of the language barrier, these were hardly the effusions of a passionate mistress, and the fact that Jefferson did not reply for over two weeks suggests a considerable cooling in his ardor. Nevertheless, he still palpably missed the physical reality of her company—perhaps if he could get her back in person it would restore the magic dissipated by her letter. "I am determined when you come next," he wrote her on November 29, "not to admit the idea that we are ever to part again." Meanwhile, he urged her to send him letters more expressive of the feelings that he still fondly hoped she harbored: "Write to me often, write affectionately and freely, as I do to you. Say many kind things and without reserve."

Instead, Maria got off a long epistle on New Year's Day that was a model of muddled vacuity. Most of the first half was a verbose complaint about not having heard from him for "a century"; the rest wavers between an account of how sensitive and "susceptible" she is, especially to "melancholy," and of how much she nevertheless enjoys her painting and her music. The whole thing was in Italian, which Jefferson could read reasonably well, though in this case he may have doubted that it was worth the effort. In any event he was unusually busy during the first part of January with stressful correspondence concerning the enormous debt that he owed to British bankers—much of it inherited from his father-in-law, John Wayles—and with his responsibilities as the American minister to France. Maria's letter was not answered.

He needed a change of scene, and by February had decided to make a long journey through southern France, partly in the hope of healing his injured wrist in the "waters" of Aix-en-Provence, but also to learn all he could about the agriculture and industry of the region. His trip was delayed by one thing and another, including important shifts in the political situation in France, which he was under some obligation to observe. The economy of the country was in a very shaky condition: there was a staggering national debt, and the government was near bankruptcy.

With a view to convincing the restive public that something was being done, the king approved the calling of an Assembly of Notables—about a hundred and fifty of the nation's supposedly most distinguished men—to discuss reforms that might avert a catastrophic economic crisis. This group was composed almost entirely of aristocrats—dukes, marquis, counts, archbishops—and it has usually been regarded by historians as one of the last maneuvers of the Old Regime in France to hang on to its power. But recently it has been argued that in fact, despite its aristocratic character, the Assembly of Notables was quite radical in the economic and political reforms that were proposed and discussed, as if its members accurately sensed that fundamental changes in the government of the nation were inevitable and imminent. Almost as a token of this, among their number was the Marquis de Lafayette, whose outspoken yearning for democracy had seriously alarmed the king and Marie-Antoinette.

Presumably it was through his connection with Lafayette that Jefferson was invited to attend the opening session, on February 22, 1787. He was eager to get started on his trip, but he did go to the session—and reported to Abigail Adams, rather skeptically: "The most remarkable effect of this convention as yet is the number of puns and bon mots it has generated." His delay also brought him, shortly before his departure, by far the longest letter he had received from Maria Cosway. Unfortunately, the length did not improve its quality: it was in labored and often incoherent English, and maundered along absentmindedly for several pages, somehow managing to convey almost nothing of interest. Jefferson set it aside, and it seems likely that it was the benumbing effect of this letter that explains his failure to send Maria a single line during a tour that lasted three and a half months, though he corresponded with many other people.

5
Sunny Interlude

————— •◆• —————

I n any event, Jefferson set out in an apparently cheerful mood
on February 28, leaving diplomatic affairs in the capable hands
of young William Short, his secretary. His itinerary was not
very unusual: down through central France and Provence to
Marseilles on the Mediterranean, along the Riviera and briefly
into northwestern Italy (crossing the Alps en route), back through
Provence, westward to Toulouse and Bordeaux, north into
Brittany, and home to Paris by way of the chateau country around
Tours. He figured the total distance as "upwards of a thousand
leagues"—about three thousand miles.

But though his itinerary was ordinary, Jefferson was a most
extraordinary traveler. Anyone interested in his character can learn
a lot from the forty-plus pages of meticulous notes he recorded as
he traveled, and from the many letters—some of them very long—
that he sent to friends and to his daughter. Patsy, disappointed at
not having heard from him after over a week had gone by, wrote
that although she hoped his wrist was better, she was "inclined to
think that your voyage is rather for your pleasure than for your
health." She was right, the more so since after numerous treat-
ments at Aix, Jefferson found no improvement in his wrist; but

what is striking is how strenuous a regimen of pleasure he prescribed for himself throughout the trip.

Dawdling was out. He was acutely aware that this was a unique opportunity "to see what I have never seen before and shall never see again," as he said in his first letter to Lafayette: "In the great cities, I go to see what travellers think alone worthy of being seen; but I make a job of it, and generally gulp it all down in a day. On the other hand, I am never satiated with rambling through the fields and farms, examining the culture and cultivators, with a degree of curiosity which makes some take me to be a fool, and others to be much wiser than I am." Then, after a detailed critique of farming methods in Champagne and Burgundy, he urges Lafayette to make a similar journey—"And to do it most effectually you must be absolutely incognito, you must ferret the people out of their hovels as I have done, look into their kettles, eat their bread, loll on their beds under pretence of resting yourself, but in fact to find if they are soft." And he closes with a farewell that is in refreshing contrast to the conventional "humble servant" formula of the period: "I content myself . . . with saying once for all that I love you, your wife and children. Tell them so and Adieu. Your's [*sic*] affectionately, Th. Jefferson."

A chief motive behind his intense interest in French agriculture is revealed in a letter to his old friend Philip Mazzei, from Marseilles early in April: "I find here several interesting articles of culture: the best figs, the best grape for drying, a smaller one for the same purpose without a seed . . . Olives, capers, Pistachio nuts, almonds. All these articles may succeed on, or Southward of the Chesapeake." As always, he was paying attention to whatever in European culture he thought might be beneficial to his own country if introduced there.

Heading his list in that regard was the olive. He was struck by its adaptability, growing well even in Alpine areas where "there is not soil enough to make bread for a single family," and he became a lifelong enthusiast for the idea of its cultivation in the American South. The wonders of virgin olive oil in garnishing salads and enhancing other culinary efforts impressed him deeply, and after his return to Monticello he imported it regularly by the gallon. (His dream of making olive orchards as common as cotton fields in America was doomed, however, by a factor he surprisingly ignored: the humidity of the southeastern states was too high for olives to flourish there.)

He was determined among other things to find out why rice from northern Italy was of better quality than that grown in America, suspecting that a better type of machine was used for cleaning it. With typical Jeffersonian tenacity, he set out across the Alps, traveling on the back of a mule through the still snowy high passes, and registering appropriate amazement at some of the snow-tipped vistas, which (it had to be admitted) were somewhat grander than anything to be seen in the Blue Ridge of Virginia. He found the best rice in Lombardy, near Milan; but the cleaning machine used was, surprisingly, "absolutely the same as ours": it was the quality of the rice itself that made the difference. Learning that exportation of this rice was forbidden "on pain of death," he decided to take the risk for his country, stuffing enough into the big pockets of his coat to send later to America for seed purposes.

But Jefferson's particular passion, during his entire journey, was to study the vineyards and wines of the regions he passed through. The record he kept of his investigation is quite amazing in its thoroughness and precision, going into great detail, for instance, with regard to the effect of different soils on the character of the local grapes and wines; the various methods of planting, supporting, and harvesting the wines; the comparative yields of one well-known vineyard and another; the fluctuation of vintage quality from one year to the next, together with probable explanations in terms of weather; the wholesale and retail prices fetched by the most acclaimed varieties of reds and whites; the cost of transportation to the most lucrative markets—and last but far from least, the crucial questions of the bouquet, body, and taste on tongue and palate attributable to each. Here, of course, the empirical approach was absolutely required, and the inquisitive American seems to have sampled so many varieties of Burgundy, Sauterne, Barsac, Médoc, Graves, Beaujolais, and so on, that it is to be wondered whether his comparative judgments were occasionally tilted one way or the other by the pleasant inebriation of the judge.

Altogether, he seems to have had a wonderful time. During most of his journey the climate delighted him: "I am now in the land of corn, wine, oil, and sunshine," he wrote William Short

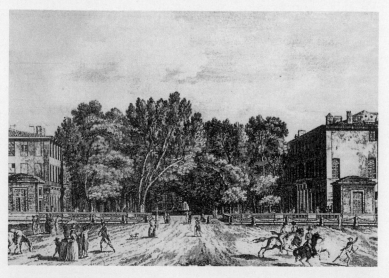

The principal entrance to Aix-en-Provence as it looked about the time of Jefferson's visit there: an engraving from the travel volume Voyage Pittoresque de la France, *c. 1784.*

from Aix-en-Provence. "What more can a man ask of heaven? If I should happen to die at Paris, I will beg of you to send me here, and have me exposed to the sun. I am sure it will bring me to life again."

Did he have any erotic encounters along the way? If so he left no hint of it, and the presumption is that he did not. In all his life, although he showed evidence of a very lively libido, he was never a man for casual, anonymous flings, and certainly the lure of the prostitute was not for him. He was by himself most of the time, but showed few signs of feeling lonely; in fact he clearly enjoyed the relative solitude. "I was alone thro the whole," he wrote a friend later, "and think one travels more usefully when alone because he reflects more." He was not, in fact, totally alone: what he meant was that he had no traveling companion of his own class. What he did have was a valet whom he hired at Dijon, who followed wherever he went and evidently kept quiet—at least Jefferson recorded nothing of any conversations, democratic or otherwise, between them. This went well with the role he apparently took pleasure in playing: the rather mysterious foreigner, on a solo mission of unknown purpose. "I have derived as much satisfaction and even delight from my journey as I could propose to myself," he wrote Short on March 15. "The plan of having servants who know nothing of me, places me perfectly at my ease."

Jefferson was, of course, one of the greatest correspondents of all time—some eighteen thousand of his letters exist—and a favorite amusement, when he was settled for the night at an inn, was to write to one of his women friends back in Paris. These for the most part were not very serious communications, and he did his best to be diverting. To Madame de Tott, a cultivated friend of the Lafayettes with whom he had discussed contemporary painting and ancient Greek literature, he got off on April 5 a long composition in the manner of Laurence Sterne:

A traveller, sais I, retired at night to his chamber in an Inn, all his effects contained in a single trunk, all his cares circumscribed by the walls of his apartment, unknown to all, unheeded, and undisturbed, writes, reads, thinks, sleeps, just in the moments when nature and the movements of his body and mind require. Charmed with the tranquility of his little cell, he finds how few are our real wants, how cheap a thing is happiness, how expensive a one pride. He views with pity the wretched rich, whom the laws of the world have submitted to the cumbrous trappings of rank . . . He wonders that a thinking mind can be so subdued by opinion, and that he does not run away from his own crouded [*sic*] house, and take refuge in the chamber of an Inn.

This idyllic scene is somewhat compromised a bit further along in his letter by a flight of humorous hyperbole revealing the actual situation at the auberge where he is chambered at the moment:

Four thousand three hundred and fifty market-women (I have counted them one by one) brawling, squabbling, and jabbering Patois, three hundred asses braying and bewailing to each other, and to the world, their cruel oppressions, four files of mule-carts passing in constant succession, with as many bells to every mule as can be hung about him, all this in the street under my window, and the weather too hot to shut it.

Madame de Tessé (the aunt of Lafayette's wife, but only a couple of years older than Jefferson) was honored by a long letter from her American friend that made (for him) the remarkable concession of seriously discussing political matters with a female—his proposal for the organization of a French national assembly. He began his letter, however, with something that he undoubtedly thought more suitable: an expression of the admiration they shared for objects of classical "antiquity," in this case those at the old Roman city of Nîmes:

> Here I am, Madam, gazing whole hours at the Maison quarrée, like a lover at his mistress . . . This is the second time I have been in love since I left Paris. The first was with a Diana at the Chateau de Laye Epinaye in the Beaujolais, a delicious morsel of sculpture, by Michael Angelo Slodtz.

This rather baroque sculpture was no antiquity, having been made less than half a century earlier, but it sharply piqued Jefferson's aesthetic sense and very likely his erotic sense as well. Commenting on it to William Short, he said that "it carries the perfection of the chisel to a degree of which I had no conception." The moment depicted, however, suggests that he may have been stirred as much by the sculpture's content as by its form: it shows the goddess Diana (or Artemis) making one of her nightly visits to her beloved Endymion, who (according to myth) fathered some fifty of her children—a neat trick, since he had been put eternally to sleep by Jupiter (or Zeus) to preserve his youthful beauty, and it all supposedly took place without waking him up.

While he was giving a lot of time and attention to his private interests and pleasures, Jefferson was not neglecting his responsibilities as the American minister to France. Short kept him well informed of what was going on in Paris, and he stayed in touch with developments in the United States through detailed accounts sent by his friend James Madison. His correspondence with Short, however, shows how much their relationship went beyond merely that of a good secretary to his superior. They shared a natural rapport as well as genuine fondness: in many ways it was almost as if

The sculpture at the Chateau de Laye Epinaye that Jefferson was so taken with, done by Michael Angelo Slodtz about 1740.

Short were the grown son that Jefferson never had. Their frequent letters were relaxed and informal and often leavened with droll or ironic asides, as for instance Jefferson's comment on a theatrical performance he attended at Aix featuring "the most celebrated actress from Marseilles . . . She is moreover young and handsome, and has an advantage over . . . some other of the celebrated ones [actresses] of Paris, in being clear of that dreadful wheeze or rather whistle in respiration which resembles the agonizing struggles for breath in a dying person."

One of Short's duties during Jefferson's absence was to visit

Patsy at her convent school and keep track of her health and disposition. It was almost unnecessary, since she sent her father several charming letters reporting on that as well as her progress—or lack thereof—in her studies. He wrote her loving replies; yet he seemed to be parentally incapable, as soon as he had put down the words "My dear Patsy," of not donning his didactic cap and delivering a quite tiresome homily on how she ought to behave:

> You know what have been my fears for some time past; that you do not employ yourself so closely as I could wish . . . Of all the cankers of human happiness, none corrodes it with so silent, yet so baneful a tooth, as indolence . . . Idleness begets ennui, ennui the hypochondria, and that a diseased body. No laborious person was ever yet hysterical . . . We are always equal to what we undertake with resolution . . . It is part of the American character to consider nothing as desperate; to surmount every difficulty by resolution and contrivance.

If Patsy had hoped for entertaining descriptions of his experiences as a traveler in a fascinating part of the country, she was repeatedly disappointed. She took it cheerfully, however, assuring him that "I have already begun to study more . . . As for the hysterics, you may be quiet on that head, as I am not lazy enough to fear them." She also exhibited a kind of biting humor rather like his own, throwing in such observations as, "There was a gentleman, a few days ago, that killed himself because he thought that his wife did not love him. They had been married ten years. I believe that if every husband in Paris was to do as much, there would be nothing but widows left." And now and then she would make a remark that must have startled and disturbed her father, such as this in a letter of May 3: "I wish with all my soul that the poor negroes were all freed. It grieves my heart when I think that these our fellow creatures should be treated so teribly [*sic*] as they are by many of our country men."

By the middle of May, Jefferson was launched upon what he soon realized was in many ways the most delightful stretch of his itinerary, the two-hundred-mile trip through the Canal of Languedoc, from the edge of the Mediterranean to Toulouse. He explained to Short:

> I dismounted my carriage from its wheels, placed it on the deck of a light bark, and was thus towed on the canal . . . Of all the methods of travelling I have ever tried this is the

Patsy Jefferson at the age of sixteen—a miniature portrait painted in Paris by Joseph Boze.

pleasantest. I walk the greater part of the way along the banks of the canal . . . When fatigued I take seat in my carriage where, as much at ease as if in my study, I read, write, or observe. My carriage being of glass all round, admits a full view of all the varying scenes thro' which I am shifted, olives, figs, mulberries, vines, corn and pasture, villages and farms. I have had some days of superb weather . . . cloudless skies and limpid waters . . . a double row of nightingales along the banks of the canal, in full song.

A few days later, having encountered at Bordeaux a Captain Gregory, who was about to sail for Virginia, Jefferson decided to send as a gift to his brother-in-law Francis Eppes "a specimen of what is the very best Bordeaux wine." He was not a man to make a parsimonious gesture: the "specimen" consisted of six dozen bottles.

6
End of an Affair

— • ◆ • —

Back home in Paris in mid-June, Jefferson found a pile of unanswered correspondence—with Maria Cosway's last letter, written four months earlier, prominently among them. He was extremely busy, but on July 1 found time to get off a kind of ex-post-facto "wish you were here" message, rather ineptly citing the pictorial delights of the Italian Alps and expressing profound regret that she had not been with him to paint the scenery. With what sounds like slightly forced joviality, he attempts to revive the ambiance of their 1786 summer romance: "Come then, my dear Madam, and we will breakfast every day a l'Angloise, hie away to the Desert [a romantic "Chinese" garden, complete with "ruins" made to fit the space], dine under the bowers of Marly, and forget that we are ever to part again." He closes by exhorting her to send him another letter—"but lengthy, warm, and flowing from the heart." Unhappily, as he was beginning to discover, this was a kind of letter Maria was incapable of, even in Italian.

What he got instead on this occasion was a note deliberately written (as she points out) on a small sheet of paper to prevent its being longer—although in fact it is quite garrulous. "Do you deserve a long letter ... No, certainly not ... How Many

Months was you without writing to me? And you felt no remorse?" She then shifts to Italian, reminding him that she is well aware of the beauties of her native Italy, and adding that her coming soon to Paris is doubtful, since it seems contrary to Mr. Cosway's inclination.

But Jefferson was too excited by something more important to pay much attention to this just then. His little daughter Polly, whom he had been longing to have with him and Patsy in Paris, had finally arrived in London and was staying with John and Abigail Adams, waiting for him to come and get her. Polly, not quite nine years old, appears to have been an exceedingly charming but rather willful sprite. She had not wanted to go to France, having been very happy with Jefferson's sister-in-law Elizabeth Eppes; yet by the time the ship reached England she was so attached to its master, Captain Andrew Ramsay, that she didn't want him out of her sight—"and indeed," the captain wrote to Jefferson from London, "I am almost the same way with her." The little enchantress soon cast her spell over Abigail too. "Her temper, her disposition, her sensibility are all formed for delight," wrote that lady of strict standards; and even sober John was moved to superlatives: "In my life I never saw a more charming Child."

Abigail, John, and Polly were all surprised and displeased to hear from Jefferson that he was not coming to London himself to get Polly, instead dispatching his French maître d', Petit, to escort her back to Paris. Abigail, hoping to change his mind, sent him a description of Polly's reaction to Petit's arrival: after "bursting into Tears," she said "that as she had left all her Friends in virginia [*sic*] to come over the ocean to see you, she did think you would have taken the pains to come here for her, and not have sent a man whom she cannot understand. I express her own words. . . ."

Jefferson was still adamant, insisting that he was too busy to come. There was probably some truth in this, but there may have been another reason. He had avoided telling Maria Cosway that Polly was in London, but as he learned from her, she had heard about it anyhow. It would have been very difficult for him to go there without dealing face to face with her. He surely did not want that complicating and delaying Polly's trip to Paris—and at this point he may have felt less than eager to see Maria at all.

By the middle of July, Polly was on the Champs Élysées—refusing to admit to any recognition of her sister, and dubious about her father, but otherwise making a quick adjustment to her strange new surroundings. Jefferson soon had her enrolled at the convent school with Patsy—considerably to Abigail Adams's Protestant disapproval—where she promptly began to enjoy herself, showing an easy aptitude for picking up French. Jefferson's weekends *chez lui* were now doubly delightful, since the girls were allowed to come home for Saturday and Sunday.

Meanwhile his relationship with Maria Cosway continued to be peppery. Shortly after her peevish "small sheet" note, he received one from John Trumbull in London that ended: "Mrs. Cosway desires me to close my letter—dinner is on table and she half starv'd. I must therefore bid you adieu." Whether or not Jefferson had realized how much time Trumbull and Maria were currently spending together, he had learned that back in October, on those very days when he was agonizing over the composition of "My Head and My Heart," the two of them had been breezing happily around Antwerp buying paintings—having met there by chance as the Cosways slowly made their way home to London from Paris.

Jealousy was a pang of the Heart that Jefferson would gladly have submitted to the domination of the Head, but he was not superhuman. Instead of answering Maria's note he answered Trumbull's, winding up curtly with "My love to Mrs. Cosway. Tell her I will send her a supply of larger paper."

John Trumbull, painted by his fellow American artist Samuel Lovett Waldo.

The record shows no further written communication between them that summer, but near the end of August, Maria appeared in person in Paris—and this time without her husband. There is evidence that she and Jefferson got together now and then during the ensuing fall, but nothing like as often as they had the previous year—"only by scraps," as he phrased it. Writing to Trumbull in November, he explained it as bad luck: "she has happened to be from home several times when I have called on her, and I when she has called on me." But something else was at work also. The drive of erotic passion, which had energized their meetings in 1786—at least on Jefferson's part—evidently had dwindled. Maria, however impassive she may have been sexually, seems to have found this disturbing, for nothing mattered more to her socially than being admired and adored. Possibly in compensation, she kept a kind of ongoing salon at her summer residence and studio, and Jefferson, when he did call on her, usually had to put up with a swarm of human lepidoptera about whom he cared nothing.

And so the autumn drifted away with the falling leaves, and

their quasi–love affair too lost its color and vitality. On the seventh of December, the night before she was to return to London, they met for a farewell evening together, but something untoward—it has never been clear just what—happened, and they parted with Maria (as she put it later) "confus'd and distracted."

At the last moment they agreed to meet the next morning for breakfast, so that Jefferson could then see her on her way. He kept the appointment, but found her already gone, leaving him only a brief note: "I cannot breakfast with you . . . to bid you adieu once is sufficiently painful, for I leave you with very melancholy ideas. You have given my dear Sir all your commissions to Mr. Trumbull, and I have the reflection that I cannot be useful to you; who have rendered me so many civilities."

They were never to see each other again. They did not know this, of course, any more than the rest of us who, unblessed (or uncursed) with foreknowledge, have watched a familiar face disappear for what turns out, unexpectedly, to have been the last time. Letters were to pass between them, sparsely and sporadically, for years to come, but the affair Jefferson-Cosway was essentially over.

7

A Big Surprise: Sally Hemings

⬧•⬧

When Abigail Adams welcomed Jefferson's eight-year-old daughter Polly into her London home in late June 1787, she was surprised to discover that the child was not accompanied by the "old Nurse" who had been expected—that is, a slave woman of mature years. Instead, there appeared a light-skinned, very pretty adolescent girl—"about 15 or 16," Abigail thought. Her name was Sally.

Mrs. Adams's reaction to Sally is interesting, especially in view of her censorious attitude toward the openly sexual ambiance of Paris and her tendency to be protective of her friend Jefferson. Like any alert American of the period, she was familiar with accounts of sexual relations between plantation masters and their slave women, and Sally's beige complexion guaranteed that there had been racial mixing in her background. Moreover, the most sensible interpretation of Abigail's overestimate of Sally's age—for she was in fact only fourteen—is that the girl was already physically a woman, with well-developed breasts that must have been obvious despite her nondescript shipboard attire. It must have made Mrs. Adams nervous to think of this nubile creature living under the same roof in Paris with a master who, she was aware, loved attractive young women and had been without a sexual partner (as far as she knew) for a long time now.

Being Abigail, she took action, or at least made a stab at it. She found a willing ally in Captain Ramsay, who had just spent over a month aboard his ship in close company with Polly and Sally—his only female passengers. After consulting with him, she sat down and wrote Jefferson to bring him up to date on Polly's state of mind, which had changed from miserable to contented overnight. "The Girl who is with her," she went on, "is quite a child, and Captain Ramsay is of opinion will be of so little Service that he had better carry her back with him." At this point Abigail must have realized that she was close to overstepping her proper role: "But of this," she quickly added, "you will be the judge. She [Sally] seems fond of the child and appears good natur'd."

Sally had explained to Mrs. Adams that she was the sister of James Hemings, the young slave who had come to France with Jefferson and his oldest daughter, Patsy, in 1784; and it is an index of Abigail's apparent apprehension about having Sally join the household in Paris that—although she was a staunch advocate of what today are called "family values"—she was so ready to block a brother-sister reunion that undoubtedly had been anticipated with approval by Betty Hemings, their mother. As for Captain Ramsay, since he had become quite familiar with Sally's attractions on the eastward crossing, his willingness to take her with him on the slow voyage back to Virginia may have had sincere motivations beyond his concern for how much she might be "of service" to Mr. Jefferson on the Champs Élysées.

But Jefferson made no move to follow Abigail's suggestion. He knew, of course, that Sally would be eager to see her brother James; and he may have had a good inkling of Captain Ramsay's

This engraving of a Gilbert Stuart portrait of Abigail Adams transmits a wonderful sense of her character.

special interest, even though Sally had been only eleven years old when Jefferson last saw her. A fond father, he must have been watching with fascination as Patsy, who was almost the same age as Sally, went through that astonishing metamorphosis that the years between eleven and fifteen bring about in a healthy young girl. What would Sally look like now?

Abigail, probably disgruntled but certainly goodhearted, accepted the failure of her ploy, and having decided that both Polly and Sally were in need of some new clothes before going off to Paris, proceeded to buy the necessary material, have the garments made, and send Jefferson a carefully itemized list of her expenses. It would have added a significant footnote to history if she had also recorded Sally's measurements.

We have no account, from Jefferson or anyone else, of Sally's first impressions of life in Paris—for despite the fact that she was literally a member of the family, being, incongruously, Patsy's and Polly's half-aunt, she was still a slave, joining her brother in those muted shadows that dim so much of American black history.

Yet this categorical disregard does not leave a total blank. In this case we know so much about the key circumstances that reasonable conjectures can be made to help visualize the scene at the Hôtel de Langeac, Jefferson's comfortable Paris mansion, in the days and weeks following Sally's arrival. It can be taken for granted that she had a lively reunion with James, with much talk about recent doings in Virginia; and Jefferson himself, who was everlastingly complaining that none of his American correspondents told him enough "facts, little facts, such as . . . every one imagines beneath notice," undoubtedly quizzed her at length along similar lines. We know that Patsy and Polly were away at boarding school five days each week, so that Sally's duties as a personal maid were minimal, leaving her free for general household chores. And we can assume, certainly, that her master, one of the most curious and observant of beings, paid close attention to the new member of his Parisian ménage.

In considering the relationship between Jefferson and Sally Hemings, most biographers have paid insufficient attention, I think, to the probability that some of her traits, of both appearance and character, were reminiscent of her half-sister, Jefferson's greatly beloved wife. Sibling similarities often tend to grow more striking as adolescence ripens childish features into adult, a process that would naturally have been in full spring during Sally's first months in Paris. Add to this picture her well-attested beauty, her evidently lively personality (she was known around her home plantation as "Dashing Sally"), and the fact that she was very light-skinned, and some idea emerges of the spell that her daily presence may have cast on her master. On top of all this, she *belonged* to him—a thought that he could hardly have kept out of his head.

It is also relevant to bear in mind that Jefferson was only forty-four when Sally arrived in Paris. Prominent biographers, led by Dumas Malone, have insisted on calling him "middle-aged" at this juncture, with the implication that his days of sexual vigor were behind him. But certainly this runs counter to most studies of human sexuality as well as to the common experience of most men in their mid-forties.

At any rate, there she was, living in his house, eating the food he provided and her brother prepared, wearing the clothes he bought her, becoming each day a more familiar part of his life as she—what?—watered plants, dusted furniture, brought refreshments on hot summer days, did some sewing, began to learn a little French, sang new Virginia songs with Polly on weekends as Patsy played the harpsichord? These are homely likelihoods; but over all there very probably hovered, for both of them, the intoxicating aura of sexual possibility.

When it comes to a question of a long sexual connection between a man and a woman, little evidence is more persuasive than the woman's concurrent production of offspring. During the thirty-six years that she lived at Monticello after their return from France and before Jefferson's death in 1826, Sally Hemings had five children whose births were noted in the plantation journal Jefferson kept, which he called his Farm Book. One of them, a boy named Madison who was freed by Jefferson's will, in 1836 moved with his wife and one child to Pike County, Ohio, where he worked as a skilled carpenter for many years. In 1873, at the age of sixty-eight, he was interviewed by the editor of a local paper, the *Pike County Republican*, for one of a series of first-person articles about the lives of "colored people," most of them former slaves, who had emigrated from Virginia. The piece resulting from this, published on March 13, 1873, contained the only direct assertion from a participant, so to speak, that Thomas Jefferson was the father of all of Sally Hemings's children.

It hardly needs saying that the Virginia historians have regarded this document with great alarm. Until Fawn Brodie republished it for the first time in a century, as an appendix to her 1974 biography of Jefferson, their tendency was either to ignore it or to say as little as possible about it—and that little was mostly derogatory. Since Brodie spotlighted it, however, any respectable discussion of the Jefferson-Hemings relationship must give careful consideration to Madison Hemings's autobiographical account.

Madison begins by explaining that his great-grandmother was "a full-blooded African" who was the property of John Wayles, and his great-grandfather a "Capt. Hemings," master of an English whaler "which sailed between England and Williamsburg, Va." The child born of this connection was Betty Hemings, who "grew to womanhood in the family of John Wa[y]les, whose wife dying she . . . was taken by the widower . . . as his concubine, by whom she had six children—three sons and three daughters . . . Robert, James, Peter, Critty, Sally and Thena. These children went by the name of Hemings."

Madison goes on to tell, with rather charming vagueness, how Thomas Jefferson became "a visitor" at John Wayles's "great house" and "formed the acquaintance" of his white daughter Martha—"I believe that was her name, though I am not positively sure"—how they fell in love and were married and "went to live at his country seat Monticello, and in course of time had born to them a daughter whom they named Martha [Patsy]. About the time she was born my mother [Sally], the second daughter of John Wa[y]les and Elizabeth [Betty] Hemings was born. On the death of John Wa[y]les [1773], my grandmother [Betty Hemings] . . . and her children by him fell to Martha, Thomas Jefferson's wife, and consequently became the property of Thomas Jefferson . . . "

Moving ahead rapidly, Madison mentions the death of Jefferson's wife and his appointment as minister to France, and how he took Patsy with him to Paris; Polly, he explains, "was left at home, but was afterwards ordered to follow him to France . . . My mother accompanied her as her body servant . . . Their stay . . . was about eighteen months." (In actuality it was a little over two years, from June 1787 to September 1789.) And now comes the quietly explosive statement:

But during that time my mother became Mr. Jefferson's concubine, and when he was called back home she was *enceinte* by him. He desired to bring my mother back to Virginia with him but she demurred. She was just beginning to understand the French language well, and in France she was free, while if she returned to Virginia she would be re-enslaved. So she refused to return with him. To induce her to do so he promised her extraordinary privileges, and made a solemn

Opposite: Madison Hemings's interview in the Pike County Republican, *March 13, 1873. This is the complete interview, word-for-word as published. The three columns on the original page of the newspaper, however, were extremely uneven in length, the middle one being more than twice as long as either of the others, so in this reproduction they have been rearranged to make three equal columns. (It's all legible, if you have good eyesight or a reading glass.)*

Pike County Republican.

WAVERLY, MARCH 13, 1873.

Life Among the Lowly.

NUMBER I.

MADISON HEMINGS.

I never knew of but one white man who bore the name of Hemings; he was an Englishman and my greatgrandfather. He was captain of an English trading vessel which sailed between England and Williamsburg, Va., then quite a port. My grandmother was a fullblooded African, and possibly a native of that country. She was the property of John Wales, a Welchman. Capt. Hemings happened to be in the port of Williamsburg at the time my grandmother was born, and acknowledging her fatherhood he tried to purchase her of Mr. Wales, who would not part with the child, though he was offered an extraordinarily large price for her. She was named Elizabeth Hemings. Being thwarted in the purchase, and determining to own his flesh and blood he resolved to take the child by force or stealth, but the knowledge of his intention coming to John Wales' ears, through leaky fellow servants of the mother, she and the child were taken into the "great house" under their master's immediate care. I have been informed that it was not the extra value of that child over other slave children that induced Mr. Wales to refuse to sell it, for slave masters then, as in later days, had no compunctions of conscience which restrained them from parting mother and child of however tender age, but he was restrained by the fact that just about that time amalgamation began, and the child was so great a curiosity that its owner desired to raise it himself that he might see its outcome. Capt. Hemings soon afterwards sailed from Williamsburg, never to return. Such is the story that comes down to me.

Elizabeth Hemings grew to womanhood in the family of John Wales, whose wife dying she (Elizabeth) was taken by the widower Wales as his concubine, by whom she had six children—three sons and three daughters, viz: Robert, James, Peter, Critty, Sally and Thena. These children went by the name of Hemings.

Williamsburg was the capital of Virginia, and of course it was an aristocratic place, where the "bloods" of the Colony and the new State met did congregate. Thomas Jefferson, the author of the Declaration of Independence, was educated at William and Mary College, which had its seat at Williamsburg. He afterwards studied law with Geo. Wythe, and practiced law at the bar of the general court of the Colony. He was afterwards elected a member of the provincial legislature from Albemarle county. Thos. Jefferson was a visitor at the "great house" of John Wales, who had children about his own age. He formed the acquaintance of his daughter Martha (I believe that was her name, though I am not positively sure) and an intimacy sprang up between them which ripened into love, and they were married. They afterwards went to live at his country seat, Monticello, and in course of time had born to them a daughter whom they named Martha. About the time she was born my mother, the second daughter of John Wales and Elizabeth Hemings was born. On the death of John Wales, my grandmother, his concubine, and her children by him fell to Martha, Thomas Jefferson's wife, and consequently became the property of Thomas Jefferson, who in the course of time became famous, and was appointed minister to France during our revolutionary troubles, or soon after independence was gained. About the time of the appointment and before he was ready to leave the country his wife died, and as soon after her interment as he could attend to and arrange his domestic affairs in accordance with the changed circumstances of his family in consequence of this misfortune (I think not more than three weeks thereafter) he left for France, taking his eldest daughter with him. He had had sons born to him, but they died in early infancy, so he then had but two children—Martha and Maria. The latter was left at home, but was afterwards ordered to follow him to France. She was three years or so younger than Martha. My mother accompanied her as her body servant. When Mr. Jefferson went to France Martha was a young woman grown, my mother was about her age, and Maria was just budding into womanhood. Their stay (my mother and Maria's) was about eighteen months. But during that time my mother became Mr. Jefferson's concubine, and when he was called home she was enciente by him. He desired to bring my mother back to Virginia with him but she demurred. She was just beginning to understand the French language well, and in France she was free, while if she returned to Virginia she would be re-enslaved. So she refused to return with him. To induce her to do so he promised her extraordinary privileges, and made a solemn pledge that her children should be freed at the age of twenty-one years. In consequence of his promises, on which she implicitly relied, she returned with him to Virginia. Soon after their arrival, she gave birth to a child, of whom Thomas Jefferson was the father. It lived but a short time. She gave birth to four others, and Jefferson was the father of all of them. Their names were Beverly, Harriet, Madison (myself), and Eston—three sons and one daughter. We all became free agreeably to the treaty entered into by our parents before we were born. We all married and have raised families.

Beverly left Monticello and went to Washington as a white man. He married a white woman in Maryland, and their only child, a daughter, was not known by the white folks to have any colored blood coursing in her veins. Beverly's wife's family were people of good circumstances.

Harriet married a white man in good standing in Washington City, whose name I could give, but will not, for prudential reasons. She raised a family of children, and so far as I know they were never suspected of being tainted with African blood in the community where she lived or lives. I have not heard from her for ten years, and do not know whether she is dead or alive. She thought it to her interest, on going to Washington, to assume the rule of a white woman, and by her dress and conduct as such I am not aware that her marriage with Harriet Hemings of Monticello has ever been discovered.

Eston married a colored woman in Virginia, and oved from there to Ohio, and lived in Chillicothe several years. In the fall of 1852 he removed to Wisconsin, where he died a year or two afterwards. He left three children.

As to myself, I was named Madison by the wife of James Madison, who was afterwards President of the United States. Mrs. Madison happened to be at Monticello at the time of my birth, and begged the privilege of naming me, promising my mother a fine present for the honor. She consented, and Mrs. Madison dubbed me by the name I now acknowledge, but like many promises of white folks to the slaves she never gave my mother anything. I was born at my father's seat of Monticello, in Albemarle county, Va., near Charlottesville, on the 19th day of January, 1805. My very earliest recollections are of my grandmother Elizabeth Hemings. That was when I was about three years old. She was sick and upon her death bed. I was eating a piece of bread and asked her if she would have some. She replied: "No; granny don't want bread any more." She shortly afterwards breathed her last. I have only a faint recollection of her.

Of my father, Thomas Jefferson, I knew more of his domestic than his public life during his life time. It is only since his death that I have learned much of the latter, except that which I have learned from books, such as his acts as a public man. But since his death, and as I have grown older, and learned more of his public life, as connected with the affairs of this country, I have the more reason to honor and respect his memory. During his life my father was in the habit of showing particular affection to us as children. We were the only children of his by a slave woman. He was affectionate toward his white grandchildren, of whom he had fourteen, twelve of whom lived to manhood and womanhood. His daughter Martha married Thomas Mann Randolph by whom she had thirteen children. Two died in infancy. The names of the living were Ann, Thomas Jefferson, Ellen, Cornelia, Virginia, Mary, James, Benj. Franklin, Lewis Madison, Septemia and Geo. Wythe. Thos. Jefferson Randolph was Chairman of the Democratic National Convention in Baltimore last spring which nominated Horace Greeley for the Presidency, and Geo. Wythe Randolph was Jeff. Davis' first Secretary of War in the late "unpleasantness."

Maria married John Eppes, and raised one son—Francis.

My father generally enjoyed excellent health. I never knew him to have but one spell of sickness, and that was caused by a visit to the Warm Springs in 1818. Till within three weeks of his death he was hale and hearty, and at the age of 83 years he walked erect and with stately tread. I am now 68, and I well remember that he was a much smarter man physically, even at that age, than I am.

When I was fourteen years old I was put to the carpenter trade under the charge of John Hemings, the youngest son of my grandmother. His father's name was Nelson, who was an Englishman. She had seven children by white men and seven by colored men—fourteen in all. My brothers, sister Harriet and myself were used alike. They were put to some mechanical trade at the age of fourteen. Till then we were permitted to stay about the "great house," and only required to do such light work as going on errands. Harriet learned to spin and to weave in a little factory on the home plantation. We were free from the dread of having to be slaves all our lives long, and were measurably happy. We were always permitted to be with our mother, who was well used. It was her duty, all her life which I can remember, up to the time of father's death, to take care of his chamber and wardrobe, look after us children and do such light work as sewing, &c.

Provision was made in the will of our father that we should be free at his death when we arrived at the age of 21 years. We had all passed that period when he died but Eston, and he was given the remainder of his time shortly after. He and I rented a house and took mother to live with us, till her death, which event occurred in 1835.

In 1831 I married Mary McCoy. Her grandmother was a slave, and lived with her master, Stephen Hughas, near Charlottesville, as his wife. She was manumitted by him, which made their children free-born. Mary McCoy's mother was his daughter. I was about 25 and she 22 years of age when we married. We lived and labored together in Virginia till 1836, when we voluntarily left and came to Ohio. We settled in Pebble township, Pike county. We lived there four or five years, and during my stay in that county I worked at my trade on and off for about four years. Joseph Sewell was my first employer. I built for him what is now known as Marksport No. 3, in Waverly. I afterwards worked for George Wolfe, Senior, and did the carpenter work of the brick building now owned by John J. Kellison, in which the Pike County Republican is printed. I worked for and with Micajah Hinson. I found him to be a very clever man. I also reconstructed the building on the corner of Market and Water streets from a store to a hotel for the late Judge Jacob Row.

When we came from Virginia we brought one daughter (Sarah) with us, leaving the dust of a son in the soil near Monticello. We have had born to us in this State nine children. Two are dead. The names of the living, besides Sarah, are Harriet, Mary Ann, Catharine, Jane, William, Beverly, James Madison and Ellen Wales. Thomas Eston died in the Andersonville prison pen, and Julia died at home. William, James and Ellen are unmarried and live at home, in Huntington township, Ross county. All the others are married and raising families. My post-office address is Pee Pee, Pike county, Ohio.

pledge that her children should be freed at the age of twenty-one years. In consequence of his promises, on which she implicitly relied, she returned with him to Virginia. Soon after their arrival, she gave birth to a child, of whom Thomas Jefferson was the father. It lived but a short time.

The Virginia historians, led by Dumas Malone and Merrill Peterson, naturally have hated the idea that Sally Hemings bore a child who must have been conceived in France, since it points so sharply to Jefferson as the probable father. Their response has been to deny that it ever happened. One piece of evidence they are fond of is the absence of any notation in Jefferson's Farm Book recording a birth to Sally in 1790, whereas her subsequent children are duly noted. But the first slave inventory that he made after returning to America was not until 1794, by which time, if what Sally told Madison was true, that infant had already died. In any case, Jefferson was uncomfortably aware that as a prominent new member of President Washington's cabinet he was now in the public limelight more noticeably than ever before. It is unlikely that at that point he would have made a written record, even in a private journal, that unquestionably would have suggested his paternity of a slave child.

Madison's listing of the rest of Sally's children—"four others, and Jefferson was the father of them all ... Beverly [a boy], Harriet, Madison (myself), and Eston"—agrees with Jefferson's Farm Book entries, except that there is also an entry for an earlier Harriet, born in 1795, who died at the age of two, and whom Madison evidently had never heard of.

Madison Hemings's reminiscences on the whole have a wonderfully direct and almost colloquial sound, calm and unsensational, and they reported much information about the Hemings family, never published before, that was later corroborated from other sources. If his interview had turned out to include a *denial* that Thomas Jefferson was his father, it surely would have been hailed by the Virginia school as a prime piece of historical evidence, instead of being disparaged as a "legend" emanating from pride or vanity on the part of Sally and Madison.

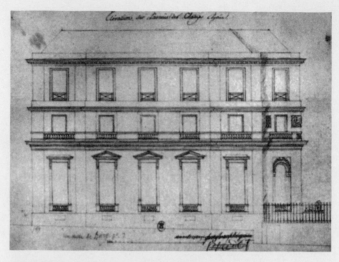

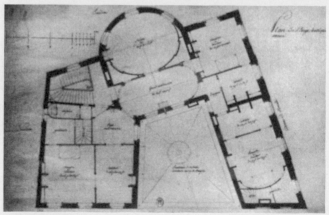

Elevation and floor plan of the Hôtel de Langeac, Jefferson's mansion on the Champs-Élysées.

8
Eros on the Champs-Élysées
———•◆•———

A
lthough the DNA evidence has made it unnecessary to speculate about whether Sally and her master had a long-term love affair, it is entertaining to think about how and why it started when it apparently did—in Paris in 1787 or '88. Certainly, the situation there was more congenial to it than it ever would be later in Virginia. For most of the two years of Sally's sojourn there, Patsy and Polly were away five days and nights a week at their convent school, and their half-aunt—Sally—was the only American servant in the household other than her brother James, and the only female who spoke English.

Of course, Sally was just on the verge of fifteen, and some of those who would deny a Jefferson-Hemings liaison have pointed to this as if it automatically demolished the idea. But in Europe and America in the eighteenth century this was considered a distinctly marriageable age—a bit on the youthful side, to be sure, but all the more fresh and attractive for that very reason. Jefferson's closest French friend, Lafayette, who came often to his house and very probably noticed the lovely new arrival, could have had no objections to her age, having himself taken a bride when she was fourteen; and in America, as noted earlier, James Madison had ardently pursued a fifteen-year-old, with his friend Jefferson cheering him on.

Another argument frequently advanced by doubters of the Sally Hemings story is that a man of Jefferson's honor and humanity, with his great respect for human dignity, could never have been, as John C. Miller puts it, "the seducer of a young, innocent, attractive colored girl, hardly out of puberty." But it is possible to agree with this and still believe that not long after her arrival in Paris, Sally Hemings and her master began an intensely sexual affair that was to last for many years. For what if *she* seduced *him*? In answering this question, it is relevant to remember that Sally's mother, Betty Hemings, had tremendously improved her lot as a slave by becoming John Wayles's consort after the death of his third wife. The master's concubine, on a Southern plantation, was a woman set apart, and in most cases, if the liaison was on a continuing basis, she could count on being treated far better than the ordinary slaves. Certainly it worked out that way for Betty and for her children too: when Wayles died in 1773, he left her and her children to his daughter Martha—who soon took them to Monticello, where they were treated even better.

Whether it was fortuitous or the result of clever maneuvering, Sally had become Polly's personal maid and playmate by the time the voyage to France was arranged. It is hard to believe that Betty Hemings failed to give her lively, pretty daughter advice on how to behave toward Master Jefferson upon entering his Paris household. She knew that he was still a single widower, and having observed the Jefferson marriage at close range for ten years—as a house servant at Monticello—she knew something about the role that Eros played in Jefferson's scheme of domestic happiness. Quite possibly the French adventure would offer a golden opportunity for Sally that might ensure her future.

As for Jefferson, he was vulnerable. His romance with Maria

Cosway was going into its twilight phase without having brought him sexual fulfillment, and now suddenly into his life had walked this young beauty whose form and face may tantalizingly have reminded him of his happy marriage. No, he was not going to overtly seduce her; that would indeed have been contrary to his nature, but what if she . . . ?

It is true, in any case, that there is little *documentary* evidence suggestive of romantic or erotic events beneath the roof of the Hôtel de Langeac during the first months of Sally Hemings's residence. There are signs that Jefferson was giving close attention to her welfare—paying a sizable doctor's bill to have her inoculated for smallpox, for instance. But this is the kind of thing he would have done anyhow, whether he was looking at Sally with lust in his heart or not.

A very interesting exhibit, however, and one that has been often ignored or misinterpreted, is a letter written by Jefferson to Maria Cosway the morning after he returned from a seven weeks' journey to Holland and Germany in the early spring of 1788. He had gone to Amsterdam with his fellow diplomat John Adams to see if a new loan could be negotiated for the young United States government, already struggling with a heavy national debt. With that mission successfully concluded after some difficulties, Jefferson decided that a vacation was called for. Acting on a recommendation by John Trumbull he set off into Germany, traveling leisurely along the beautiful Rhine valley through Düsseldorf and Heidelberg to Strasbourg, stopping off along the way to see the local sights, sample the food and wine, and occasionally visit an art gallery. (At Strasbourg, to cite an inconsequential but amusing detail, he was awarded a gratuitous honor by the clerk at his hotel, who headed his final bill with the inscription: "Mons. Le Général Jefferson.")

Back in Paris on April 23, he found a letter from Maria expressing something closer to fury than to love: he had not written her for three months. "Your long silence is impardonable," she wrote. "[M]y intention was only to say, *nothing*, send a blank paper; as a Lady in a Passion is not good for Any thing."

Jefferson was in a rare mood when he sat down to answer this on April 24. He seems to have been in a slight daze, intending to make amends to Maria, yet unable to quite keep his mind on it. He assures her:

> At Dusseldorp I wished for you much. I surely never saw so precious a collection of paintings. Above all things those of Van der Werff affected me the most. His picture of Sarah delivering Agar to Abraham is delicious. I would have agreed to have been Abraham though the consequence would have been that I should have been dead five or six thousand years.

What was poor Maria to make of this? There is nothing on record to suggest that she had ever been to Düsseldorf, knew anything about van der Werff, or had ever read or heard the Old Testament story of Abraham and Sarah and Hagar ("Agar"). It was almost as if he were making a diary entry about his trip rather than writing a letter. And what was the point?

Well, you can look it up (Genesis 16); and you can look at the picture (opposite), which survives with undimmed luster after two centuries. The essence of the Bible story is this: Hagar was an Egyptian slave ("bondwoman") belonging to Sarah, Abraham's wife, and Sarah said to him, "Behold now, the LORD hath restrained me from bearing: I pray thee, go in unto my maid . . . And Sarah, Abraham's wife, took Hagar . . . and gave her to her husband . . ." This is the poignant moment depicted in the painting that so enraptured Jefferson—and it is a highly erotic scene,

Sarah Delivering Agar to Abraham, *by Adriaen van der Werff*

what with the naked Abraham waiting, eagerly ready, in the rather rumpled bed; the lissome Hagar, succulently modest but with her thin gown just slipping off one breast; and Sarah handing her into the bed with that "this is a far better thing" expression of pious self-sacrifice. But the punch line, so to speak, is Jefferson's: "I would have agreed to have been Abraham though the consequence would have been that I should have been dead five or six thousand years." (The fact that in the painting Abraham has red hair and a rangy, muscular build like his own surely did nothing to deter him from seeing himself in the role.)

He wasn't through with his letter yet. Acknowledging to Maria that he wasn't much of an art connoisseur, he adds a sentence that should give some pause to the many devotees of Jefferson as a steely, unwavering rationalist: "I am but a son of nature, loving what I see and feel, without being able to give a reason, nor caring much whether there be one." And as if to give further proof of this he goes on, after a feeble attempt to describe a scenic view on the Rhine at Heidelberg:

> At Strasbourg I sat down to write to you. But for my soul I could think of nothing at Strasbourg but the promontory of noses, of Diego, of Slawkenburgius his historian, and the procession of the Strasburgers to meet the man with the nose. Had I written you from thence it would have been a continuation of Sterne upon noses . . .

What was *this* all about? He was talking to himself again, rather than to Maria, letting his mind run where it would. The very specific allusion, of course, is to *Tristram Shandy*, and though less obviously than the van der Werff painting, the cited passage is hardly less sexual. Sterne, who spends a great deal of time in his lengthy novel making comedy about human genitalia, whether explicitly or by innuendo and metaphor, begins his "Book 4" with a mysterious tale of a stranger who arrives in Strasbourg one summer evening and immediately sets the entire town in an uproar because of the hugeness of his nose. Everyone is in a frenzy to see it and—especially the women—to touch it, and gradually, as the story meanders along, the conviction dawns on the reader that what's being talked about is not really a nose, but a penis.

Maria Cosway understood none of this—she quite likely had never read a word of Sterne—and sent Jefferson a squawk of outrage by way of reply: "How could you . . . think of me . . . and not find one word to write, *but on Noses?*" It was a good question; and it leads to another one: What was going on at the Hôtel de Langeac that he should have composed such a letter?

The circumstantial context of the letter suggests some clues. Jefferson had just come from a seven-week trip, and naturally would have been glad to get back to the comforts of home. He got in after nightfall, and the house was probably quiet: it was a Wednesday, and his daughters were away at their boarding school. Sally, however, was presumably there—young, beautiful, and not unhappy to greet him after their first long separation since her arrival in France ten months earlier.

And where had Sally come from? She had been Martha Jefferson's slave girl, and just as the biblical Sarah had given *her* slave Hagar to Abraham, Martha had given Sally to Jefferson— not, of course, to be his concubine; but Martha was gone forever, and no longer could bring children to him any more than Sarah could to Abraham, nor the joys and solace of the spousal bed either. He could take Sally to his bed, moreover, without violation of his promise to Martha that he would never marry again.

The fact that Jefferson had van der Werff's painting so vividly on his mind as his letter to Maria indicates, suggests that the picture may have struck him as a kind of epiphany: almost as a sanction for a sexual affair that may have begun shortly before he went on his tour, or perhaps began on the night of his return. That he felt a compulsion, either consciously or unconsciously, to hint this—however metaphorically—to Maria Cosway, the woman who apparently had failed to match his eager libido, is psychologically quite fascinating. She missed the point, but at least he had managed to get it off his chest.

Whether one is of the pro party or the con, with regard to the validity of the Hemings-Jefferson liaison, it would seem ridiculous to claim, after reading Jefferson's letter to Maria, looking at the van der Werff painting, and browsing through the relevant passage in *Tristram Shandy*, that the letter writer was a man of cold detachment who no longer had a personal interest in sex. Yet Dumas Malone, at the end of his chapter on Jefferson's "sentimental adventure" with Maria Cosway, asserts with certainty that "her middle-aged admirer," his passion for her evaporated, "embarked on no romantic adventure with anybody else" for the rest of his life. It doesn't sound much like the man, just turned forty-five, who—humorously but with obvious conviction—declared his willingness to have been in Abraham's shoes, or rather his bed, with a beautiful young slave girl, and never mind the consequences.

With spring burgeoning in Paris and Jefferson in a lusty mood, the ambiance in the house and gardens of the Hôtel de Langeac must have been invigorating. There was an additional contributing factor too. One of the best friendships Jefferson had developed in France was with the Duc de La Rochefoucauld, in whom he found very compatible interests both politically and intellectually. The two had spent many an afternoon or evening talking about such things as the chances for a constitutional monarchy, Jefferson's idea for a greatly improved plow, or the philosophical relationship of deism and democracy. William Short, Jefferson's handsome young secretary, had often been in on these congenial discussions, but it became increasingly obvious that his attention was distracted. The duc's second wife, Rosalie, was only in her early twenties, and like so many second wives of affluent men, she

William Short, by Rembrandt Peale.

was strikingly beautiful as well as vivacious. (In this case she also happened to be the duc's niece.) Short was totally lovestruck.

Rosalie, it seems, was equally smitten, and since La Rochefoucauld was either unobservant or remarkably tolerant, and they were able to spend a considerable amount of time together, a romance was soon in the making. Jefferson was aware of what was going on, and does not appear to have had moral objections, but he felt that ultimately there was little chance of a permanent connection for the young couple. It probably was his urging plus distress over what had begun to look like a hopeless love affair that sent Short off, late the following summer, on a continental tour that lasted for months. In the meanwhile, however, love was wonderfully in bloom on the Champs-Élysées.

It remains true, nevertheless, that for the rest of Jefferson's time in France the evidence for a liaison with Sally is mostly inferential—perhaps implicit, for instance, in the way he let his connection with Maria Cosway atrophy into little more than a garland of fond memories and conventional expressions of affection. It also might be inferred from the fact that for these months some of his friends noticed his growing tendency to avoid the whirl of Parisian society and spend a great deal of his leisure time at home. Gouverneur Morris, the American politician and gallant who was to follow him as minister to France, found him during this period altogether too domesticated to be a congenial companion.

A few odd sparks did fly up from the embers of his love for Maria. He wrote her no letters for months, but now and then there was a bit of secondhand communication via John Trumbull. In August 1788, for instance, he sent Trumbull one of his "commissions"—that is, requests that were almost commands—this time to have a new carriage built for him in London to typically detailed specifications ("3 feet 2 inches wide within . . . the steps to shut within . . . venetian blinds . . . oval backlight of 2 feet diameter . . ." and so on) At the end there is this: "Kneel to Mrs. Cosway for me, and lay my soul in her lap." It was rather peculiar language under the circumstances, and to some might sound a distant echo of Hamlet's sarcastic question to Ophelia at the play-within-the-play: "Lady, shall I lie in your lap? I mean, my head upon your lap?" Jefferson may have been cheerfully recovered, with Sally's help, from his bitterness about Maria's failure to reciprocate his passion, but he was not above throwing a barb or two.

The late months of 1788 rolled along into the early months of 1789, bringing with them a winter unpleasantly unlike anything Jefferson had ever seen in Virginia: the ice on the Seine was so thick that carriages crossed on it, and thousands of Parisians shivered from a scarcity of fuel for their fires and bread for their bellies. The many hearths of the Hôtel de Langeac were kept adequately ablaze, yet, writing at last to Maria, Jefferson complained, "Surely it was never so cold before. To me who am an animal of a warm climate, a mere Oran-ootan, it has been a severe trial." If Maria's acquaintance with *Notes on the State of Virginia* was good enough, this may have triggered a disquieting memory. There, expressing anthropological opinions for which he has been castigated ever since, Jefferson had insisted on the preference of blacks for whites as sexual partners "as uniformly as is the preference of the Oranotan for the black woman over those of his own species." It could be argued that putting himself metaphorically in the "Oran-ootan" category constituted in some measure a tribute to the comforting warmth of Sally Hemings, for however light her complexion, he was still inevitably aware of her status as a slave and thus theoretically a "black."

Spring came at last, and with it harbingers of the great upheaval that was to turn France upside down: Louis XVI's reluctant convoking of the Estates General, their self-transformation into the National Assembly followed by the king's failed attempt to dissolve that body; the ballooning anger of the people along with steady price rises and bread shortages; sporadic confrontations between citizens and some of the soldiers the king was bringing into Paris whole troops at a time; and in July the bloody event that forever after would symbolize the start of the French Revolution, the storming of the Bastille. The minister of the United States observed and reported all these events carefully, but without great alarm. As something of an expert, he even helped Lafayette draw up a Declaration of the Rights of Man for France that not surprisingly had several important phrases almost paraphrasing the Declaration of Independence; they both hoped the adoption of this would help to cool things down and avoid a political conflagration.

Meanwhile, on the domestic front, he had been faced with the threat of a little rebellion himself. He had enrolled Patsy in the convent school in 1784 with the understanding that there would be no efforts to convert her to Catholicism, and despite his lifelong enmity toward authoritarian religion he had assured skeptical friends like Abigail Adams that his daughter was safe from intellectual corruption there. He must have been correspondingly shocked, therefore, when in mid-April 1789 a letter came from Patsy asking her father's permission to become a nun. (The letter has not survived, and may have been torn up on the spot; but Patsy, according to her children, passed the story down, and it became part of the family history.) Patsy knew her father very well, and she could hardly have been surprised when he abruptly appeared at the school, conferred briefly with the abbess who ran it, and drove off with both Patsy and Polly and all their belongings. Even though there is evidence that the nuns had indeed tried to convert Patsy, and that she had given them some hope of success, it is tempting to conclude that she had had enough of the school, and was aware that there was no quicker way than this to get away from it.

There may have been a more particular reason. It is not unusual for a sixteen-year-old girl who is intensely fond of a widower father—as Patsy certainly was—to be jealous of his interest in other females. Patsy had shown no fondness for Maria Cosway, and now she may well have become aware that Jefferson's concern for Sally, whose flourishing sexual attractions were so obvious, went far beyond that ordinarily shown by a master to a maidservant. This would have been disturbing to Patsy on many levels. Very probably she knew that Sally was the half-sister of her adored mother, which added an aura of almost incestuous betrayal to the situation; she also, of course, knew that sexual relations between a plantation master and a slave woman were—theoretically, at least—taboo. Patsy was of an age when young ladies of her social status began to think seriously of marriage: was her desirability as a bride to be compromised by whispers that her famous father was involved in miscegenation with a slave girl younger than Patsy herself, yet (almost paradoxically) also her half-aunt? Whatever was going on at the Hôtel de Langeac, from day to day and night to night, could certainly be much better observed right there than from the exasperating remove of the Abbaye de Panthémont, her school.

One entertaining sidelight on this scene of familial rivalry is that shortly after Patsy came home Jefferson made entries in his account book showing a big splurge of expenditures for dressmaking materials—linen, silk, cambric—as well as for shoes and other

The Grille de Chaillot, the western limit of the main part of Paris when Jefferson lived there: The view here is directly down the Champs-Élysées. One end of his residence, the Hôtel de Langeac, can be glimpsed on the left.

accessories. Earlier in April, before her return, he had recorded a substantial sum—almost two hundred francs—for "clothes for Sally." While there was no question who was the grandest lady in the Easter parade at the Hôtel de Langeac, Sally was obviously not going around in rags.

Having been abroad for nearly five years, Jefferson had applied for a six-month leave. He wanted to get back to Monticello for at least a couple of months to check on the state of his plantation and put things in order, he wanted to survey the American political situation at first hand, and he wanted to place Patsy in a social milieu favorable to her marriage prospects—after all, she was now nearly seventeen. As for himself, he ardently hoped to return to his post in France, and he was confident that William Short would handle official business capably while he was away.

There were many things to be attended to before he sailed for America, of course. Even though he expected to come back, there was a truly astounding amount of stuff that he wanted to take home—books, pictures, sculpture, furniture, tableware, many cases of wine—and it all had to be carefully packed. He had to bid proper adieu to his French diplomatic contacts, and he had to give a large farewell dinner to important Americans who were in Paris. This last he did on the Fourth of July, 1789—just ten days before the fall of the Bastille—including on the guest list Gouverneur Morris, Joel Barlow (the poet), and that dual citizen Lafayette. A congratulatory address was made to the host, with a graceful and modest acknowledgment from Jefferson followed by a large number of patriotic toasts.

What about Madison Hemings's assertion that his mother, as the days drew near to the time of departure for Virginia, threatened to stay in France, where she knew she would be free, unless Jefferson made "a solemn pledge" to free any children she might have by him when they reached the age of twenty-one?

In judging the likelihood of this, it's a good idea to remember that sixteen-year-old Sally had her big brother James, now twenty-four, right there to advise and support her. James Hemings is a most interesting figure, an insider from early childhood on life at Monticello, and from his adolescence a trusted servant to Jefferson. Intelligent and self-reliant, he was often given surprising responsibilities for his age—for example, when Jefferson and Patsy were en route from Le Havre to Paris, after their arrival in France in 1784, James (then nineteen) would be sent ahead by several hours to make sure they had good accommodations awaiting them when they pulled into a town for the night. Now, five years later, he had learned French and learned a great deal about expert French cooking in Jefferson's kitchen—and beyond question he had also learned a lot about his status in France as compared with his status in America.

Jefferson, legal scholar that he was, understood the situation exactly. In a quite startling passage of a letter to another American in Paris who had brought in a young slave, he wrote:

The laws of France give him freedom if he claims it . . . Nevertheless I have known an instance where a person bringing in a slave, and saying nothing about it, has not been disturbed in his possession. I think . . . in your case . . . the boy is so young that it is not probable he will think of claiming freedom.

No chance of this existed in the case of the smart, fully adult James Hemings. To be fair to Jefferson, it must be remarked that in any event he probably planned to free James eventually. It was not to be forgotten that he was a Hemings and a half-brother to Jefferson's late wife; and indeed he was freed a few years later. But Thomas Jefferson was not a man to give up something highly valued for nothing. A consummate gourmet, he very much wanted to transport James and his culinary skills back to Virginia—and a pledge of freedom in his native land was a bargaining chip the young man would have had a hard time resisting.

As for Sally, it seems dubious that she felt any deep urge to stay in France, even though she might easily have found employment with the Lafayettes or the La Rochefoucaulds. A point often overlooked is that by this time she may have been much in love with her master, and not desirous of being anywhere except with him, freedom or no freedom. On the other hand, if she had now been in effect his mate for over a year, she quite likely had come to understand something of the bargaining power conferred upon a slave woman by that rank. It was an advantage that might never be exercised if she remained in France, but would almost certainly be hers if she went back to Virginia. And there were, of course, her mother and the many other sweet attractions of home awaiting her at Monticello, all of them no doubt subjectively enhanced if she was indeed pregnant.

At any rate, when all the complicated preparations for the voyage to America had finally been made, in the last days of the summer of 1789, both Sally and James Hemings were on the passenger list.

9
Return of the Natives

————•◆•————

The travelers—Jefferson, Patsy, Polly, Sally, and James, plus Petit, who was to see them as far as Le Havre—left Paris on September 26, 1789, en route for America. It happened to be the day before Patsy's seventeenth birthday, though there is no record of a celebration.

Left in charge of American interests in France was William Short, who could be counted on to do a good job if he wasn't too distracted by the delightful Rosalie. As for the superheated political scene from which Jefferson was taking a holiday, the American minister seems to have felt remarkably optimistic: he wrote Tom Paine in England that there was "no possibility now of anything's hindering . . . final establishment of a good constitution" for France. (At just about this time a clever member of the National Assembly, Dr. Joseph-Ignace Guillotin, was sketching designs for a machine that could, he claimed, make capital punishment by decapitation far more humane and democratic: it guaranteed swift and uniform efficiency. But it was to be another two years before this device became the bloody tool and symbol of the Terror.)

The Jeffersons took with them an enormous quantity of personal baggage, since Patsy and Polly were leaving for good, and they suffered the eighteenth-century equivalent of a blowout—a broken wheel rim; otherwise the overland trip apparently was uneventful. Unhappily, Jefferson had been unable to find a seagoing ship sailing directly from Le Havre at the right time, and they were forced to make a choppy Channel crossing to the Isle of Wight before embarking on the Atlantic. (Significantly, during a ten-day layover there, Jefferson wrote a farewell note to Maria Cosway, but made no effort to see her though she had begged him to visit on the way to America.) Finally, on October 22, they boarded the merchantman *Clermont*, and by the end of the month were on the open sea with sunny weather and favorable winds. They joyfully stepped onto American soil at Norfolk on November 23, and managed to make it home to Monticello just before Christmas.

Jefferson had been surprised and not much pleased to learn at Norfolk that President George Washington had nominated him to be secretary of state, and that the Senate had already confirmed the appointment. His dream of a few more years in France was suddenly gone with the wind—hindsight might say luckily, in view of the political hurricane that was about to engulf that country. He wrote with slight hope to Washington that his own preference would be to remain as minister to France, but the president made it clear that he felt Jefferson's presence in the cabinet was crucial.

The consolation was that Jefferson was back on his much loved plantation and in the great house he had so thoughtfully designed and could now set about repairing and improving. And he was once again very much the lord of the manor. Patsy Jefferson later wrote of the tremendous excitement with which his slaves had greeted him when they arrived at Monticello that Christmas: "When the door of the carriage was opened they received him in their arms and bore him to the house, crowding round and kissing his hands and feet—some blubbering and crying—others laughing." While a portion of this enthusiasm must have been for James and Sally Hemings, the only world travelers among the slave contingent at Monticello, there is no doubt that it was also one of many recorded expressions of affection for a master known to be kinder and fairer to his human chattels than most.

The family had hardly unpacked and settled in when rumors of an unexpected coming event began to circulate around the plantation: Miss Patsy was planning to marry in the very near future. The prospective bridegroom was Thomas Mann Randolph, Jr., a not very distant cousin, and by all accounts a romantically attractive figure—tall, handsome, dark-haired, and a marvelous horseman. Jefferson seems to have been extremely pleased when his daughter told him of her love for this "young gentleman of genius, science, and honorable mind," as he later described Randolph. It would be a quintessentially Virginia marriage, further interweaving two eminent families who were already connected (Jefferson's

Thomas Mann Randolph, Jr., who married Jefferson's elder daughter, Patsy, shortly after her return to Virginia from France.

mother was a Randolph); and it took place with all the material trappings of such: Jefferson gave the young couple one thousand acres of his plantation plus about twenty-five slaves, a dowry balanced by the bridegroom's father with a house, 950 acres, and forty slaves on an estate called Varina. None of this did anything to undermine the institution to which Jefferson had often applied such adjectives as "infamous" and "abominable."

The wedding was on February 23, 1790, just two months after the Jeffersons' return to Monticello—and it is an interesting question why Patsy rushed so quickly into it. She could not have known Randolph well, having been in France since she was twelve (though flimsy evidence suggests that he may have paid a brief visit to Paris in 1788 after studying at Edinburgh). A few weeks after the marriage Jefferson wrote her: "It is a circumstance of consolation to know that you are happier; and to see a prospect of its continuance in the prudence and even temper of both Mr. Randolph and yourself." What had she been less happy about?

If Sally was pregnant when they embarked from England in October 1789, and Patsy had not known about it before, it is altogether likely that she became aware of it during the weeks of intimate living together aboard ship. The prospect of Sally giving birth to a practically white baby, soon enough after their arrival at Monticello to make it clear that the child had been conceived in Paris, was a dismaying one. It was bound to be a spicy item in the gossip mill that whirred away among the slaves at Monticello as at every big plantation—and an acute mortification to the eldest daughter of the house, just at a time when she expected to be entertaining suitors for her hand, and family respectability would be at a premium.

In eighteenth-century America, there was only one accepted way for an upper-class girl of seventeen to escape from a domestic situation that she found intolerable, and that was to get married.

She would thereby instantly become the mistress of her fortune, free—indeed, expected—to leave her father's home for one of her own. In Patsy's circumstances very rapid action must suddenly have seemed to be essential, and she had the good luck to find a highly suitable bridegroom ready and waiting.

As things turned out for her and her husband, the house at Varina that his father had given them was not yet ready, and they remained at Monticello for some time after the marriage and after Jefferson had gone to New York in March to begin his service as secretary of state. Probably they were there when Sally gave birth to her first child. But Patsy was now Mrs. Thomas Randolph, and no longer obliged to stay at Monticello if at any time things became uncomfortable for her there. In the meantime the newlyweds got started on a family of their own—quite a formidable project, for Patsy was eventually to give Jefferson twelve grandchildren.

Jefferson's reaction to the birth of Sally's child can only be guessed at. On the assumption that he had planned to take both James and Sally with him when, as expected, he returned to Paris, the discovery that she was pregnant of course cast a new light on their future together. It would have been conspicuously awkward to take her back on the long trans-Atlantic voyage when she was nursing a baby a few months old. On the other hand, once her impending motherhood became apparent, Washington's decision to keep Jefferson in America as his secretary of state may have struck him as less disagreeable than it might have otherwise. Sally would be with him, and on a plantation like his that had a large population of young slave mothers, one more infant would not be very remarkable—or so he may have hoped.

It is notable, given Jefferson's generally enthusiastic attitude toward human breeding, that Sally produced only six offspring during about twenty-five years (1790–1815) of presumed fecundity, as compared to Patsy's twelve in approximately the same period of time; or to Jefferson's record, with his wife, of six in ten years. This could be partly explainable by his long absences from Monticello—but also by the obvious fact that the fewer "nearly as white as anybody" kids who looked like him were running around Monticello, the less talk there was going to be about it. Sally must have been keenly aware of this, and it is not unlikely that she practiced a certain amount of rhythm birth control, and that Jefferson may have been less given to carefree dalliance than he might have been otherwise.

In any event, she was exempt from the sort of hard-boiled calculation that Jefferson expressed when, writing to his daughter Polly's husband in 1820, he said, "I consider a [slave] woman who brings a child every two years as more profitable than the best man on the farm."

How did Thomas Jefferson treat these near-white children and their beautiful mother, the half-sister of his beautiful wife, as the years went by at Monticello and the glamorous days in France gradually faded into a tapestry of exotic memories? Madison Hemings had a few things to say in his autobiographical interview:

> About his own home he was the quietest of men. He was hardly ever known to get angry, though sometimes he was irritated when matters went wrong, but even then he hardly ever allowed himself to be made unhappy any great length of time ... He occupied much of the time in his office, engaged in correspondence and reading and writing. His general temperament was smooth and even; he was very undemonstrative. He was uniformly kind to all about him. He was not in the habit of showing partiality or fatherly affection to us children. We were the only children of his by a slave woman. He was affectionate toward his white grand-

children, of whom he had fourteen, twelve of whom lived to manhood and womanhood . . . My father generally enjoyed excellent health . . . Till within three weeks of his death he was hale and hearty, and at the age of 83 years he walked erect and with stately tread . . .

When I was fourteen years old I was put to the carpenter trade under the charge of John Hemings, the youngest son of my grandmother . . . My brothers, sister Harriet and myself were used alike. They were put to some mechanical trade at the age of fourteen. Till then we were permitted to stay about the "great house," and only required to do such light work as going on errands. Harriet learned to spin and to weave in a little factory on the home plantation. We were free from the dread of having to be slaves all our lives long, and were measurably happy. We were always permitted to be with our mother, who was well used. It was her duty, all her life which I can remember, up to the time of father's death, to take care of his chamber and wardrobe, look after us children and do such light work as sewing, &c. Provision was made in the will of our father that we should be free when we arrived at the age of 21 years. We had all passed that period when he died but Eston, and he was given the remainder of his time shortly after. He and I rented a house and took mother to live with us, till her death, which event occurred in 1835.

Jefferson had earlier fulfilled the rest of the pledge that, Sally told Madison, he had made to her in France. Her first child to survive, the boy named Beverly, was noted in Jefferson's Farm Book as "run away 22" (that is, let go, presumably in 1822, when he was twenty-three years old); according to Madison, he "went to Washington as a white man. He married a white woman in

Part of a page from Jefferson's Farm Book noting the departures from Monticello of his children Beverly and Harriet ("run away 22" and "run 22") in 1822.

Maryland . . . ." In 1801 came a baby girl, Harriet, who grew into the young woman described by the Monticello overseer Edmund Bacon as "nearly as white as anybody, and very beautiful." She too was allowed to leave in 1822: Bacon said, "by Mr. Jefferson's direction I paid her stage fare to Philadelphia and gave her fifty dollars . . . don't know what became of her." Brother Madison kept track of her, however; he said she "married a white man in good standing in Washington City . . . I am not aware that her identity as Harriet Hemings of Monticello has ever been discovered." Madison himself, as he noted in his memoir, and his brother Eston were assured of their freedom by Jefferson's will—two of the only five Monticello slaves so blessed.

The three others emancipated were also blood relatives of Sally: John Hemings, her half-brother, who had been Monticello's master carpenter and the teacher in that trade of Beverly and Madison; Burwell Colbert, a half-nephew who had been trained as a glazier but had actually served for several years as Jefferson's butler; and another half-nephew, Joe Fossett, an expert blacksmith.

It would be fascinating to have some knowledge of Sally Hemings's reaction to the visit paid to Jefferson near the end of his life by Lafayette, whose stop at Monticello was a highlight of his lavishly celebrated trip to America in 1824. The two old heroes spent about a week and a half together, drinking good wine and talking about the two great revolutions that had so preoccupied their lives, about old friends in Paris, about slavery and the necessity of somehow ending it, and about more personal matters. Lafayette had now, like his host, been a widower for many years, and he had with him—to the prudish alarm of many American ladies—the young avant-garde feminist and radical social reformer Fanny Wright, who was planning the integrated white-black, freethinking community that she actually established later at Nashoba, Tennessee. Jefferson found her extremely impressive, and an encouraging letter he wrote her in 1825—less than a year before the death foreseen by him ("one foot in the grave, and the other uplifted to follow it," he told her) suggests that she at least nudged his conviction that such a project was bound to fail. (It did, in fact, fail rather quickly, which would not have surprised him had he lived to see it.)

• • •

Fanny Wright, the extremely avant-garde young feminist who visited Monticello with Lafayette in 1824. Many years later, this picture was used by Susan B. Anthony as the frontispiece for a book on woman suffrage.

Thomas Jefferson, as nearly everybody knows, died on the Fourth of July, 1826, exactly a half-century after the adoption of the Declaration of Independence. John Adams, with whom he had been corresponding delightfully for about a decade—the political acrimony of their presidential years blown away by their intellectual compatibility—managed to hang on to life with equal respect for the anniversary, and died the same distinguished day.

Sally Hemings's name was conspicuously absent from the short list of slaves emancipated by Jefferson's will, the probable reason being that if she had been on it, it would have been even more conspicuous—and surely would have revived the gossip about a liaison with her master that so agitated Patsy Jefferson. A rather heartbreaking fact is that when the appraisers came to Monticello after the master's death to make a list of the property assets, including of course the slaves, Sally Hemings was described as "an old woman worth $50." She was fifty-six. Allowed to go by

Patsy—and it was undoubtedly an emotional moment for both of them—she found a home with her two younger sons for several years, as Madison tells us, and died in 1835 at the age of sixty-two.

She had lived, for an American slave, an unparalleled life. It must have been strange to spend so many years at Monticello, so close to Jefferson yet knowing that he would never openly acknowledge his special relationship to her and her children, at least in front of other family members or visitors. But she had the quiet assurance that neither she nor her children would ever be sold, that they would always be amply fed and sheltered, that finally they would go free—and that the children had been left an invaluable bequest: a passport to white America by reason of their virtually white skin.

One of the saddest afflictions of old age, for many people, is having no one left to remember old times with—to verify the past, and savor over again particular moments of surprise, poignancy, or joy. There must have been many occasions, in Jefferson's later years, when (except for a few other servants) he and Sally were alone together in the big house. It is pleasant to picture them, in the comfort of their long familiarity, recalling the happy years in Paris when life had been so fresh and open. "Paris is the only place," he wrote wistfully to William Short in 1815, "where a man who is not obliged to do anything will always find something amusing to do"; and his nostalgia for it shows in the very few letters he sent to Maria Cosway as time went by. But at least Sally was always near him whenever he was home at Monticello, no doubt quickly responsive if something unexpectedly triggered a "Remember that time in Paris . . . "

10

On the Bridge of the Ship of State

———•✦•———

It was the summer of 1774, and the American Revolution was on the verge of being born. A meeting of delegates from each of the thirteen colonies, to be called the Continental Congress, had been set for September in Philadelphia: its purpose, to discuss and consolidate American grievances about unfair taxation and other annoyances, and express them clearly and strongly so that King George III and the British Parliament would understand the solidarity of American discontent and resistance.

Without being authorized or asked, thirty-one-year-old Thomas Jefferson sat down and wrote an essay that he called "A Summary View of the Rights of British America," and sent it hopefully off to Williamsburg as a kind of instructional guide for Virginia's delegation to the Congress. Despite his youth and, thus far, lack of any great distinction as a statesman, his language was so lively, lucid, and cogent that it caused a notable stir, and "A Summary View" was quickly printed and widely distributed.

"Let those flatter who fear: it is not an American art," wrote Jefferson, brashly addressing George III directly. "Kings are the servants, not the proprietors of the people . . . The great principles of right and wrong are legible to any reader; to pursue them requires not the aid of many counsellors. The whole art of government consists in the art of being honest . . . The god who gave us life, gave us liberty at the same time: the hand of force may destroy, but cannot disjoin them."

A few months later, the Congress having met and not only sent off firm petitions to King George but declared a general boycott on British imports, another young American published a pamphlet in New York, defending their actions against a scalding attack penned pseudonymously by a conservative Anglican clergyman. The defender's name (although he too concealed his identity) was Alexander Hamilton, and readers puzzling over who it might be would have been amazed to learn that he was a teenager—a student at King's College (soon to be renamed Columbia). Though articulate, he was extraordinarily verbose, reeling off what amounted to more than fifty printed pages, citing British and European history as if he were a learned professor, and he soon followed this with an equally wordy sequel pamphlet. Along with the prolixity, however, he was very cocky, and his confidence in the superiority of everything American offered no clue to the fact that he had emigrated from the West Indies only two years earlier. Moreover, his ardor for the Colonial cause easily matched Jefferson's, and now and then he got off a passage that almost echoed the Virginian: "The sacred rights of mankind are not to be rummaged for, among old parchments, or musty records. They are written, as with a sun beam, in the whole *volume* of human nature, by the hand of the divinity itself; and can never be erased or obscured by mortal power . . . I consider civil liberty . . . as the greatest of terrestrial blessings. I am convinced, that the whole human race is intitled [*sic*] to it; and that it can be wrested from no part of them, without the blackest and most aggravated guilt."

It would have seemed quite appropriate, in 1774, to suggest that these two young patriots ought to get together and share their clearly compatible ideas and enthusiasms. But fifteen years went by before their fates converged, and when they finally did get together, although it was under the benign and fatherly auspices of President George Washington, there was sharp friction and mutual suspicion almost from the start.

By that time Hamilton, now a well-known figure on the American scene, had made himself a reputation as a young and gallant artillery officer in the Continental Army and as an aide on Washington's staff, and later as a highly successful lawyer in New York. He had also greatly enhanced his social standing by marrying Elizabeth Schuyler, the lovely daughter of one of the most distinguished blue-blood "patroon" families of upstate New York. Jefferson, meanwhile, had staked a claim on immortality by writing the Declaration of Independence, and had served as governor of Virginia and as the United States minister to France. With Hamilton as his secretary of the treasury and Jefferson as secretary of state, Washington had reason to think in 1789 that the two most important posts in his cabinet had been filled by the best possible choices.

Yet before they had finished their service as cabinet officers, Jefferson was calling Hamilton (in a letter to Washington) "a man whose history . . . is a tissue of machinations against the liberty of the country"; and Hamilton was calling Jefferson (in a newspaper piece) "the promoter of national disunion, national insignificance, public disorder and discredit."

There were particular reasons for this alienation, having to do with problems of policy facing the infant nation that demanded immediate attention, and on which the two men stubbornly opposed each other. But in the end, what it came down to was two distinctly different visions of the kind of society each man believed

Alexander Hamilton as secretary of the treasury, by James Sharples.

Thomas Jefferson as secretary of state, by Charles Willson Peale.

to be the right paradigm which the country should strive for in order to fulfill its promise as a new nation, bringing its citizens health and happiness.

Hamilton's dream focused primarily on economic development: the steady expansion of manufacturing and merchandising, with a vigorous flow of commercial enterprise aided by a strong central government and appropriate legislation, the whole system essentially run by a powerful elite consisting of the wealthy, well-educated, and privileged. Although he had argued cogently, in his contributions to the *Federalist* papers, for ratification of the new Constitution, he never felt that the federal government was given enough "general authority" over the states. He also never abandoned his belief that, all things considered, a constitutional monarchy would have been preferable to a democratic republic, and that the British government was the best in the world. His faith in the ability of common people to make the right choices on matters of national policy was feeble, and it did not strengthen as time went by: shortly before his death in 1804 he wrote to a friend that what really ailed America was "the poison" of democracy. Not surprisingly, he was always an advocate for a large standing army, and for the use of military force to quell any antigovernment disturbance to the peace. (In 1794 hundreds of farmers in Pennsylvania, whose main source of income was whiskey made from their grain, raised a fierce rumpus over a new tax on that commodity. Hamilton then persuaded George Washington to let him lead some twelve thousand militiamen to put them down. By the time the troops got there, the trouble had cooled off—but Hamilton had the soldiers arrest over a hundred farmers and march them to Philadelphia—where they were soon let go.)

Jefferson's dream focused above all on a free society, with firm protection of states' rights against federal encroachment, and with individuals guaranteed the right to think as they pleased, and to do as they pleased to the greatest possible extent consistent with civil peace and safety; with the views of the people, openly expressed, as the final test of what was right for the nation. The ideal representative democracy was seldom out of his mind. He understood, of course, that the welfare of a nation was much dependent on the health of its economy, but he clung to his old image of a predominantly agricultural society, serviced by many small, independent shopkeepers and tradesmen. He believed that communities well-ordered by democratic participation in local government would have little need for a large army, or even for a large police force. But they would very much need, in his view, excellent public schools as well as wide access to colleges and universities, since only a well-informed public would be able to make good decisions on public policy.

The differences between Thomas Jefferson and Alexander Hamilton were profound, and had many ramifications: whole books have been written on the subject. But Jefferson himself once epitomized them in an anecdote. Hamilton, he said, came to call on him in his rooms at Philadelphia, and noticed portraits of three men on the wall. When he asked who they were, Jefferson said, "They are the three greatest men the world has ever produced: Sir Francis Bacon, Sir Isaac Newton, and John Locke"—the first renowned for his application of the empirical method in science and philosophy; the second for fundamental discoveries in mathematics, physics, and astronomy; and the third for advancing ideas in political science that were seminal in the European Enlightenment. Hamilton was not impressed. "The greatest man that ever lived," he said, "was Julius Caesar"—the exemplar of dictatorial power and military conquest.

And in fact, there is evidence that for much of his life Hamilton dreamed of being commander-in-chief of the army and heroically leading the nation to forceful acquisition of additional territory—for example, Spanish Florida, or even Mexico. In 1798, during the presidency of John Adams, he actually became, briefly, the top general, achieving this as a result of a fit of national paranoia that swept the country when it was widely but mistakenly believed that Napoleon Bonaparte was on the verge of launching a French invasion of America. (Abigail Adams, observing Hamilton's jingoistic maneuvering, got off one of her peppery comments: "That man would in my mind become a second Buonaparty [sic] if he was possessed of equal power.") Jefferson, who at the time was suffering the absence of power and even influence so often the lot of American vice presidents, was appalled by the entire situation, but could do little to counter the war hysteria. It could be argued that one of the few benefits to the country of the 1798 war panic was its contribution toward convincing Jefferson that if America was to be saved from the blunders and antidemocratic plans of the Federalists, they would have to be ousted from the national leadership and replaced by good Democratic-Republicans—like himself.

One sharp quarrel between Jefferson and Hamilton, as cabinet members back in 1790, had to do with how the government was to deal with the problem of financing itself and putting the national economy on a prosperous course. A big issue was whether the debts piled up by the individual colonies during and since the war with England should, in the spirit of "*e pluribus unum,*" be assumed by the central power. Hamilton argued that assumption of these debts was necessary to make the Union a credible, operating reality, worthy of trust in seeking loans from other countries, and of support from what he called "the monied men"—wealthy Americans who had made loans to state governments, and who had in many instances not yet been repaid.

Hamilton's view of debt on a national scale was far from negative: he held the then radical opinion that it actually could be a very good thing. "A national debt," he wrote, "if it is not extreme, will be to us a national blessing. It will be a powerful cement of our Union. It will also create a necessity for keeping up taxation to a degree, which, without being oppressive, will be a spur to industry." Together with the establishment of a national bank, which he also vigorously recommended, it would "erect a mass of credit that will supply the defect of monied capital, and answer all the purposes of cash . . . offer adventurers [that is, investors] immediate advantages, analogous to those they receive by employing their money in trade . . . not only advance their own interest and secure the independence of their country; but, in its progress, have the most beneficial influence upon its future commerce, and be a source of national wealth and strength."

All this was anathema to Thomas Jefferson. The idea that the national debt could be "a blessing" struck him as absurd if not evil. "We are ruined," he wrote to his friend James Monroe in the spring of 1791, "if we do not over-rule the principles that 'the more we owe, the more prosperous we shall be,' 'that a public debt furnishes the best means of enterprize,' 'that if ours should once be paid off, we should incur another by all means however extravagant' &c. &c." He was sure that a national bank would hugely increase the national debt, and be of benefit mostly to speculators, stockbrokers, and unscrupulous businessmen, thus wedging ever wider the gap between the rich and the poor; and that the more the debt was allowed to inflate, the greater the likelihood of an expensively large standing army and of the temptation to use it in wasteful and dangerous international entanglements. "Debt" was for him, as we might put it today, a four-letter word in the worst sense.

Jefferson, to many Americans already an icon, was of course much less than godly in his private life, and (like most of us) often influenced in his view of national affairs by his personal situation.

Having started his career as a wealthy plantation owner, he had expected to remain prosperous and to leave his beloved daughters decidedly well-off when he died. Instead, as the years went by, he found himself trapped in a web of relentlessly growing debt. Much of it, he belatedly discovered, had been inherited from his father-in-law, John Wayles, and this was increased by further borrowing, as well as by substantial loans he generously but misguidedly made to friends who never paid him back. Meanwhile, his income from the cultivation and sale of tobacco, cotton, and wheat was often painfully less than anticipated, subject as it was to unpredictable vicissitudes of weather and the market.

Ironically aggravating all this was Jefferson's unwavering devotion to good—indeed lavish—living, exemplified by his fondness for the very best in gourmet food and fine wines, his pleasure in always acting the role of the openhanded convivial host, and his endless determination to keep remodeling Monticello to suit his architectural dreams regardless of the cost. By the time he came back from France and was appointed secretary of state, at the age of forty-six, until his last octogenarian years, he was haunted by the perennial specter of heavy personal debt from which he might never—and as it turned out, never did—escape. Projecting his own situation onto the national scene, it seemed axiomatic to Jefferson that a long-extended or perpetual national debt would mean the destruction of the happy republican society that he envisaged for his country.

An odd proclivity of this American *philosophe* who prided himself on adherence to realistic and practical solutions to life's problems, was sometimes to propose, for social problems that happened to be, in effect, magnifications of his personal dilemmas, solutions so fanciful as to be dubious at best. Mulling over the herculean burden of his indebtedness, just before returning to America from France in September 1789, he wrote to James

Madison that he had come to realize the tremendous importance of a principle that, though "self-evident," had been much neglected: "*that the earth belongs in usufruct to the living*; that the dead have neither powers nor rights over it." It was possibly a bit unfortunate, with regard to clarity, that a key word in the statement is rare enough to send even Ph.D.'s to their dictionaries. There they find (or are reminded) that "usufruct" derives from the Latin word meaning "use and enjoyment."

What Jefferson had his mind on, above all, was the evil (as he saw it) of inherited debt—the legal obligation of a man to pay off loans borrowed not by himself but by a parent or other ancestor, and, on a national scale, for one generation of citizens to be saddled with debts incurred by another. This all seems reasonable enough, but when it came to working out the details, Jefferson got rather quirky. On the basis of some French actuarial tables he had studied, he concluded that the average length of a generation is nineteen years, and that this should be the basis for limiting the length of a debt. Then, with Jeffersonian logic, he applies this limit, in theory, very widely: "every constitution . . . and every law, naturally expires at the end of 19 years," to ensure that people are not being governed, in effect, by the dead rather than by themselves.

His friend Madison, while generally agreeing with him on the evils of a national debt, observed that, having only recently labored prodigiously to produce a new and good constitution for the U.S.A., he did not plan to start all over again in, say, 1806. Jefferson then conceded that this part of his theory was not practicable, and recognized that the constitutional provisions for repeal and amendment were an acceptable substitute. But he was not about to give in on the debt question, as witnessed by his fierce opposition to Hamilton's plans for the government.

One interesting aspect of Jefferson's now-famous principle that "the earth belongs to the living" is that, like many of his ideas, it involves a profound ambiguity. Although it asserts that one generation has no right to impose obligations or rules on the next, it also implies, by the word "usufruct," that in one important respect there is an endless obligation that each generation inherits from the one before: the obligation not to abuse the earth, but, while enjoying its fruits in their time, to conserve it for the enjoyment of generations to come. The dictionary definition of "usufruct" helps to clarify this: "The right to utilize and enjoy the profits and advantages of something belonging to another so long as the property is not damaged . . ." This is not, understandably, the chief emphasis Jefferson puts on the idea in his discussions of it; two hundred years ago the suggestion that there would ever be such hordes of people crowding the earth—especially in America!—and such industrial pollution as to threaten a shortage of commonplace wonders like clean air and pure water, to say nothing of redwood forests and edible fish, would have seemed absurd.

If he were alive today, Jefferson surely would have much to say along this line, but in his ongoing contention with Hamilton, the national debt was the salient point. That controversy heated up nearly to an explosive temperature in the spring of 1790, with many angry speeches in Congress on both sides of the debt-assumption question. Jefferson's views were eloquently argued by Madison, with equally vociferous rhetoric in Hamilton's favor from leading Federalist congressmen like Fisher Ames of Massachusetts. It was clear that there was a sharp split geographically as well as ideologically: the Southerners were nearly all against assumption, the Northerners for it. Madison and Jefferson both began to worry that the impasse might disastrously disrupt the still fragile Union—and, reluctantly, they decided to compromise.

So it was that on a June evening in 1790, Alexander Hamilton was surprised by an invitation to dine at Jefferson's New York lodging, along with Madison; and while the after-dinner wine (or perhaps, more appropriately, a cordial) was being sipped, the trio made an interesting bargain. Madison would arrange for a few Southern votes in the House of Representatives to switch to the pro-assumption side, and Hamilton would throw his powerful support to selecting the banks of the Potomac as the projected permanent site for the nation's capital.

The immediate political crisis was thus defused. The squabbling between Hamilton and Jefferson, however, went on in lively fashion for another three years, until Jefferson, worn out and disgusted, retired to Monticello at the end of 1793—temporarily, as it turned out.

Meanwhile, there had raged a particularly bitter fight over the proper American attitude toward the French Revolution, which epochal event had been moving spasmodically from admirable through dubious to terrifying, ever since Jefferson's return from Paris in 1789. Having left it with almost ecstatic hopes that France was about to establish, peacefully, an essentially self-governing constitutional monarchy, he was inevitably disturbed by the reports of murderous turmoil, mayhem, and wholesale beheading that he got from his former secretary, William Short, who was still abroad. But as a man to whom "the right of the people to alter or to abolish" any government destructive of individual liberty was sacred, he remained firmly supportive of the revolution in France, convinced that despite the horrors of the guillotine, the cause of human freedom would benefit in the long run. "My own affections have been deeply wounded by some of the martyrs to this cause," he told Short in a private letter in January 1793, "but rather than it should have failed, I would have seen half the earth desolated. Were there but an Adam and Eve left in every country, and left free, it would be better" than if it had failed. Perhaps a little embarrassed by his own rhetoric, he quickly added, "I have expressed to you my sentiments, because they are really those of 99 in an hundred of our citizens"—and as a matter of fact, popular sentiment in America at the time was wildly enthusiastic about the overthrow of the French monarchy, with much celebratory feasting and drinking.

It was probably just as well for Jefferson, nonetheless, that his rhetorical exuberance was not witnessed by either Washington or Hamilton, for it could almost be said that the basic struggle in France was being played out in microcosm in the increasingly nasty donnybrook between Jefferson and Hamilton. As a devotee of English law, order, and commercial enterprise, and a committed skeptic on popular sovereignty, Hamilton saw nothing but chaos and disaster when he looked at what was going on in France, and Jefferson's attitude struck him as despicable. Each of them did his best to incline President Washington toward his side of the dispute, and each of them carried it into the public realm by vitriolic use of journalism. Hamilton had virtual editorial control of the Federalist newspaper, the *Gazette of the United States*, which launched in 1792 a series of articles depicting the secretary of state as a snake in human form and a Francophile revolutionary; the *National Gazette*, whose editor, Philip Freneau, was a protégé of Jefferson's, replied blow by blow, accusing the secretary of the treasury of being a closet Tory and monarchist whose monetary policies were subverting the morality of the American people. (Hamilton, who never could resist the temptation to write another pamphlet or article, was himself the author, under a series of pseudonyms, of most of the Federalist pieces, while Jefferson preferred to exercise remote control—partly so that he could tell Washington without blushing that he had not published a word against Hamilton.)

With Jefferson's departure from the cabinet at the end of 1793 and Hamilton's in 1795, and with the French Revolution blundering toward its end after the dictatorial rise of Napoleon Bonaparte, that particular battle was over; but the Hamilton-Jefferson animosity was never to be quite laid to rest.

Yet Jefferson, who was often more doctrinaire in theory than in action, gradually came to see that his dream of a nation of happy farmers, who cultivated their crops by day and read great books at night, was mostly utopian fantasy, and that to a large extent there was truth in Hamilton's vision of an industrialized America. On the other hand, during his two terms as president he rigorously applied to the government the pay-as-you-go formula that he had been unable to follow in his private life, and—with the expert assistance of his astute treasury secretary Albert Gallatin—he accomplished a drastic reduction in the national debt that has never been matched by any other administration. He felt, with some justification, that Hamilton's idea of a perpetual national debt as a good thing had been convincingly refuted, and that the entire tendency of the Federalist programs to betray the republican principles on which, as he saw it, the nation had been founded, had been powerfully countered if not destroyed.

His good friend James Madison had argued, however, that, under special circumstances, it could be beneficial to the country to temporarily incur a heavy debt; and in 1803 this proposition was unexpectedly embodied by what was surely one of the most astonishing windfalls of all time. Napoleon Bonaparte, having acquired the vast territory of Louisiana in a secret deal with Spain, was entertaining grandiose thoughts of colonizing the middle of the North American continent, and Jefferson was made aware of this shortly after the start of his first term. He was greatly alarmed in general by the prospect of a huge French establishment adjacent to the United States, and particularly by the likelihood that American

The Louisiana Purchase, *by Constantine Brumidi (fresco in the U.S. Capitol). James Monroe and Robert Livingston are given the surprise of their lives by François de Barbé-Marbois, Louis XVI's finance minister, 1803.*

commercial use of the Mississippi might be corked off by French control over New Orleans. He therefore dispatched James Monroe to Paris with instructions to try to buy New Orleans and West Florida from France for two million dollars, and to up the ante by several million more if necessary.

In the meantime Napoleon, who had been losing both men and money at an appalling rate in unsuccessful attempts to squelch the slave rebellion in Santo Domingo, had decided that he would cancel his American project if it would net him enough cash. Monroe and Robert Livingston, then the American minister to France, were thus seized by enormous surprise when they were asked how much they were willing to give not just for New Orleans, but for the land that ultimately would become the states of Louisiana, Arkansas, Missouri, Iowa, Oklahoma, Kansas, Nebraska, and South Dakota, plus big chunks of North Dakota, Minnesota, Colorado, Wyoming, and Montana. The American diplomats, no doubt nervous because they were going far beyond their mandate and—telegraph, telephone, and Internet being as yet not quite available—unable to communicate immediately with Jefferson, took (presumably) a big gulp and closed the deal for about fifteen million dollars. Jefferson, when the news reached him, was more than gratified, and for once entirely willing to take on the consequent debt, although he did worry some about the constitutionality of the unprecedented bargain—and sure enough, some of the Federalists in Congress, suddenly become scrupulously frugal, complained that it was indeed unconstitutional as well as egregiously extravagant.

Looking back, as the millennium turns over, to the long contention between the Federalists and the Democratic-Republicans, and their respective heroes, Hamilton and Jefferson, a pattern of American history emerges that prevails even now, in what has been called lately "the culture war." The lineaments of the opposing sides in this "war" are not always clearly defined, and the dividing line between them is sometimes blurred, but essentially it can be characterized as the political right vs. the political left (or, if you prefer, conservative vs. liberal). Their social goals sometimes converge, as, for example, in the case of Medicare, but on the most divisive issues—for instance, welfare, abortion, gun control, separation of church and state, government support and/or censorship of the arts, grounds justifying presidential impeachment—the kernel of the disagreement seems to come down to absolutism vs. relativism. Citizens who believe that human behavior should be directed by eternal moral and ethical rules that are determined and dictated by the Bible or some other source of unchallengeable authority, with a heavy emphasis on law and order, an extremely powerful military establishment, tax breaks for the affluent, and less permissiveness for individuals than for corporations, are likely to line up with the political right—in recent times meaning the modern Republican Party—and Alexander Hamilton is likely to be their patron saint.

On the other hand, citizens who believe that the individual human conscience is the only valid source of moral judgments, and in a pluralistic, relativistic society, with as much mutual tolerance as possible, with a military clearly subject to civilian control, tax breaks for the middle class, and constant protection of civil liberties, are likely to line up with the political left—usually meaning the Democrats—and Thomas Jefferson is their guiding light. Despite all his contradictions and compromises, he struggled throughout his life to make his Enlightenment ideals dovetail with reality, or when possible vice versa—and the rallying cry, always, was *liberty*.

Is America today more Hamiltonian or more Jeffersonian? It is, of course, an amazing mélange of the two—and that may be the secret of its greatness as a world leader.

11

Slave Master—and Racist

————•◆•————

Taking note of the rebellious agitation among Virginia's political leaders against British imposition of the new taxes in the late 1760s, Dr. Samuel Johnson, the quirky London pundit, got off a derisive question: "How is it that we hear the loudest *yelps* for liberty among the drivers of negroes?"

It was a shot that rather bounced off Thomas Jefferson, for though he had joined George Washington and others in signing a resolution to boycott British imports as a "yelp" against the taxes, and was like all of them a slaveholder, he was at the same time outspoken in his condemnation of slavery. Already—as a new member of the Virginia legislature in 1769—he had drawn up a bill to permit an owner to free a slave at will, without government consent. It was quickly defeated, but the young devotee of the Enlightenment was not discouraged. In 1770 he helped a mulatto youth sue for his freedom on the grounds of his descent from a white woman. Going out on what the judge saw as a very fragile limb, Jefferson argued that "under the law of nature, all men are born free, and every one comes into the world with a right to his own person, which includes the liberty of moving and using it at his own will"—a proposition that obviously challenged the whole

Virginia system. The case was peremptorily dismissed, and the young man remained a slave.

But this was before Jefferson had begun to court Martha Wayles, and committed himself to the life of a large plantation owner. He had started a promising career as a lawyer, and undoubtedly could have supported a wife and children quite handsomely as a member of that profession. It is tantalizing to try to imagine the difference that choice might have made in his life, to say nothing of the history of the country. Without the need for more than three or four house servants, the number of his slaves might have been reduced to few or even none. It seems certain that this would have put him in a much stronger posture to lead a movement toward emancipation in Virginia, which incidentally at that time held more than half of the slave population in America.

But might-haves do not alter the course of historical reality, and the reality was that Jefferson at twenty-seven was under heavy pressure to become the operator of a substantial plantation. There was the example of his much admired father, who had left him about fifty slaves and several thousand acres of good land, and there was the fact that Martha, whom he ardently hoped to make his wife, had been raised on a big plantation and probably expected nothing less as a bride. There was also, of course, his own love of country living, his conviction that agriculture was the best of all possible occupations, and his intense ambition to build a home on the grand scale that would be not only unparalleled in America for its classical beauty but a suitable residence for a gentleman of highly enlightened and sophisticated tastes—himself. By the time Martha had agreed to marry him the construction of Monticello was well under way, and Jefferson's determination to become a successful planter was presumably irrevocable.

This meant, regrettably, that Thomas Jefferson was doomed to be a slaveholder—for slave labor was the sine qua non of this enterprise. It was the only readily available source of cheap and controllable labor for raising tobacco and cotton on the huge plantations of Virginia and the Deep South, and these were the principal commercial products of the region. Thus the lavish lifestyle of the white elite was inseparably dependent on black muscle and sweat. From birth to death and from morning to night, the life of the typical Southern planter was conditioned by his close involvement with the lives of those who (as Jefferson once put it) labored for his happiness.

It has been a puzzle to many people how a man made world-famous by his passion for human freedom could have adapted to a prominent role in a system of involuntary servitude that he frequently denounced as evil. The answer in part is that he didn't have to adapt: he had been born into the culture of slavery, and knew from earliest memory how it all worked; it was as familiar to him as blue sky and green grass. Once it had become necessary to his livelihood, moreover, he practiced it with a great deal of composure and few outward signs of guilt, regardless of the inner doubts and turmoil that it caused him.

Admirers of Jefferson have often stressed that although he was a slave master, he was a kind and generous one. A reasonable case can be made for this in comparison with the typical Virginia planter of the period, but it is a claim easily overstated. Lucia Stanton, chief research historian at Monticello, has shown in an important recent monograph that while he always tried to keep his slaves healthy, fairly well fed, and contented within the limits allowed by their tasks, he was nonetheless a demanding taskmaster. A striking illustration is the nailery that he established on his mountaintop in 1794, to augment Monticello's income. The workers, as Jefferson explained unabashedly to a correspondent, were "a dozen little boys from 10 to 16 years of age" who were taught to hammer hot iron into nails at anvils grouped around four fires in a building on Mulberry Row, not far from the big mansion. Their hours of labor were long: the master who prided himself on rising every day with the sun required his slaves to do the same, and to keep going until sunset. With his penchant for measuring everything, he kept close track of the number of pounds of nails produced daily by each boy, including exactly how much iron was wasted by each in the process. On the other hand, he rewarded his young workers with extra food rations, and prizes in the form of new suits of clothes for those who were the most productive. The nailery also served as a selective screen enabling Jefferson to choose the most talented boys for further training useful both to the plantation and to themselves: several of them later became expert in such skills as blacksmithing and carpentry.

When it came to punishing slaves for misbehavior, Jefferson usually preferred to do it through his overseers rather than personally. He is not known to have flogged a slave himself, but sometimes ordered flogging as a deterrent to other slaves. Jamey Hubbard, one of the nailers, was caught stealing nails and at first got off with only a lecture on morals from his master, but after he subsequently ran away and was eventually captured and returned to Monticello, he was "severely flogged in the presence of his old companions," as Jefferson described it. When this kind of chastisement was not enough and a slave continued to be recalcitrant, there was a disagreeable but clear-cut solution: he was sold. Jefferson was well aware of how devastating this could be to the culprit, and how intimidating to the Monticello slave community. While he was in Washington during his first presidential term, his son-in-law Thomas Mann Randolph sent him a letter reporting a near-murder at the nailery: a youth named Cary had deliberately slugged a coworker with his hammer, badly fracturing his skull. Jefferson's fierce reply ordered that Cary should be sold to "negro purchasers from Georgia" or "any other quarter so distant as never

RUN away from the subscriber in *Albemarle*, a Mulatto slave called *Sandy*, about 35 years of age, his stature is rather low, inclining to corpulence, and his complexion light; he is a shoemaker by trade, in which he uses his left hand principally, can do coarse carpenters work, and is something of a horse jockey; he is greatly addicted to drink, and when drunk is insolent and disorderly, in his conversation he swears much, and in his behaviour is artful and knavish. He took with him a white horse, much scarred with traces, of which it is expected he will endeavour to dispose; he also carried his shoemakers tools, and will probably endeavour to get employment that way. Whoever conveys the said slave to me, in *Albemarle*, shall have 40 s. reward, if taken up within the county, 4 l. if elsewhere within the colony, and 10 l. if in any other colony, from
THOMAS JEFFERSON.

Jefferson's advertisement, shocking today, was run-of-the-mill when it was printed in the Virginia Gazette *for September 14, 1769.*

more to be heard of among us," and it would seem to the other boys "as if he were put out of the way by death."

There were, however, relatively benign ways to exercise the owner's property rights over his human possessions. In general, Jefferson tried to keep slave families together, and occasionally would make sales or purchases with that as the primary object rather than any material advantage to Monticello. He did, however, encourage his slaves to find mates right there rather than on other plantations, so that their interests and his would be in accord. "There is nothing I desire so much," he wrote to one of his overseers in 1815, "as that all the young people in the estate should intermarry with one another and stay at home. They are worth a great deal more in that case than when they have husbands and wives abroad."

Despite his humane inclinations, Jefferson was painfully aware after his return from France in 1789 that Monticello was sliding steadily into debt, and economic considerations could not be ignored in dealing with his slaves. From a modern point of view, he was especially harsh with regard to teenaged children: he viewed them as capable of productive work by that age, and often gave them assignments that separated them from their parents.

And in the end, all of this "good" master's solicitude for the welfare of his slave "family" (as he called it) was virtually canceled by the ineluctable workings of the slave system itself. Burdened with a huge debt by the time of his death in 1826, he could not, as George Washington did, arrange that they should all go free; as we have seen, only a few of the privileged Hemings family were granted that boon. Less than a year later, his grandson Thomas Jefferson Randolph put all the rest—130 men, women, and children—up for auction. They brought good prices.

Lucia Stanton has woven the narrative of her monograph on slavery at Monticello around the very poignant story of Joe and Edy Fossett, two of the most outstanding of Jefferson's slaves. Joe, whose mother was Betty Hemings's oldest daughter and Sally Hemings's half-sister, was from the age of fourteen one of the cleverest of the crew at the nailery, and after further training became first an assistant and finally, in 1807, the plantation's head blacksmith. Meanwhile he had fallen in love with Edy, a teenager, who, judging from the intensity of Joe's passion for her, must have been extremely attractive. When Jefferson went to the White House for the first term, he took Edy with him for training in French cuisine, and she continued in this tutelage until her master's retirement in 1809. Although there is no way to prove it, it would seem that she and Joe must have gotten together now and then—perhaps during visits to Monticello—for by 1807 she had two small children, and there is no knowledge of any other father.

There was, however, a rumor of close attention to her by some other man in Washington, conveyed to Joe by one of Jefferson's White House servants when the president came home briefly in the summer of 1806. Very shortly thereafter, Joe Fossett disappeared from Monticello—much to Jefferson's dismay, since Joe had "never in his life received a blow from any one," and was looked upon as a model slave. But the master had been remarkably inattentive about the whole business, for evidently he knew that Joe and Edy had been "formerly connected." Now, having learned that Joe was last seen heading for Washington, he finally put two and two together and instructed the man sent in pursuit of Joe to check with Edy at "the President's house." And there, indeed, Joe was apprehended and sent back to Monticello, but not before the young couple had patched things up between them. If this were a fairy tale, their ultimately goodhearted master would have sent them back together, with his cheerful blessing; but this was Thomas Jefferson, and he was not about to curtail Edy's education in gourmet cooking for the sake of a romance that he probably assumed would survive a few more months of separation. And sure enough, when Edy finally came back in 1809 and was made Monticello's head cook, the loving couple became mates for life, and raised a total of eight children.

But their adventures were not over. Jefferson's will directed that Joe Fossett should be given his freedom, effective in July 1827—presumably because he was a favorite slave as well as Sally Hemings's half-nephew. Six months before that, however, he had suffered the trauma of seeing his wife and his children sold to the highest bidders at the auction of Monticello's "negroes." It could have been worse: Edy and their two youngest children were bought by Jesse Scott, a well-known Charlottesville professional fiddler who was actually Joe's brother-in-law, having married his sister Sally Bell. Two teenaged daughters were also sold to Charlottesville residents, and when the sorry business was over, the Fossett family had survived the Monticello auction with only three of the children lost to an unknown fate. And ten years later Joe Fossett, free Negro, having by hard work and various financial maneuvers managed to *buy back* his wife Edy and the children still living with her, performed an act that could be said to put to shame the whole system of American slavery: he legally emancipated them.

Looking at Thomas Jefferson in action as a plantation operator at least offers some consolation to a person disturbed by the fact of his having been a slaveholder: it becomes clear why, if he was going to be the one, he had to be the other. It does not reduce, however, the surprise at his vehemence against the system in such a passage as this from his *Notes on Virginia:*

> The whole commerce between master and slave is a perpetual exercise of the most boisterous passions, the most unremitting despotism on the one part, and degrading submissions on the other. Our children see this, and learn to imitate it . . . The parent storms, the child looks on, catches the lineaments of wrath, puts on the same airs in the circle of smaller slaves, gives a loose to the worst of passions, and thus nursed, educated, and daily exercised in tyranny, cannot but be stamped by it with odious peculiarities. The man must be a prodigy who can retain his manners and morals undepraved by such circumstances.

This excoriation, which might almost have come from the pen of a militant abolitionist, was written by Jefferson when he had already been an active slave master for ten years. It consequently takes on by implication something of the quality of a confession, a mea culpa. Like most confessions, however, it also seeks to a degree to expiate—at least verbally—the sins it admits to. Not a few observers, comparing this man's words with his actions, have raised the cry of "Hypocrite!"—but it's as if Jefferson had replied, "Yes, I acknowledge the painful contradiction, but as you see, I have already condemned myself for it. Cease to chide me."

To live with such a contradiction on one's conscience, nevertheless, is a heavy psychological burden, and the man would indeed "be a prodigy" who would not look for some way to lighten it in his own mind. Jefferson found it by summing up, in *Notes on Virginia*, the conclusions he had reached, through many years of observation, about the physical, mental, and emotional character of blacks, as compared with whites.

"The first difference which strikes us," he says, "is that of color . . . And is this difference of no importance? Is it not the foundation of a greater or less share of beauty in the two races? Are not the fine mixtures of red and white, the expressions of every passion by greater or less suffusions of color in the one, preferable to that eternal monotony, which reigns in the countenances, that immovable veil of black which covers the emotions of the other race? Add to these, flowing hair, a more elegant symmetry of form . . ." Other "physical distinctions proving a difference of race" are cited: blacks are said to sweat more than whites do, "which gives them a very strong and disagreeable odor." They "seem to require less sleep," the master notes, and—apparently unaware of the light it throws on the recreational starvation imposed by the work regimen of the slave—gives this by way of picturesque illustration: "A black after hard labor through the day, will be induced by the slightest amusements to sit up till midnight, or later, though knowing he must be out with the first dawn of the morning."

This leads to further rumination on the psychological characteristics of blacks, again tending to the conclusion that they are simpler folk, and seeming to imply that they are therefore probably better suited to a life of captivity than whites.

They are at least as brave, and more adventuresome. But this may perhaps proceed from a want of forethought, which prevents their seeing a danger till it be present . . . They are more ardent after their female; but love seems with them to be more an eager desire, than a tender delicate mixture of sentiment and sensation. Their griefs are transient. Those numberless afflictions, which render it doubtful whether heaven has given life to us in mercy or in wrath, are less felt, and sooner forgotten with them.

Finally, in the faculty of reason, blacks are "much inferior" to whites, and in imagination they are "dull, tasteless, and anomalous," so that in the whole range of the arts—with the possible exception of music—their meager productions are pitiful.

Despite this catalogue of negatives, Jefferson finds one important attribute in blacks that is decidedly positive. "Whether further observation will or will not verify the conjecture," he says, "that nature has been less bountiful to them in the endowments of the head, I believe that in those of the heart she will be found to have done them justice . . . we find among them numerous instances of the most rigid integrity, and as many among them as among their better instructed masters, of benevolence, gratitude, and unshaken fidelity."

Jefferson is anxious in all of this to take the stance of the disinterested scientist, and ends his discussion with a rejection of dogmatic certainty: "The opinion that they are inferior in the faculties of reason and imagination, must be hazarded with great diffidence . . . I advance it, therefore, as a suspicion only, that the blacks, whether originally a distinct race, or made distinct by time and circumstances, are inferior to the whites in the endowments both of body and mind." Unfortunately, his claim of detachment has been undercut by his extensive and anything but diffident recital of particular points on which he finds blacks to be clearly inferior, as well as by occasional generalizations, such as the following, which seem to leave no room for argument: "The improvement of the blacks in body and mind, in the first instance of their mixture with the whites, has been observed by every one, and proves that their inferiority is not the effect merely of their condition of life."

It has been suggested above that Jefferson's low opinion of blacks' physical and mental "endowments" was in large measure an attempt to narrow, in his own mind, the ironic gap between his proclaimed loathing for slavery and his lifelong role as a slave master, and thus alleviate his sense of guilt. Obviously, on the assumption that his slaves were less than bright, his role as their owner might be viewed to some extent as that of a charitable patriarch taking care of his family. But this in the end is a further irony, since the basic rationale for the "peculiar institution" had always been the assumption of black inferiority.

Although the figure of Thomas Jefferson as slave owner has long been so conspicuous as to be known to the American public in general—calling for nervous explanations, no doubt, on the part of countless public school history teachers—his deeply rooted racial bias has been much less exposed, and even less familiar is the fact that he was all his life an implacable segregationist. Indeed, this has been such a touchy point since the American civil rights movement began to gain real momentum that in some important instances it has been deliberately concealed. A striking example is the Jefferson Memorial in Washington, where thousands of tourists every year read his stirring words on the future of black Americans: "Nothing is more certainly written in the book of fate, than that these people are to be free"—unaware that the sentence has been chopped off midway, and that the startling unseen second half is: "nor is it less certain that the two races, equally free, cannot live in the same government."

This unequivocal declaration was made in his *Autobiography*, written just a few years before his death, but it reprised a view that he had expressed no less forcefully more than thirty years earlier in *Notes on Virginia*, where he proposed that all slaves should be emancipated at birth, but as children

> brought up, at the public expense, to tillage, arts, or sciences, according to their geniuses, till the females should be eighteen, and the males twenty-one years of age, when they should be colonized to such place as the circumstances of the time should render most proper . . .

This reads so matter-of-factly that it takes a moment to realize that the great champion of human liberty is talking about a program of forced training and deportation designed to ultimately rid America of its black population altogether. It was a phantasmagorical scheme even presupposing its political feasibility (which was nil), given its enormous expense, and the guaranteed resistance both of the South's slaveholders and of the slaves themselves. But Jefferson never quite relinquished it as an idea, to the end of his days refining his calculations about it: it would take fifty vessels annually to remove from the country the sixty thousand or so young blacks who were born each year, and so on, and so on.

What compelled a man of Jefferson's humanity, rationality, and sense of justice to advocate such a monstrously authoritarian and utopian plan? He explains it in *Notes on Virginia:*

> Among the Romans emancipation required but one effort. The [white] slave, when made free, might mix with, without staining the blood of his master. But with us a second is necessary, unknown to history. When freed, he is to be removed beyond the reach of mixture.

This, of course, gives an instant clue to Jefferson's insistence on segregation and, if possible, deportation. The point was to avoid the social disaster of miscegenation: the contamination of the pure white strain of the typical Anglo-American with Negro blood. It was a cardinal point for him, and he clung to it all his life—writing to a neighboring Virginian in 1814, for example, "The amalgamation of whites with blacks produces a degradation to which no lover of his country, no lover of excellence in the human character, can innocently consent."

Jefferson had a reason even more worrisome than miscegenation for his dream of getting rid of America's black population. Anticipating challenges to his scheme of emancipation, training, and deportation, he said in *Notes on Virginia*:

> It will probably be asked, Why not retain and incorporate the blacks into the States . . . ? Deep-rooted prejudices entertained by the whites; ten thousand recollections, by the blacks, of the injuries they have sustained; new provocations; the real distinctions which nature has made; and many other circumstances, will divide us into parties, and produce convulsions, which will probably never end but in the extermination of one or the other race.

This ominous passage began to assume a prophetical aspect in the 1790s, when the blacks of Santo Domingo (now Haiti and the Dominican Republic) rose in fierce rebellion against their French masters. By 1797, under the brilliant leadership of the former slave Toussaint L'Ouverture, they were largely in control of the island after much bloody fighting. The prospect of an independent black republic so close to the United States sent alarm through the South for fear that American slaves might catch the revolutionary spirit. It reconvinced Jefferson that the only adequate solution to the problem of slavery would be to somehow get all the blacks out of America. "If something is not done, and done soon," he wrote to a friend, "we shall be the murderers of our own children." He was by no means reassured when a French army sent by Napoleon in 1802 to reconquer Santo Domingo was nearly destroyed by the insurgents, even though Toussaint himself was treacherously captured and sent to France as a prisoner—where he died in 1803. And the struggle ended in 1804 with a horrendous massacre of nearly all the whites who were left on the island.

Not enough attention has usually been given to the potent mixture of guilt and fear about slavery that existed at some level in Jefferson's mind for much of his life. The fear component grew as the years went by, but even in the 1780s when he was writing and revising his *Notes on Virginia,* he already, as has been seen, was having bad dreams about a lethal racial war if the blacks were not gotten out of the country. Not surprisingly, as the likelihood of realization for his deportation plan grew steadily dimmer, his youthful enthusiasm for emancipation subsided along with it. The success of the Revolution intensified the abolishment of slavery in the Northern states, but the invasion of the South by the British in 1781, while Jefferson was governor of Virginia, had brought the scary spectacle of thousands of slaves (including about thirty of Jefferson's) absconding to the enemy—sometimes, of course, under great pressure from the British.

The threat of slave rebellions had also been magnified. One that stirred tremendous alarm flared up in the summer of 1800, just months before Jefferson became president. A young Richmond blacksmith named Gabriel Prosser, a free black who persuaded slave acquaintances to arm themselves and strike for freedom by citing the Declaration of Independence, planned the initial attack for the night of August 30. Someone had betrayed

This illustration for a nineteenth-century biography of Toussaint L'Ouverture shows the moment at which—called to a "parley" with the French commanders agaist whom his black soldiers had been fiercely fighting—he realizes that he has been tricked and is about to be taken prisoner.

the scheme, however, and Governor James Monroe quickly called out the militia in large numbers. Gabriel and some twenty of his followers were arrested and summarily hanged. Jefferson, though no doubt disturbed by the rebellion, was equally disturbed by the punishment: he had argued for deportation of the culprits, but to no avail.

In 1784 Jefferson had sponsored a nearly successful congressional bill to outlaw slavery in any new state. But in 1820, at the crux of the controversy over whether Missouri should be admitted to the Union as a slave state or free, he argued firmly in favor of permitting slavery. His basic argument was that a large number of independent small farmers, each having only a few slaves, would be more likely to treat them kindly, and more willing to let them go if and when the time came for emancipation. Thus, he maintained, the "diffusion" of slavery would both humanize it and hasten its end—and, he no doubt hoped, also lessen the likelihood of a mass rebellion.

Among his close friends, Madison and Monroe—both slave owners—tended to agree, but Lafayette was unable to comprehend how spreading slavery around the United States was going to contribute to the cause of human freedom. For many Virginia planters, the idea of diffusion had economic appeal, quite aside from (or in spite of) its "humanitarian" gloss. Virginia at this period had an enormous population of surplus slaves, so selling them to buyers in other states was becoming a profitable business. It looked as if Missouri might offer a good expansion for this market.

While Jefferson refrained from commenting on this aspect of the debate, he was surely well aware of it. As for the political aspects, he came down unequivocally on the Southern side, expressing the view that allowing the federal government to dictate the prohibition of slavery within a state violated states' rights and the Constitution. It would be a likely precursor, he feared, to a federally mandated national emancipation (with no provision for deportation)—"in which case," he wrote to his former secretary of the treasury, Albert Gallatin, "all the whites within the United

States south of the Potomac and Ohio must evacuate their States, and most fortunate those who can do it first." This, though phrased with something like bitter humor, was another projection of his serial nightmare—the specter of perhaps a million unfettered blacks wreaking revenge on their former masters.

At the same time, he was much upset by the compromise that Congress worked out on the Missouri problem: that state would be permitted to have slavery, but territories north of an extension of the Mason-Dixon line and west of Missouri would be free ground. The news of this, he wrote to a congressman in April 1820, aroused him "like a fire bell in the night . . . I considered it at once the knell of the Union." He believed that this legalized North/South division on such a sensitive question would exacerbate the growing political and economic rivalry between the two sections of the country, and might split the nation with a civil war. Once again, he referred to his utopian plan of emancipation and "expatriation," but he was no longer hopeful of its realization—"as it is," he said, with a metaphor that has gone down in history, "we have the wolf by the ear, and we can neither hold him, nor safely let him go."

Through all of this, Jefferson never gave up his conviction that slavery was an evil that must eventually be wiped out. On the personal level, however, he seems to have accepted complacently that he was destined to live out his days as a slaveholder, and now and then he made observations that were decidedly mellow compared to his execration of slavery in *Notes on Virginia*. The slaves, he pointed out to a correspondent in 1814, in addition to being well fed and given decent shelter, "have the comfort of numerous families in the midst of whom they live without want or fear of it, a solace which few laborers of England possess." It sounded almost enviable.

· · ·

Now that the sexual liaison between Jefferson and Sally Hemings has been generally accepted as true, it is interesting to consider the effect that the relationship may have had on his thinking about slavery. He had been intricately involved with the "peculiar institution" all his life; but no matter how well a master knew favorite slaves such as his personal servants, there was bound to be an impenetrable barrier of status that made true intimacy impossible. If Sally had been merely a convenient concubine, summoned occasionally to satisfy her master's surges of lust and nothing more, that barrier would have remained intact; but there are many reasons to believe that their love affair went far beyond that. Its endurance over a period of at least twenty years and seven pregnancies, resulting in at least four children who were given names drawn from Jefferson's family history, and who were well cared for until they grew to adulthood and were allowed to go free, speaks not of a master's ruthless exploitation of living property, but of a genuinely conjugal relationship despite the quasi-secrecy that surrounded it.

It is altogether likely, I believe, that Thomas Jefferson learned more about the actualities of his slaves' lives, about their hopes and fears and joys and sorrows—in short, about their human sensibilities—from Sally than from any other source he ever had. She was raised differently from most of them, of course, being not just the daughter of a favored house servant but also a blood relative of Jefferson's beloved wife. Yet Betty Hemings, her mother, was surely in close touch with the entire black community at Monticello, and Sally herself was by no means isolated from it. If Jefferson had done his revision of *Notes on Virginia* a couple of years *after* Sally had settled in at his mansion in Paris in 1787—the only English-speaking female under his roof most of each week—instead of a couple of years before, I suspect that his characterization of blacks would have been far less derogatory and far more realistic than it was. Indeed, having a beautiful slave as a lover, and producing bright and beautiful children with her, quite probably helped to alter his own retrospective view of that characterization, so that he was able to write to a correspondent a number of years later, "My doubts were the result of personal observation on the limited sphere of my own State, where the opportunities for the developing of their genius were not favorable . . . On this subject they are gaining daily in the opinions of nations, and hopeful advances are making towards their re-establishment on an equal footing with the other colors of the human family." *Amor vincit*, it seems—well, perhaps not *omnia;* but a great deal.

A few well-meaning attempts were made to persuade Jefferson that he ought to bring his principles and his practice into better alignment. One of his Virginia neighbors was a young man named Edward Coles, who enormously admired Jefferson and had been James Madison's private secretary for several years. Coles was ardently antislavery, and in the summer of 1814 he sent Jefferson a letter respectfully urging him to exercise his great prestige in leading a strong public movement toward emancipation in Virginia. He himself had recently become the reluctant owner of about twenty slaves by inheritance, but had been deterred from freeing them by the Virginia law forcing them to leave the state once freed. He had therefore (he explained in a follow-up letter) made the drastic decision to sell his Virginia land and take his slaves with him to Illinois, where he planned to free them and set them up as tenant farmers.

Innocently unaware that emancipation without deportation was anathema to his idol, he must have been sharply disillusioned by the response he got. Jefferson not only declined to actively take up the cause, on the ground that he was too old for the role, but tried to dissuade the young idealist from carrying out his plan.

The blacks, he said, having unfortunately been made unfit for freedom by their years of slavery ("incapable as children of taking care of themselves"), probably never would succeed as tenant farmers. Better for Coles, Jefferson advised, to stay in Virginia and himself become a missionary for emancipation and "softly and steadily" inculcate its acceptance among the state's educated class.

But Edward Coles was too young and too bold to be satisfied with any such vague program. He did indeed sell his Virginia property, take his slaves to Illinois, free them, and get them started as independent farmers. Not only that, but in 1822 he was elected governor of Illinois on an antislavery platform, and in 1824 successfully defeated an attempt by the proslavery forces to pass a state constitutional amendment legalizing slavery—a true early hero in the struggle to free American blacks.

12

Blinkered Historians

———•✦•———

J efferson's popular reputation, after his death, ebbed and flowed with the decades, but without much attention to Sally Hemings until the second half of the twentieth century, when the awakening civil rights movement began to focus sharply on the split between his often avowed hatred of slavery and his lifelong ownership of hundreds of slaves. Already elected to the American pantheon because of his indelible association with the Declaration of Independence, which was unforgettably confirmed by Lincoln's citation of "all men are created equal" in the Gettysburg Address, Jefferson became an increasingly difficult figure for history teachers to explain as rumors began to circulate among their students about a black mistress who was young enough to be his daughter.

This all sprang into wide public view with the publication in 1974 of Fawn M. Brodie's *Thomas Jefferson: An Intimate History*. Brodie, a well-known UCLA history professor and biographer, firmly took the position that Sally and her master had been lovers for more than thirty years, starting when they were together in France in 1787–1789, and resulting in the births of all of Sally's children. Despite its academic origin, the book was written in a lucid and lively style and quickly became a bestseller with many reprintings. It was, however, immediately and ferociously attacked by a posse of professorial critics and reviewers, led by the eminent Virginia biographers Dumas Malone and Merrill Peterson.

It is arguable that the most important thing about the recent scientific confirmation of the Sally Hemings story is the light it throws on one of the most striking and persistent derelictions of scholarly integrity ever seen in American historiography: the ignoring, misconstruing, distorting, and denying of very strong circumstantial evidence supporting the story by the country's most distinguished Jefferson biographers. It is a complicated tale, but for purposes of epitome a look at just three scholars will do. Malone and Peterson, both of whom produced renowned studies based on many years of research, clearly qualify; and Joseph J. Ellis, by dint of winning the 1997 National Book Award, makes a good third man.

The question comes down to this: how could these highly trained scholars have so unequivocally rejected the story in the face of several salient and undisputed pieces of evidence that have been conspicuously available for many years?

First there is the undisputed fact that despite his prolonged absences from Monticello during his service as secretary of state, vice president, and president, Thomas Jefferson was invariably there when Sally conceived each of her six known children, and, conversely, she never conceived when he was not there. Second, there is contemporary word-of-mouth evidence that her three male offspring who survived into adulthood bore a startling resemblance to Jefferson himself. Third, Jefferson saw to it that all four of Sally's surviving children, as well as she herself, escaped from slavery—a blessing he bestowed upon no other slave family among the scores he owned during his life. (As noted earlier, the two eldest Hemings children, Beverly and Harriet, simply departed from Monticello with his help soon after coming of age; Madison and Eston were freed by his will; and Sally was allowed to join them by Patsy, after his death.) The children were all octoroons, and presumably (and by report) very light-skinned.

Finally, there is the fascinating fact, accepted by nearly all Jefferson biographers, that Sally Hemings's father was the slave trader and lawyer John Wayles, who was also the father of Martha, Jefferson's wife: they were half-sisters. This could be used (and has been) either to explain Jefferson's extraordinary favoritism toward Sally and her children (regardless of who sired them) or to support the idea that sisterly resemblance between Sally and Martha, who was passionately loved by her husband for the ten years of their marriage, aroused Jefferson's love and desire after Martha died and Sally grew into a reputedly beautiful young woman.

It is a historical irony that Malone, who was devoutly interested in showing that Jefferson was "innocent," spent a lot of time unwittingly compiling documentary evidence putting Jefferson at Monticello at just the times of Sally's conceptions. This certainly was far from Malone's intention, which was simply to provide, as part of the apparatus for each of the five volumes of his biography after the first, a careful chronology of the great man's activities, including of course his movements to and from his mountain estate in Virginia. This made it almost absurdly easy for Fawn Brodie, in the 1970s, to compare Jefferson's sojourns at Monticello with the dates, as noted by him in his Farm Book, of the births of each of Sally's offspring, and by subtracting the magic number nine from those dates to arrive at the strikingly consistent correlation. (There was a late flurry of suspense at Monticello in 1993 when Lucia Stanton, the senior research historian, found a hitherto unnoticed reference, in a letter of Jefferson's, to an unnamed child of Sally's who died soon after it was born in 1799. Would the date of its conception confirm or contradict the evidence of his having always been there at the appropriate times for impregnation? It turned out that he was right there that time too, upping the odds for Jefferson as the likely father of all of her offspring to a level that, it might be supposed, would convince even a skeptical gambler.)

Neither Malone nor Peterson saw fit to make any comment on the remarkable chronological correlation, however—an instance of their inclination to don historical blinkers when reality loomed up and threatened their fond vision of Thomas Jefferson. Nevertheless, if Jefferson had not furnished the necessary sperm, some other candidate had to be found—and he had to fulfill certain requirements. He had to have been a white man, and he had to have been related closely enough to Jefferson to produce children who obviously resembled the master.

It is another wonderful irony that the most outspoken witness on the matter of the close resemblance of some of Sally's children to Jefferson was his grandson, Thomas Jefferson Randolph, who was also his most fervent defender—as "immaculate a man as God ever created," he said—against allegations that his grandfather had sired those children. In 1868 pioneering biographer Henry S. Randall related to the younger biographer James Parton that some ten years earlier he had conversed with Randolph about "the Dusky Sally story." According to Randall, Randolph remarked, "There was a better excuse for it than you might think: she had children which resembled Mr. Jefferson so closely that it was plain that they had his blood in their veins." But despite his embarrassment at having the obvious resemblance "blazoned to all the multitudes who visited Monticello," Randolph insisted that "there was not the shadow of suspicion" that his grandfather had ever "had commerce" with Sally or any other female slave. The explanation of the close likeness, he said, was the "notorious" fact that Sally was "the mistress" of Peter Carr, Jefferson's nephew, and that Peter had actually confessed to Randolph (with "tears coursing down his cheeks") that he had fathered at least some of Sally's children.

So much has been made of this explanation by leading biographers, including Malone and Peterson, that it has become the mainstay exhibit against all the circumstantial evidence on the other side of the controversy. Yet it was an egregiously slender thread to hang that burden on. It has usually been overlooked, in the murk of the argument, that Thomas Jefferson Randolph was the lone source of the claim that Peter Carr was the responsible man. There is no evidence that Carr on any other occasion ever admitted having anything to do with Sally Hemings, or that anyone other than Randolph ever accused him of it. The tearful-confession story, moreover, was thirdhand hearsay evidence relayed after a very long lapse of time: Parton was passing along, in his biography of Jefferson, what he had heard from Randall about a story *he* had heard from Randolph about ten years earlier, about an incident that had supposedly occurred at least forty years before that.

(Randolph's wispy story, incidentally, has been completely blown away by the DNA tests: blood samples from Carr descendants were tested along with those from Jefferson descendants—and no correlation between the Carr and Hemings blood samples was found.)

The reaction of Malone and Peterson to the basically unarguable items of circumstantial evidence supporting the probability of the Jefferson-Hemings liaison was typically either to look the other way or turn to some flimsy explanation such as Thomas Jefferson Randolph's. There were few clues to the motivation behind their denials of the relationship other than their strong feeling that Jefferson simply was not the kind of man who would have done such a thing. But with the publication in 1974 of Fawn Brodie's book, this quickly changed. Although it was a comprehensive biography, covering all aspects of Jefferson's life, what quickly focused the attention of these scholars was Brodie's emphasis on the Hemings connection. This generated a storm of lacerating epithets in reviews and articles: "nonsense," "slander," "psychological speculation," "a tissue of surmises," "sexually obsessed," and so on. But repeat printings of the book continued to pour out, and in 1979 CBS Television revealed a plan for a Sally Hemings miniseries. Greatly agitated, both Malone and Peterson wrote indignant letters to CBS officials deploring a project that would promote (Malone said) "a tawdry and unverifiable story."

Although the plan for the television series was eventually dropped for one reason or another, the level of Malone's and Peterson's animus against Fawn Brodie did not subside. They were particularly disturbed by her resurrection of Madison Hemings's 1873 memoir. The inclusion of it as an appendix to her biography was its first reprinting since its original publication—an admirable service to Jefferson studies, but one that the Virginia historians were exceedingly loath to honor. Merrill Peterson, who had been aware of the document when he wrote his well-known study *The Jefferson Image in the American Mind* (1960), allowed that Madison's recollections of Monticello were "vivid and accurate," and briefed them reasonably well—though he mistook Madison's brother Beverly to have been a girl. He even quoted one significant sentence, about Sally: "It was her duty, all her life which I can remember, up to the time of father's death, to take care of his chamber and wardrobe, look after us children and do such light work as sewing, &c." But he summarily disposed of the claim that Jefferson was Madison's father with the remark that "no serious student of Jefferson has ever declared his belief" in this "legend"— a fine example of begging the question. A generation of hot debate on the subject failed to change Peterson's mind, except that, in an essay published in 1993, the "legend" had become "the hoary legend," and Fawn Brodie, who is charged with having "revived" it, is identified as "a latter-day abolitionist."

Dumas Malone, galvanized by what he regarded as the outrageous success of Brodie's biography and by the new prominence she had given to Madison's memoir, conducted some research on the circumstances of its original publication, and declared in a *Journal of Southern History* article in 1975 that it had been "solicited and published for a propagandist purpose" by the editor of the *Pike County Republican*—that is, to make Thomas Jefferson look bad as a "Democratic" slaveholder who had kept his own son in bondage. Beyond that he made no analysis of Madison's account, simply stating that it was "unacceptable in important respects." What he did do, however, was to reprint an 1873 editorial from a fierce Democratic rival of the *Republican*, the weekly *Watchman*, sarcastically attacking the veracity of Madison's memoir. It is, the editorial asserts, "a well known peculiarity of the colored race" to "lay claim to illustrious parentage . . . A perusal of Hemings' autobiography reminds us of the pedigree printed on the numerous stud-horse bills that can be seen posted around . . . No matter how scrubby the stock or whether the horse has any known pedigree, the 'Horse Owner' furnishes a full and complete pedigree of every celebrated horse in the county . . ," Malone has no word to say about the blatant racism of this critique, and the uncomfortable feeling arises that he may have found it rather agreeable. Having detected nothing specifically assailable in Madison's memoir, however, he evidently decided that oblivion was the best place for it: in the final volume of his own Jefferson biography, which came out in 1981, his only reference to it is a bibliographical note listing his *Journal of Southern History* article. As for Fawn Brodie, her name is not to be found anywhere in Malone's biography or in his bibliography.

The failure by both Malone and Peterson to make any scholarly analysis of Madison Hemings's obviously important memoir, or to look closely at the items (cited above) of essentially undisputable evidence in favor of the truth of the Jefferson-Hemings liaison, unfortunately adds up to a strong impression of a disheartening myopia on the whole subject. It raises a faint but clear echo of the old Virginia law—now long gone, but kept on the books with Jefferson's endorsement when the state constitution was being revised in the late 1770s—decreeing the testimony of Negroes, whether enslaved or free, to be inadmissible in court. The two scholars seem to have constructed an image of their hero pleasantly consonant with their view of themselves as liberal-minded but socially conservative Virginia gentlemen, and judged his relationship with Sally Hemings accordingly. As Malone expressed it, "it is virtually inconceivable that this fastidious gentleman . . . could have carried on through a period of years a vulgar liaison which his own family could not have failed to detect." Such sentiments plus the utterly contemptuous tone of their epithets for Fawn Brodie's work, together with their habitual reverence for their notoriously white-supremacist icon, create a distinct aura of racial bias, whether conscious or unconscious.

The role of Joseph Ellis in the Sally Hemings wrangle is unique. Early in his prize-winning biography he strikes a magisterial posture and declares that "the available evidence on each side of the controversy is just sufficient to sustain the debate but wholly insufficient to resolve it one way or the other. Anyone who claims to have a clear answer to this most titillating question about the historical Jefferson is engaging in massive self-deception or outright lying." He briefly reprises this Solomon-like stance at the end of the book in an appendix called "A Note on the Sally Hemings Scandal," balancing Madison Hemings's memoir against Thomas Jefferson Randolph's odd little tale of Peter Carr's confession of having fathered Sally's children, as if they were equally convincing. (Ellis confuses the record at this point, stating that it was Martha Jefferson Randolph (Patsy) whom Carr confessed to rather than Thomas Jefferson Randolph—for which there is no historical evidence.) He cites the fact that "the timing of her [Sally's] pregnancies" was "compatible" with Jefferson's presence at Monticello, but nonetheless proceeds to veer into a line not sharply divergent from that of his much admired seniors, Malone and Peterson: the likelihood of the liaison is, he says, "remote."

Then comes the stunner. Ellis has developed a theory about Jefferson's character that is a radically original contribution to American history. Our third president, he has decided, "for most of his adult life, lacked the capacity for the direct and physical expression of his sexual energies . . . Jefferson consummated his relations with women at a more rarefied level, where the palpable realities of physical intimacy were routinely sublimed to safer and more sentimental regions." In plainer and less elegant words, Jefferson was impotent for most of his life.

One person who surely would have been astonished to hear this was Martha Wayles Jefferson, the young wife whom Jefferson kept almost incessantly pregnant during the ten years of their tragically brief marriage. During that time she bore him six children, and there are indications of at least one miscarriage besides. Mr. Ellis knows this, of course, but still reaches the unqualified conclusion that after Martha's death in 1782 Jefferson lost the ability as well as the desire to make physical love: "His most sensual statements were aimed at beautiful buildings rather than beautiful women."

A slight difficulty with this hypothesis is the well-documented story of Jefferson's ardent but abortive pursuit of Maria Cosway, the beautiful and talented Anglo-Italian whom he met in 1786 during his service as minister to France. But this is seen by Ellis as an illustration of his theory that Jefferson "sublimed" his sexual urges from physical to sentimental. He refers to the couple as "lovers," but says that "the abiding character of their lengthy correspondence makes it abundantly clear that Jefferson preferred to meet his lovers in the rarefied region of the mind rather than the physical world of his bedchamber." Apparently Ellis had never noticed the letter (quoted in Chapter VIII) Jefferson wrote to Cosway in April 1788, after returning from his trip along the Rhine valley, extolling Van der Werff's "delicious" painting showing Sarah offering her slave girl Hagar, suitably undressed, to her naked husband, and Jefferson's immortal comment, "I would have agreed to be Abraham though the consequence would have been that I should have been dead five or six thousand years."

Though preposterously dubious, Ellis's theory of Jefferson's impotence did offer a solution to the question, mostly shied away from by the mainstream biographers, of why a man whose passionate sexuality for the first half of his life was so obvious should have abruptly shifted to monklike abstinence for the second half. But of course this was never a problem for anyone who believed in the Jefferson-Hemings liaison, and with the clincher of the DNA evidence it has vanished into the stratosphere. This may be as good a place as any to mention that with the announcement of that evidence, Ellis instantly leaped to the other side of the fence, and has now become a sturdy proponent of the validity of the liaison—though as far as I know he has had nothing further to say about his impotence theory.

To those on the "denial" side of the debate, a source of comfort has been that Madison's testimony largely repeated the assertions made in 1802 by James Callender, "the most unscrupulous scandalmonger of the day," as John C. Miller summed it up—thus associating Madison with their favorite scapegoat, a man to whom, as they saw it, vicious lies and slander were bread and butter. This characterization of Callender became a kind of cliché of Jefferson biography, and prevailed with little or no challenge until 1990, when Michael Durey's study of Callender's career, *"With the Hammer of Truth": James Thomson Callender and America's Early National Heroes*, was published. This revealed a far more complex personality, a radical idealist who was so fervently devoted to "pure" democracy that he turned his pen—which did seem naturally to exude vitriol—successively against George Washington, the Constitution, Alexander Hamilton, John Adams, and Thomas Jefferson, because none of them lived up to his utopian notions of what good government should be. He believed that his mission as a journalist was to expose to the American people the corruptions of their leaders so that corrections could be made through elections, which in his opinion should be held annually.

Jefferson was well aware that Callender had a genius for scalding satire that often veered into defamation; but as long as it was directed against Jefferson's enemies, it struck him as politically useful. He had become friendly with the Republican pamphleteer in Philadelphia in 1797, when Callender was busy exposing some of Alexander Hamilton's sins, sexual and professional, and in 1798 the two exchanged several amicable letters discussing Callender's prolific efforts on behalf of Jefferson's political interests. In addition to strong verbal encouragement, Jefferson sent the chronically impoverished writer fifty dollars to keep him going, and Callender understandably began to look on the vice president as an admired mentor as well as a politician amazingly free of the vices he usually attributed to men in powerful positions.

So it was that as the presidential election of 1800 drew near, Jefferson quietly helped Callender in the preparation of a work entitled *The Prospect before Us*, a ferocious attack on John Adams and his administration, paying him another fifty dollars in advance for copies of it, reading proofs of some pages, and supplying the journalist with additional information. The tract, published early in 1800, was widely read and caused a considerable stir—not least among the Federalists, who had been waiting for a chance to hit Callender. They shortly got him indicted for violating the Sedition Act by publishing false and malicious statements about President Adams, and in May 1800 he went on trial in Richmond.

There was little doubt about the outcome: the judge was a belligerent Federalist, and all twelve members of the jury were of the same political persuasion. Moreover, the Republican defense lawyers exerted no great effort to save Callender, instead seeking to drag out the trial so as to make the judge seem even more biased than he actually was, and to attack the Sedition Act itself as unconstitutional. As for Callender, he was content to sacrifice himself for his hero Jefferson and for the good of the Republican party in the forthcoming election. He clearly expected that in the martyr's role he would be amply rewarded by the party and, especially, by Jefferson's gratitude, which he fondly hoped would take the form of some sort of government appointment after the election. The job of postmaster at Richmond, he thought, would be just right.

Sentenced to nine months in prison plus a fine of two hundred dollars, Callender managed to make the best of his incarceration in the ramshackle Richmond jail, turning out scores of newspaper columns defending Jefferson on every point the Federalists picked for verbal assault, and directing the publication of a sequel to *The Prospect before Us.*

But, although he received commiserating visits from such leading Republicans as James Monroe—then governor of Virginia—and Jefferson's old friend George Wythe, Jefferson himself did not appear, nor did a single letter arrive to answer several Callender sent him. By the time Callender got out of jail in March 1801, Jefferson was president of the United States, and the martyred ex-convict specifically asked to be appointed as Richmond postmaster.

Jefferson, however, like other newly elected presidents, had decided to lean more to the political center in his administration, and Callender was by now a notorious champion of the Republican left. Desperate to salvage something from his years of risky labor for the cause, Callender went to Washington to plead his case, but was not even admitted to see Jefferson, and got a cold shoulder from Secretary of State James Madison. The shattering reality now dawned on him that he was to get nothing at all from the leader he had so ardently supported.

Full of bitterness that was marinating into hatred as the months went by, Callender started writing for a supposedly nonpartisan paper, the *Richmond Recorder*, but soon was clamorously feuding with his former friends in the Republican press. What finally triggered his explosive attack on Jefferson was a venomous piece in the Philadelphia *Aurora* late in August 1802, accusing Callender of having caused his wife's death by infecting her with venereal disease, and of shamefully neglecting his children. Aiming directly at the man who now seemed to him to be the prime cause of his misery, Callender fired off his notorious claim, on September 1, 1802, that the president "keeps, and for many years past has kept, as his concubine, one of his own slaves. Her name is SALLY."

Durey's summation of the Callender/Jefferson tangle was not one to elicit delight from the Virginia historians and their cohorts. "Contrary to the opinion of Jefferson's admirers," he says, "Callender was not an incorrigible liar. His interpretations of facts frequently were strained and exaggerated, but there is little, if any, evidence of his purposeful invention of stories or falsification of

The paragraph that stunned readers of the Richmond Recorder on the morning of September 1, 1802, and started a controversy that was to last two hundred years, wasn't even on the front page. Callender, its embittered author, had earlier composed a long, rambling complaint about Jefferson's colossal ingratitude, unmatched in history, for the years of ardent work he, Callender, had performed to ensure a Jefferson victory; and it was after that had already been typeset for the first page that the journalist's anger and hatred finally erupted and resulted in the immortal accusation about Sally Hemings, appearing without fanfare or warning on the second page. Callender made some factual mistakes (which he corrected later) after the first two sentences; but the impact of those two would make him famous (or infamous, if you prefer) in American history.

facts. When his published facts, rather than opinions, were found to be false, he usually publicly corrected them ... What is surprising is not Callender's penchant for falsification, but his ability to uncover facts that have later been found to be true."

Looked at more fully and unblinkingly than nearly all Jefferson's biographers have been willing to do, his relationship with Callender throws an unflattering light on Jefferson's character. Not only did he coldly abandon Callender after encouraging and approving his pamphleteering against the Federalists, but he later tried to conceal the extent of his involvement by describing (to Abigail Adams and others) the money he sent to Callender as "charity" toward a needy writer, rather than payments for political propaganda, and protesting falsely that "nobody sooner disapproved of his writing than I did." To Mrs. Adams he added that society must in the end judge him "by a regard to the general tenor of my life. On this I am not afraid to appeal to the nation at large, to posterity, and still less to that Being who sees himself our motives, who will judge us from his own knowledge of them." It was the kind of blanket self-endorsement that Jefferson used several times in his life, sidestepping specific denials, to smother suspicions that he might have done something wrong.

The tone of racial bias in the fervor of leading Southern biographers to deny the Jefferson-Hemings liaison would be compatible with a relatively tolerant attitude toward Jefferson's own racism. This proves to be true for Dumas Malone, who treats Jefferson's discourse on the inferiority of blacks in *Notes on Virginia* gently, and with emphasis on the tentativeness of his conclusions. "His comments," wrote Malone ". . . represented the tentative judgments of a kindly and scientifically minded man who deplored the absence of sufficient data and adequate criteria." But it is notable that he does not quote Jefferson's specific listing of the blacks' deficient characteristics as compared to the whites', so that the powerful impact of the original text—almost producing the effect of a diatribe—is utterly lost. Merrill Peterson, on the other hand, although he credits Jefferson with having been "honest" and "disinterested" in his observations, declares that his opinion of blacks "was also a product of frivolous and tortuous reasoning, of preconception, prejudice, ignorance, contradiction, and bewildering confusion of principles." And he goes on to an eloquent indictment of Jefferson's profound bias and self-delusional posture of objectivity: "Many of his observations, paraded as scientific, were but thinly disguised statements of folk belief about Negroes." This is surprising in view of the disgust and contempt that Peterson voices with regard to allegations of validity for the Jefferson-Hemings affair and, ironically enough, is reminiscent of the very sort of intellectual confusion that he is denouncing in Jefferson.

In any event, there was one corollary of Jefferson's racial bias that did strikingly fit the purpose of denying the Hemings connection. His horror of miscegenation between whites and blacks seemed to offer a strong reason for believing that, regardless of any supposed evidence to the contrary, Thomas Jefferson never would have indulged in a sexual affair with a slave girl. "A miscegenous relationship," Merrill Peterson confidently remarks, would have "revolted his whole being"; John C. Miller agrees that it would have been "in utter defiance of . . . his loathing of racial mixture."

But this is a prime instance of the disinclination of these historians to look searchingly at certain pieces of evidence that cast doubt on their conclusions. There is no challenging the fact of Jefferson's disgust for miscegenation in general. Yet he had given much thought to the genetics that were involved, and had worked out precise calculations on the subject. His results were summarized in his response to a query from an acquaintance in 1815 as to "what constituted a mulatto by our law." ("Mulatto," as Jefferson used the term, meant a person with enough Negro blood to be considered legally black.) Drawing up a chart of various black/white combinations, he concludes that if a person of one-fourth Negro blood (a "quarteroon," Jefferson called it; the more usual term is "quadroon") were to cross with a "pure white," their offspring, "having less than 1/4 of . . . pure negro blood, to wit 1/8 only, is no longer a mulatto, so that a third cross clears the blood."

Think what this means when applied to Sally Hemings. She was a quadroon, a person of one-fourth Negro blood, having had a white father (John Wayles) and a half-breed mother (Betty Hemings). She was legally a slave, and by Virginia law any children she had, of whatever skin color, would automatically be slaves also. If she mated with a black man, the chances of those "colored" children ever escaping from the yoke of slavery would be very slight. But if she mated with Thomas Jefferson—a "pure white" if there ever was one—her children would be "no longer . . . mulatto." They would still legally be slaves, but they would almost certainly be white enough to pass for white; and with a father who was master of the plantation and a man eager to decrease the black population of Virginia and increase the white, their chance for freedom would be very good indeed.

Considering all this in Paris in 1787, Jefferson may well have felt that a heaven-sent obligation had descended upon him. If Sally, young, fresh, and deliciously nubile, were to go back to Monticello at sixteen or seventeen, unattached and available, every young black male on the plantation would be after her, and the consequences, from Jefferson's point of view, would be highly regrettable. His antipathy for miscegenation had almost surely been intensified by the discovery that his father-in-law, John Wayles, had breached the color line with Betty Hemings: the results of that miscegenation, as embodied in Sally and James Hemings, had been undeniably admirable in a sense; yet on principle it could not be condoned, for it had dishonored and contaminated the family pedigree. Here was an opportunity to rectify, in part, that contamination: it would in effect *rescue* Sally's children from "amalgamation," and constitute, on a small but meaningful scale, an act of benign ethnic cleansing. (That phrase does not seem to have existed in eighteenth- and nineteenth-century discussions of the subject, but I think Thomas Jefferson would have found it extremely apt.) He was thus in the pleasant position of being able to enjoy Sally's enticements with a sense of performing a decidedly noble deed.

And indeed, with regard to the fate of Sally's children, things worked out just as Jefferson's genetic chart predicted: they were (as the Monticello overseer put it) "nearly as white as anybody," so that as young adults they were basically equipped to step out of the black world into the white. Three of them—Beverly, Harriet, and Eston—actually did it. The fourth, Madison, although presumably light enough to pass for white, chose to marry Mary McCoy, a free woman whose grandmother had been a slave. She herself was evidently at least one-fourth black—possibly rather close in color to Madison's mother, Sally. His decision not to join the white community may have been partly a defiant rejection of Jefferson's theory that "the two races, equally free, cannot live in the same government." But whatever his reason was, it very probably would have severely annoyed his late master.

One aspect of Jefferson's view of life that has been held to cast doubt on the Sally Hemings story is his great fondness for the idea of family. From the days of his youthful dreaming about a domestic future when he and a good wife and children might create an ideal household, perhaps even teaming up with a close friend like John Page—a joyful center of love, learning, cultivation of the arts, and good living in general—through the many years of striving to make Monticello a castle of domestic felicity, the image of family as the wellspring of happiness was never far from Jefferson's mind. "It is in the love of one's family only," he wrote his daughter Polly in 1801, "that heartfelt happiness is known"; and to Patsy a few years later, "I long to be among you where I know nothing but love and delight."

Not surprisingly, this intense affection for hearth and home has been cited by biographers like Malone and Peterson as obvious evidence that an extramarital intimacy would be just too much to believe—"virtually inconceivable," in Malone's words, for "this fastidious gentleman whose devotion to his dead wife's memory and to the happiness of his daughters and grandchildren bordered on the excessive."

A neutral observer, however, might note the fact that Sally Hemings was, after all, literally a member of the Jefferson family, and had been part of the Jefferson household for her whole life. The head of that household, nostalgically envisaging the Monticello scene while he was away in Philadelphia or Washington, could hardly have left her out of the picture.

Historian Jan Lewis, who has written extensively and perceptively on Jefferson's domestic life, has observed that "it was only after he returned to the United States from Paris" that he explicitly "began linking his happiness to his family." "The first time Jefferson said that his happiness derived from his family," she notes, "was in June 1791 when, writing to his daughter Maria [Polly] from Philadelphia . . . he exclaimed, 'Would to god I could be with you to partake of your felicities, and to tell you in person how much I love you all . . . '" It is by no means unimaginable that "all," in Jefferson's mind, included Sally Hemings, who at this point may quite possibly have been nursing their first child, conceived in Paris.

13
The Heart of the Matter

—◆—

Jefferson's very long, labored epistle to Maria Cosway after she
went back to London from Paris in the autumn of 1786, which
he described as a "dialogue between my Head and my
Heart," has generally been regarded by biographers as offering
deep insights into his character, and has been given corresponding
attention. The Head/Heart dichotomy is too neat an imposition
on the complexity of the human psyche: rational and emotional,
objective and subjective phenomena are in real life often (if not
always) intertwined, and it is hard to tell where one leaves off and
the other begins. Nevertheless, it reveals a lot about an individual
to look at his or her own perception of the balance—or contest—
between them, as to what functions are at least theoretically
assigned to each, and the circumstances under which one or the
other is seen as dominant.

A brief summary of Jefferson's letter was given earlier in this
book, with the conclusion that to a neutral observer the Heart
would seem to be the clear winner of the debate—not only
because it is granted, unrebutted, the entire last four pages of the
dialogue, but because the Heart is put in charge of morals, as
opposed to calculation and logic. ("Morals were too essential to

the happiness of man to be risked on the incertain combinations of the head.")

But Merrill Peterson amazingly concludes that the Head emerges triumphant: "Reason and sentiment might divide life between them, yet, for him [Jefferson], one was the master, the other the servant." Peterson's friend at Princeton, Julian Boyd—the first editor of the ongoing edition of Jefferson's papers—was even more insistent: for Jefferson, he said, "reason was not only enthroned as the chief disciplinarian of his life but also . . . was itself a sovereign to whom the heart yielded a ready and full allegiance, proud of its monarch and happy in its rule." This judgment is printed as a footnote to the dialogue itself, but no explication is offered as to how it might be derived from the text.

Dumas Malone, on the other hand, although in general he was much averse to the idea that Jefferson was ever at the mercy of passion, and especially sexual passion, took an unblinkered look at "My Head and My Heart" and decided that "the most significant conclusion that emerges from the dialogue is that this highly intellectual man recognized in human life the superior claims of sentiment over reason." It is a valid perception.

Not that reason ranked low in Jefferson's list of important human attributes: he saw it, among other things, as the essential means for attaining the ends chosen by sentiment, as well as the means of forseeing the consequences of a given end after it is attained. But as the Head vs. Heart dialogue shows, he was more inclined to sentimental judgments than would be expected from a man who so often has been characterized as primarily a rationalist. It is closer to the truth to say that frequently he was remarkably romantic.

"Nature" was a key word in Jefferson's vocabulary, having powerful meanings ranging from his cosmological and scientific views to his views on human society and morality; but with reference to the noncivilized, nonhuman world around him—mountains and forests and rivers and animals and birds and bees and flowers and fruits and vegetables and beautiful scenery of any sort—the word often carried romantic connotations for him. Consider his paean to his beloved American home in his long letter to Maria:

And our own dear Monticello, where has nature spread so rich a mantle under the eye? mountains, forests, rocks, rivers. With what majesty do we there ride above the storms! How sublime to look down into the workhouse of nature, to see her clouds, hail, snow, rain, thunder, all fabricated at our feet! And the glorious Sun, when rising as if out of a distant water, just gilding the tops of the mountains, and giving life to all nature!

This lush description was a projection of the romantic impulse that moved Jefferson to choose a mountaintop as the best site for his dream house in the first place. Among the thousands of acres that his father left him was a splendid stretch along the Rivanna River a few miles from Charlottesville. There he could have constructed a mansion like Monticello at far less expense and effort, yet with a delightful vista of the river and its wooded opposite shore, easy access to the town and to river transportation, and readily available drinking water. Instead, he selected a small but steep mountain more than eight hundred feet high that to begin with had to be lopped off at the top to make level ground for his foundation—requiring hundreds of man-hours (that is, slave-hours) of digging and wheelbarrowing—and which to be reached by wagons and carriages demanded the construction of a road through thick forest and underbrush up a severe incline. A productive well, he found, could be practicably dug only a considerable way from the top. All of these obstacles, however, Jefferson stubbornly confronted and overcame for the sake of one romantic thing: the magnificent view from the mountaintop, with all the romantic associations that view brought to his mind and heart.

An equally striking hint of the romantic thread in Jefferson's psychic weave was his lifelong love of the Natural Bridge, a ninety-foot limestone arch about two hundred feet high that some vagary of erosion had carved out eighty miles or so southwest of Charlottesville. This phenomenon, which seemed to indicate that Nature or Nature's God possessed among an infinity of other powers the skills of a construction engineer, so intrigued him that in 1774 he bought it, together with 157 surrounding acres. The bridge served no practical purpose in the eighteenth century (today a highway runs across it), but it always excited Jefferson, and he was forever urging friends and visitors to go and see it. "It is impossible," he wrote in *Notes on Virginia*, "for the emotions

The Natural Bridge, as painted by Frederick Edwin Church.

arising from the sublime to be felt beyond what they are here; so beautiful an arch, so elevated, so light, and springing as it were up to heaven! The rapture of the spectator is really indescribable!"

In a letter to John Adams in 1812, Jefferson recalled how a Cherokee chief, Ontasseté, had stirred him when, in Williamsburg, the distinguished Indian made a farewell oration to his followers just before starting on a famous trip to England in 1762. Jefferson wrote:

> The moon was in full splendor, and to her he seemed to address himself in his prayers for his own safety on the voyage, and that of his people during his absence; his sounding voice, distinct articulation, animated action, and the solemn silence of his people at their several fires, filled me with awe and veneration . . .

That was not quite the end of Jefferson's description, however: the final clause is "altho' I did not understand a word he uttered."

This almost capsulizes his attitude toward the American Indians, who—whether one understood their language or not—seemed to him to be nature's noblemen, endowed with intelligence, courage, honesty, ingenuity, strength, grace, dignity, love of freedom, and whatever other virtues humanity was capable of. His estimate of their qualities was based to a considerable extent on personal observation, since Cherokees and members of other tribes sometimes stopped at Shadwell, his father's plantation, on their way from their camps to various negotiations at Williamsburg, and his curiosity also led him to much study of what was available on Indian history, tribal organization, customs, geographical distribution, and languages. This last was a special interest for Jefferson, and he actively encouraged the compilation of word lists and dictionaries of the many different tongues of the Eastern woodland tribes, under the impression that eventually they might be found to be merely dialects of a very few earlier linguistic sources. (This enterprise was much hampered by the fact that none of the tribes had any written language; and Jefferson must have been further confounded by the discovery of Lewis and Clark, as they pushed westward, that nearly every new tribe they encountered spoke a distinctly different language from the one before.)

But the most significant thing about Thomas Jefferson's attitude toward aboriginal Americans was his conviction that, unlike the blacks, they were not essentially inferior to whites: with them, somehow, miscegenation was not a degrading "amalgamation," but might even have positive value. He made this notably explicit in an address to a delegation of Delawares and Miamis who came to Washington during his second term as president: "You will mix with us by marriage, your blood will run in our veins, and will spread with us over this great land." His basis for this inclusive view was less empirical and scientific than it was a matter of sentimental prejudice: American Indians, in addition to what he took to be their innate nobility, were, after all, undeniably *American*, and in the mind of this enthusiastic patriot there was no higher recommendation. There was also the fact, of course, that he had never held any Indians as slaves.

Jefferson's hope was that most of the Indians would perceive the advantages of merging into the American mainstream, so that the "Indian problem" would gradually just disappear. As time went by, however, and that peaceful vision appeared to be less and less realistic, it became manifest to him that the tribes as such must give way to white settlement. When Indian resistance took the form of hostile raids, slaughter, and scalpings, his generally benevolent feelings toward them turned into ferocity: "If ever we are constrained to lift the hatchet against any tribe, we will never lay it down till that tribe is exterminated, or driven beyond the Mississippi."

Such antipodes of demeanor were part of Jefferson's character, and suited to the occasion. He could vary, for example, from almost childish delight in a pet mockingbird to icy ruthlessness toward pet dogs if they threatened his property. Margaret Bayard Smith related how, while he was president, he would let his favorite mockingbird fly around his study, "and it would perch on his shoulders and take food from his lips . . . How he loved this bird!" But at about the same time, having heard from his Monticello overseer Edmund Bacon that dogs belonging to the slaves were killing some of his sheep, he commanded: "To secure wool enough, the negroes' dogs must all be killed. Do not spare a single one. If you keep a couple yourself it will be enough for the whole land."

Jefferson's taste in literature, by and large, was conventional: he bought for his library, and presumably read, works that any well-educated gentleman of the late eighteenth century would be familiar with—Shakespeare, Milton, Pope, Dryden, Swift, among others, and including, of course, Greek and Roman classics like Homer and Virgil. But he has the odd distinction of having chosen as his most favorite authors two who are quite possibly looked upon in the twentieth century as, respectively, the least and the most interesting writers of Jefferson's own time.

The least was Ossian, supposedly a Celtic bard of about the third century, whose epic poetry was "discovered" and "translated" from the Gaelic by James Macpherson, a minor Scottish poet who was a few years older than Jefferson. It turned out, upon investigation, to have been mostly invented by Macpherson himself, but that did not prevent its being taken up rapturously by large numbers of his contemporaries in England, France, Germany, and not least in America. Ossian's works, as presented by Macpherson, were very heady stuff, well attuned to a culture that was beginning to veer toward romanticism as a kind of antidote for overemphasis on reason, restraint, and order. Ossian told, in florid phrases, of rough but passionate warriors of titanic strength and courage who would engage in violent combat with one another without much urging, whether over the favors of "white-bosomed" maidens or some insult to their honor, and subsequently celebrate their heroic victories around roaring campfires or at sumptuous feasts in their fortresses, with copious draughts of ale and many noble toasts, not only to themselves but to their fallen opponents. These events took place amid very picturesque and rugged scenery, with a lot of descriptive attention, for some reason, to the moon and its eerie light on desolate heaths and moors. And at appropriate junctures there would be poetically lugubrious reflections on the transience of it all:

How long shall we weep on Lena; or pour our tears in Ullin? ... The mighty will not return ... The valiant must fall one day ... Where are our fathers, O warriors! ... They have set like stars that have shone, we only hear the sound of their praise ... Thus shall we pass, O warriors, in the day of our fall. Then let us be renowned when we may; and leave our fame behind us, like the last beams of the sun, when he hides his red head in the west.

This—one of the passages that Jefferson copied into his literary commonplace book—could easily have passed for a speech attributed to some eloquent American Indian chief, and it raises the suspicion that some of the young Virginian's admiration for this "ancient" poetry may have hung on a feeling that the Indians, if they could have been magically equipped with broadswords and breastplates and transported back about fifteen centuries, might have fitted in admirably with the Gaelic clans celebrated by Macpherson/Ossian.

A glimpse of Jefferson's bedazzlement with Ossian was left by the Marquis de Chastellux in his report of an evening he spent at Monticello in 1782. He and his host discovered to their mutual delight that they were both Ossian devotees, and, over a bowl of punch after supper, they got to reciting "passages of those sublime poems which had particularly struck us . . . Soon the book was called for . . . and placed beside the bowl of punch. And before we realized it, book and bowl had carried us far into the night." It is an entertaining picture: these two eminent sons of the Enlightenment tipsily declaiming chunks of verse so romantic that they might have made Keats, Shelley, and Byron raise their eyebrows in unison.

Jefferson's other favorite author was a very different phenomenon. Laurence Sterne (1713–1768) was an English clergyman who was never cut out to be one. But when he was graduated from Cambridge University in 1737, after an undergraduate career spent in good part by entertaining fellow students with readings of witty and ribald satires, he took advantage of family connections and became the vicar of a small church in Yorkshire. This left him plenty of time to read and write, and in 1759 the first volume of *The Life and Opinions of Tristram Shandy, Gentleman* was published in London. When Thomas Jefferson entered the College of William and Mary in 1760, the first two volumes (later called "books") were out and much talked about. It seems likely that his freethinking professor, William Small, recommended them to him, and by the time he married Martha Wayles, in 1772, he had purchased the entire set, as well as *A Sentimental Journey Through France and*

Italy, Sterne's last work (1768). Before starting out on his tour of southern France in 1787, Jefferson bought a new set of Sterne's works in a format small enough for a volume to be slipped into one of the large pockets of a typical suit coat of the period; it seems evident that he did not want to be without *A Sentimental Journey* or *Tristram Shandy* while he was on the road, so that he could reread pertinent passages as he went along.

Sterne is delightful reading under almost any circumstances, but he offers, I think, a particular reward for anyone interested in Jefferson's cast of mind. A person's literary enthusiasms often reveal a good deal, especially if the favored books are as distinctly *sui generis* as Sterne's. Turning certain pages of *Tristram Shandy* and realizing how fondly Jefferson quite probably did the same, a reader may suddenly feel that the opportunity has magically arisen to share an evening with the great man himself. And when the wonderful book is finally closed, the sense that you understand Jefferson better than you did before is almost, I find, unavoidable.

More attention has been paid by critics of modern literature to

Laurence Sterne, author of
Tristram Shandy.

Tristram Shandy than to any other work of fiction published in the eighteenth century. Sterne has been compared, not unfavorably, to James Joyce, Marcel Proust, Thomas Mann, Franz Kafka, and Samuel Beckett. He was avant-garde—by about a century and a half—with regard to many things. There was his obvious disdain for orderly, chronological plot, for instance: the storyline loops, stalls, goes temporarily backward, leaps ahead, and loops some more, in an endless series of digressions, some of them several chapters long, and including even a digression on digressions. Time is elastic: a great deal can happen in a short chapter (some consist of only one or two sentences), or it may take several chapters to get Tristram's father and his Uncle Toby down a staircase, because they pause on nearly every step to go off into tangential discussions aroused by the proliferating association of ideas. To make sure the reader understands how intentional all this is, Sterne throws in a blank page now and then, or numbers chapters out of sequence, and doesn't get around to writing his preface until Chapter XX of Book III. There is an almost continual feeling of unpredictability, which is one of the things Sterne is after: "I set no small store by myself upon this very account," he tells us; ". . . if I thought you [were] able to form the least judgment or probable conjecture to yourself, of what was to come on the next page—I would tear it out of my book."

"I wish," *Tristram Shandy* begins, "either my father or my mother, or indeed both of them, as they were in duty both equally bound to it, had minded what they were about when they begot me . . ." This is followed by a couple of hundred words on the importance, for the character imparted to their offspring, of the "humors and dispositions" that were uppermost in his parents' minds at the moment of conception; and finally the eager and possibly impatient reader is let in on exactly what was going on: "'Pray, my Dear,' quoth my mother, 'have you not forgot to wind up the clock?' 'Good G—!' cried my father, making an exclamation but taking care to moderate his voice at the same time . . . 'Did ever woman, since the creation of the world, interrupt a man with such a silly question?'" The reader is then (as he or she frequently will be in the book) brought into the narration: "'Pray, what was your father saying? —Nothing." And thus ends the first chapter.

Long before Freud declared that for every physical event there is a psychological concomitant, Sterne put it this way: "A man's body and his mind, with the utmost reverence to both I speak it, are exactly like a jerkin and a jerkin's lining—rumple the one,—you rumple the other." This idea makes him extremely interested in what today we call body language. Tristram's father, Walter Shandy, observes:

> There is a certain mien and motion of the body and all its parts, both in acting and speaking, which argues a man well within . . . There are a thousand unnoticed openings . . . which let a penetrating eye at once into a man's soul; and I maintain . . . that a man of sense does not lay down his hat in coming into a room, or take it up in going out of it, but something escapes, which discovers [that is, reveals] him.

Sterne had read John Locke attentively and accepted Locke's view that all human knowledge comes to the mind through the senses. He is constantly aware, however, that since we are all individual organisms, the real world as perceived by one person is likely to differ from the real world as perceived by someone else. Tristram says of his father:

> The truth was his road lay so very far on one side, from that wherein most men travelled—that every object before him

presented a face and section of itself to his eye, altogether different from the plan and elevation seen by the rest of mankind. In other words, 'twas a different object, and in course was differently considered. This is the true reason, that my dear Jenny and I, as well as the world besides us, have such eternal squabbles about nothing.

It is all, it seems, a question of subjective relativity.

These idiosyncrasies of perception, in addition to spawning endless disagreements, often frustrate communication. People mean one thing and are taken to mean something else, and their habitual mental preoccupations may be so incompatible that it's a wonder they can get along together at all. Tristram's Uncle Toby, a former military man who has never gotten over it, thinks almost constantly in terms of his campaigns in Flanders: attacks, retreats, bombardments, and especially (since he was seriously wounded by a rock blown off a parapet by an enemy fusillade) fortifications. His brother Walter, Tristram's father, is a speculative logician who tries to reduce any subject whatever to a complex system of hypotheses, inferences, and conclusions, supported every step of the way by learned allusions to often very recondite authorities, ancient and modern. Yet these two brothers spend hours nearly every day in each other's company, smoking their pipes and conversing about anything and everything without (the reader feels) much mutual comprehension; and nonetheless, as many incidents reveal, they are intensely fond of each other. A marvelous chorus to their amicable disputations is provided occasionally by Tristram's mother, who has only one thing to contribute. As Tristram explains it, with a tone of some exasperation, it was her way "never to refuse her assent and consent to any proposition my father laid before her merely because she did not understand it, or had no ideas of the principal word or term of art, upon which the tenet or proposition rolled." "To be sure, Mr. Shandy," is her all-purpose response.

The *actuality* of human life—which above everything else it was Sterne's fervent desire to convey in his writing—is thus presented as hodgepodge without end. "But mark, madam," he has his narrator say at one point (this madam being evidently the reader) "we live amongst riddles and mysteries—the most obvious things which come in our way have dark sides, which the quickest sight cannot penetrate into; and even the clearest and most exalted understandings amongst us find ourselves puzzled and at a loss in almost every cranny of nature's works; so that this, like a thousand other things, falls out for us in a way, which tho' we cannot reason upon it—yet we find the good of it, . . . and that's enough for us."

Jefferson, like Sterne, was a highly cerebral man, and it cannot be doubted that he hugely enjoyed the needle-sharp wit displayed so liberally in *Tristram Shandy*, and Sterne's constant probing of the ordinary—often banal—events of upper-middle-class life to poke out their simultaneously ridiculous yet somehow endearing qualities. And despite his stubborn belief that, all things considered, the world was run by natural laws ordained by a benevolent Providence, Jefferson knew by hard experience, from his youth on, that it was also teeming with unforeseeable mischance, which all too easily could escalate into grievous disaster. Mutual sympathy was much needed by beings inhabiting such a world, and Laurence Sterne—living and writing with the knowledge of his not-distant death from consumption—was hypersensitive in this regard. He called it sentiment or sentimentality—we would be more likely today to use the word "empathy"—and Jefferson recognized it as a nonrational, impulsive human characteristic that was essential to a civilized and happy society.

Sterne found life full of intriguing paradox, and he saw to it that this was amply reflected in *Tristram Shandy*—another attraction the book probably held for Thomas Jefferson. Its most "sentimental" character is Uncle Toby, the nostalgic retiree from the world's most tough-minded and deadly profession. Full of sympathy and compassion for his sidekick Corporal Trim, for his brother Walter, and for all other members of the Shandy circle—not to overlook the widow Wadman, down the road, who throughout the narrative is none too subtly sizing him up as a possible mate—Toby is nothing if not softhearted.

Uncle Toby's war wound, as the reader is constantly reminded, was somewhere in his groin; but its precise location is a matter for much speculation, especially by the widow. There is a delightful scene near the end of *Tristram Shandy* where Toby, having finally mustered up the courage to propose to Mrs. Wadman, responds to a pointed query from her meant to determine once and for all just what damage the wound has done:

And whereabouts, dear Sir, quoth Mrs. Wadman, a little categorically, did you receive this sad blow?—In asking this question, Mrs. Wadman gave a slight glance towards the waistband of my uncle Toby's red plush breeches, expecting naturally, as the shortest reply to it, that my uncle Toby would lay his forefinger upon the place.

Whereupon Toby, who had in front of him a large map of the battle that had occasioned his injury, took *her* finger in his hand and placed it upon the exact spot on the map where he stood when he was wounded.

This kind of comic sexual titillation suffuses both *Tristram Shandy* and *A Sentimental Journey*. That it was much appreciated by Jefferson is attested by the fact that, while he recommended Sterne's works in general to friends as models of good writing and moral sensitivity, the two most prominent passages from Sterne among the very few that he ever cited specifically were both extremely sexual. One of them is the nose/penis digression (the longest in the book) from *Tristram Shandy;* the other, the bedroom scene that ends *A Sentimental Journey*, is almost a preview of a renowned situation in the classic film *It Happened One Night*—except that the nocturnal "barrier" between the narrator and the lady in question, instead of being a blanket, turns out to be the lady's maid, "as brisk and lively a French girl as ever moved."

Some of Sterne's contemporaries (including Dr. Samuel Johnson), and later many Victorian critics, sniffed and sneered at him as vulgar and prurient. But Sterne perceived, openly and without moral judgment, that for most people in the world, much of the time, sex is just offstage in the theater of their minds, ready to make an entrance on an infinity of cues—and that human life might long ago have died out if it were otherwise.

It is very difficult to identify the Thomas Jefferson who so enjoyed the world according to Laurence Sterne with the austere and aloof rationalist admired by the deans of the Virginia school of historians, or for that matter with the sexually traumatized individual imagined by more recent biographers.

Incidentally, though it is a speculative game, it is diverting to leaf through Sterne's pages trying to guess which passages struck Jefferson most arrestingly. But now and then comes one that scarcely requires guessing, as for example this from Book IX, Chapter VI of *Tristram Shandy*, in which Corporal Trim tells Toby a story involving "a poor negro girl" in a sausage shop who is "flapping away flies—not killing them" with a bunch of feathers on the end of a long cane:

'Tis a pretty picture! said my uncle Toby—she had suffered persecution, Trim, and had learnt mercy— . . .

—A negro has a soul? an' please your honor, said the corporal (doubtingly).

I am not much versed, corporal, quoth my uncle Toby, in things of that kind; but I suppose, God would not leave him without one, anymore than thee or me—

—It would be putting one sadly over the head of another, quoth the corporal.

It would so, said my uncle Toby.

Why then, an' please your honour, is a black wench to be used worse than a white one?

I can give no reason, said my uncle Toby—

—Only, cried the corporal, shaking his head, because she has no one to stand up for her—

—'Tis that very thing, Trim, quoth my uncle Toby,—which recommends her protection—and her brethren with her; 'tis the fortune of war which has put the whip into our hands now—where it may be hereafter, heaven knows!—but be it where it will, the brave, Trim, will not use it unkindly.

—God forbid, said the corporal.

Amen, responded my uncle Toby, laying his hand upon his heart.

The confusions—and sometimes the distortions and silences—with regard to Thomas Jefferson's essential character, on the part of certain scholars who spent years of their lives studying him, seem to point to an inadequate understanding of his moral philosophy. It was an area of investigation in which he was keenly interested from the days of his youth, when he read the classics as well as seventeenth- and eighteenth-century philosophers like John Locke, Francis Hutcheson, and Henry St. John Bolingbroke, and struggled to work out some basic principles of ethics and morality. How could a human being determine good behavior from bad?

One thing that is quickly impressive, from the selections Jefferson chose to copy into his notebooks in his early years, is his strong inclination to favor philosophers who did not believe that any authoritarian sanction was necessary to validate a moral code. Both the Epicureans and the Stoics of ancient Greece and Rome, for instance, held that human beings were capable of making moral decisions without directives from gods or other supernatural sources, and Jefferson's lifetime rejection of biblical revelation goes back to this formative period during his adolescence and young adulthood. He was not disturbed, evidently, by the usually assumed opposition between the two ancient moral creeds, and saw no reason why the Epicurean principle of pleasure as the highest good could not be combined with the Stoic exhortation to use rationality and self-discipline in choosing particular pleasures, with sharp attention to consequences in order to avoid pain.

His admiration for the teachings of Epicurus was to last through his life—with some modification. Writing to William Short in 1819, when he was seventy-six, he declared himself still "an Epicurean"; and although he made it clear that at that age he was more inclined to emphasize the "tranquility" that came with satisfied desires than the pleasurable activity involved in satisfying them, he took the occasion to remind Short that the pursuit of happiness was not compatible with laziness. He wrote:

> I take the liberty of observing that you are not a true disciple of our master Epicurus, in indulging the indolence to which you say you are yielding. One of his canons, you know, was that "that indulgence which prevents a greater pleasure . . . is to be avoided." Your love of repose will lead, in its progress, to a suspension of healthy exercise, a relaxation of mind, an indifference to everything around you, and finally to a debility of body, and hebetude of mind, the farthest of all things

from the happiness which the well-regulated indulgences of Epicurus ensure . . .

And Jefferson enclosed with his letter a "syllabus of the doctrines of Epicurus" that he made "some twenty years ago," in which he defines "active pleasure" as not happiness in itself, but "the means to produce it," and gives an example: "Thus the absence of hunger is an article of felicity; eating the means to obtain it." The analogy with sexual desire and sexual activity could not have been lost upon Short, whose passion for the lovely Rosalie de La Rochefoucauld had never been completely fulfilled.

The philosophical essays of the late Lord Bolingbroke, the remarkable British politician and intellectual, were first published in 1754 and were being widely read and commented on by the time Jefferson got to William and Mary in 1760. He probably was unaware of the free publicity bestowed on these essays by Dr. Samuel Johnson, who called them "a blunderbuss against religion and morality"; but even without that advertisement Jefferson found them fascinating, and copied into his commonplace book extracts amounting to over ten thousand words—much more than from any other author. It was Bolingbroke who gave him the essentials of deism, the "natural" religion that asserted the existence of a Creator as a rational deduction based on observation of the laws of physics and astronomy—a God who, having designed the universe, stepped back and let his creation run by itself, without further divine intervention, and without access to knowledge of his will except through close study of natural phenomena, including human nature. Young Jefferson was charmed not only by Bolingbroke's fluid and lucid prose style, but by his cool, ironic tone, as in this typical extract comparing revealed with natural religion:

The missionary of supernatural religion appeals to the testimony of men he never knew, and of whom the infidel he labors to convert never heard, for the truth of those extraordinary events which prove the revelation he preaches . . . But the missionary of natural religion can appeal at all times, and everywhere, to present and immediate evidence, to the testimony of sense and intellect, for the truth of those miracles which he brings in proof: the constitution of the mundane system being in a very proper sense an aggregate of miracles.

One problem for deism, however, since it denied the authority of such "revealed" rules of behavior as the Ten Commandments, was to discover some natural human attribute that would serve as a guide to morality. The moral philosophers of England and Scotland in the seventeenth and eighteenth centuries, from John Locke (1632–1704) through Francis Hutcheson (1694–1746) and David Hume (1711–1776), agreed that the biblical doctrine of orig-

Henry St. John, Lord Bolingbroke.

inal sin was a slander on human nature, and that mankind was naturally good. They also agreed that human goodness was controlled by an inborn faculty they usually called "the moral sense," though they differed somewhat in their particular definitions of it and how it operated. In any case, it was emotional and appetitive, not rational; as Hume put it in *A Treatise of Human Nature* (1740), "The approbation of moral qualities is not derived from reason, or any comparison of ideas; but proceeds entirely from a moral taste, and from certain sentiments of pleasure or disgust which arise upon the contemplation and view of particular qualities or characters." Driving this point home more bluntly, in another passage he says: "Reason is, and ought only to be, the slave of the passions; and can never pretend to any other office than to serve and obey them."

Jefferson, no doubt with William and Mary's William Small as his mentor, owned and studied the works of these philosophers, and it is possible to trace his beliefs about the moral sense back to them fairly specifically. For an understanding of his mind and character, however, the important thing is to look at his own formulation of the theory, and luckily he summed it up more than once in personal letters. To his nephew Peter Carr he wrote from Paris in 1787:

Man was destined for society. His morality, therefore, was to be formed to this object. He was endowed with a sense of right and wrong, merely relative to this. This sense is as much a part of his nature, as the sense of hearing, seeing, feeling, touch; it is the true foundation of morality . . . The moral sense, or conscience, is as much a part of man as his leg or arm. It is given to all human beings in a stronger or weaker degree . . . It may be strengthened by exercise, as may any particular limb of the body. This sense is submitted, indeed, in some degree, to the guidance of reason; but it is a small stock which is required for this . . . State a moral case to a ploughman and a professor. The former will decide it as well and often better than the latter because he has not been led astray by artificial rules.

The example of the perspicacious plowman immediately explains part of the appeal of the moral-sense theory to Thomas Jefferson: its usefulness as a basis for the validation of democracy. It promised that a majority of mankind, well informed and given the opportunity to make a choice on any significant question, would make the right one just by following the moral impulse with which they are naturally endowed. Note that the function of reason is merely "guidance": the moral sense, which is nonrational, chooses ends and goals; the reason may help in achieving them. But for Jefferson morality is socially oriented, in any event; it is not selfish but basically altruistic: "These good acts give us pleasure, but how happens it that they give us pleasure? Because nature hath implanted in our breasts a love of others, a sense of duty to them, a moral instinct, in short, which prompts us irresistibly to feel and to succor their distresses." The use of terms like "a sense of duty" and his occasional identification of the moral sense with "conscience" has led some to suppose that Jefferson was modifying his insistence on the supremacy of feeling and sentiment over reason, but he countered that explicitly from time to time. "A man owes no duty," he wrote to an inquiring friend in 1814, "to which he is not urged by some impulsive feeling."

The conviction that the moral sense was essentially altruistic to some extent accounts for Jefferson's rather surprising decision, during his first term as president (1801–1805), to draw up what he called a "syllabus" of the merit of the doctrines of Jesus compared with those of ancient philosophers such as the Epicureans and the Stoics, as well as those of the Jews, all of which he now found to put insufficient emphasis on unselfish behavior. He also believed that the teachings of Jesus had been "mutilated" and "misstated" by the writers of the Gospels and followers like St. Paul, but that when cleared of their "corruptions" they would be "a system of morals . . . the most perfect and sublime that has ever been taught by man." Jefferson had been painfully stung, during the presidential campaign, by Federalist accusations that he was an infidel and atheist, and his syllabus was obviously intended to show that these charges were unjustified. He sent copies to his daughters and to a few carefully selected friends—carefully because he knew that many would find his reading of "Scripture" (which was not a word he used himself) far too radical. To Dr. Benjamin Rush, an eminent Philadelphia physician and fellow signer of the Declaration of Independence, he sent a letter along with the syllabus, explaining his basic stance: "I am a Christian, in the only sense he [Jesus] wished any one to be; sincerely attached to his doctrines, in preference to all others; ascribing to him every *human* excellence; and believing he never claimed any other."

The reply Jefferson got from Dr. Rush, while not hostile, was not exactly encouraging. Rush thanked him politely, but quickly added that in his opinion, nobody who denied the divinity of Christ was entitled to be called a Christian.

Nonetheless, Jefferson proceeded, early in 1804, to make a forty-six-page document that was in effect an expurgated Gospel. Working his way through a King James version of the New Testament, scissors in hand, he cut out any passage that struck him as being, probably, an authentic saying of Jesus, while leaving behind all that seemed spurious because of references to something supernatural. The "authentic" passages he then pasted into a copybook, which when finished he called "The Philosophy of Jesus."

It was a decidedly Jeffersonian abridgment: he had eliminated a large percentage of the very things that were most indispensable, from the point of view of a conventional Christian of any denomination whatever. Gone was any statement or implication that Jesus was divine, or a Messiah to whom God's will had been specially revealed; gone was any account of miracles, including the Virgin birth; gone was any indication that belief in these things would bring salvation; gone was any reference to the Holy Ghost or the Trinity; gone was the story of Christ's resurrection and ascension to heaven. Gone, in short, was a great deal of what is usually found in a formal definition of "Christian," and Jesus had turned out to be, of all things, what today would be called a secular humanist—one, indeed, of great wisdom, sensitivity, and eloquence, but on the whole a man with a close intellectual resemblance to Thomas Jefferson.

Although not much resulted immediately from this remarkable contribution to Bible study, and Jefferson quietly filed it away, he did not forget about it. In 1819, in a letter to his old protégé William Short, he reverted to the idea that a more careful and more biographical "abstract from the Evangelists of whatever has the stamp of the eloquence and fine imagination of Jesus" might in time "effect a quiet euthanasia of the heresies of bigotry and fanaticism which have so long triumphed over human reason . . ." He was, he said, too old for the project. But in fact, at seventy-six and retired at Monticello, he had time on his hands; and shortly thereafter he began to construct a much more elaborate version of an expurgated Gospel that he called "The Life and Morals of Jesus of Nazareth." It must have required many painstaking sessions in his study with scissors and paste, for it consisted of carefully chosen clippings from *four* New Testaments, one in Greek, one in Latin, one in French, and one the King James version in English. After selecting an appropriate passage in English, he then located the corresponding passages in the three other tongues, clipped them all out, and pasted them in parallel columns on two facing pages of a blank copybook—Greek and Latin on the left-hand page, French and English on the right, in that order. (Presumably, the object was to let a sufficiently learned reader compare different shades of meaning from one language to another.)

The result, while quite fascinating to a religiously detached observer, would make a biblical fundamentalist's hair stand on end, for in addition to nimbly skipping over the miracles and anything else that he regarded as theological nonsense, Jefferson did not hesitate to combine on a given page clippings from two or more of the Gospels, evidently in the interest of clarity or rhetorical grace, or, sometimes, to emphasize a point of "morals." For example, after pasting in the first twelve verses of Matthew 5 (the Beatitudes), he interrupts it with three from Luke 6 (the "woe unto you" verses), before going back to Matthew 5:13.

Despite such drastic editorial surgery, Jefferson eschews word editing, so that some statements attributed to Jesus inevitably include ideas that the editor (Jefferson) does not agree with ("not free from objection," as he put it). He was modern enough in his study of the Gospels to know that they had all four been written many years after the crucifixion, and by men who had never personally known Jesus, so that they were necessarily an imperfect record; and in any case, since Jefferson's insistent view was that Jesus was only human, any particular point in his moral code was open to either agreement or disagreement. The Sermon on the Mount, for instance, with its often severe reinforcements of the Ten Commandments, is included intact in Jefferson's compilation,

Opposite: A right-hand page from Jefferson's "The Life and Morals of Jesus of Nazareth," showing parallel versions of New Testament passages in French and English.

CHAPITRE V.

Sermon sur la Montagne.

JÉsus voyant tout ce peuple,monta sur une montagne ; et s'étant assis, ses Disciples s'approchérent de lui.

2. Et ouvrant sa bouche, il les enseignoit, en disant :

3. Heureux les pauvres en esprit; car leRoyaume des cieux est à eux.

4. Heureux ceux qui pleurent ; car ils seront consolés.

5. Heureux les débonnaires ; car ils hériteront la terre.

6. Heureux ceux qui sont affamés et altérés de la justice ; car ils serout rassasiés.

7. Heureux les miséricordieux ; car ils obtiendront miséricorde.

8. Heureux ceux qui ont le cœur pur ; car ils verront Dieu.

9. Heureux ceux qui procurent la paix ; car ils seront appelés enfans de Dieu.

10. Heureux ceux qui sont persécutés pour la justice ; car le Royaume des cieux est à eux.

11. Vous serez heureux, lorsqu'à cause de moi on vous dira des injures, qu'on vous persécutera , et qu'on dira faussement contre vous toute sorte de mal.

12. Réjouissez – vous alors , et tressaillez de joie, parce que votre récompense sera grande dans les cieux ; car on a ainsi persécuté les Prophètes qui ont été avant vous.

24. Mais malheur à vous, riches, parce que vous avez déjà reçu votre consolation.

25. Malheur à vous , qui êtes rassasiés ; parce que vous aurez faim. Malheur à vous , qui riez maintenant ; car vous vous lamenterez et vous pleurerez !

26. Malheur à vous , lorsque tous les hommes diront du bien de vous ; car leurs pères en faisoient de même des faux Prophètes !

13. Vous êtes le sel de la terre ; mais si le sel perd sa saveur, avec quoi le salera-t-on ? Il ne vaut plus rien qu'à être jeté dehors, et à être foulé aux pieds par les hommes.

14. Vous êtes la lumière du monde : Une ville située sur une montagne ne peut être cachée.

AND seeing the multitudes, he went up into a mountain : and when he was set, his disciples came unto him :

2 And he opened his mouth, and taught them, saying,

3 Blessed are the poor in spirit : for their's is the kingdom of heaven.

4 Blessed are they that mourn : for they shall be comforted.

5 Blessed are the meek : for they shall inherit the earth.

6 Blessed are they which do hunger and thirst after righteousness : for they shall be filled.

7 Blessed are the merciful : for they shall obtain mercy.

8. Blessed are the pure in heart : for they shall see God.

9 Blessed are the peace-makers : for they shall be called the children of God.

10 Blessed are they which are persecuted for righteousness' sake : for their's is the kingdom of heaven.

11 Blessed are ye when men shall revile you, and persecute you, and shall say all manner of evil against you falsely, for my sake.

12 Rejoice, and be exceeding glad ; for great is your reward in heaven: for so persecuted they the prophets which were before you.

24 But woe unto you that are rich ! for ye have received your consolation.

25 Woe unto you that are full ! for ye shall hunger. Woe unto you that laugh now ! for ye shall mourn and weep.

26 Woe unto you when all men shall speak well of you ! for so did their fathers to the false prophets.

13 Ye are the salt of the earth : but if the salt have lost his savour, wherewith shall it be salted : it is thenceforth good for nothing, but to be cast out, and to be trodden under foot of men.

14 Ye are the light of the world. A city that is set on an hill cannot be hid.

but it's difficult to believe that he (no Jimmy Carter) accepted "I say unto you that whosoever looketh on a woman, to lust after her, hath committed adultery with her already in his heart."

It is interesting that in adopting "the morals of Jesus" as superior to those of the classical philosophers of Greece and Rome, he contradicted his early mentor Bolingbroke, who had explicitly argued that a system of ethics derived from the New Testament would be less "entire" and "coherent" than one derived from such "antient heathen moralists" as Seneca and Epictetus. Jefferson probably accepted this view as a young man, but now he found that these writers were "short and defective" in "developing our duties to others." Jesus, he said, surpassed them, "inculcating universal philanthropy, not only to kindred and friends, to neighbors and countrymen, but to all mankind, gathering all into one family, under the bonds of love, charity, peace, common wants and common aids."

This heavy emphasis on *inclusive* altruism, empathy, and benevolence became a cardinal point in Jefferson's philosophy rather late in his life. But it certainly conditioned his vision of an ideal democratic republic: the moral doctrines of Jesus, he believed, if generally put into practice, would go far to ensure the social harmony requisite for a successful self-governing nation. It seems likely that it must also have affected his feelings about slavery and his own guilt-ridden involvement in that "abomination," for (as his relationship with Sally Hemings could hardly have failed to remind him daily) there was no way that "the whole family of mankind" could exclude one whole race of humanity.

One of the most curious aspects of Jefferson's laborious project of editing the Gospels is that he kept the whole thing a close secret. He did have the extracts bound by a professional, but there is no evidence that anyone else saw them before his death six years later, shortly after which his daughter Patsy (Martha) found the surprising volume among his papers.

The image of the old patriarch—of his country as well as his family—working away behind the closed door of his study on the Gospel according to Thomas Jefferson, for so many of his later days (or nights), is a rather moving one. He had met with little but sharp disapproval for his abbreviated version of fifteen years earlier, and he must have realized that his vision of a democratic America, freed of superstition and converted to "natural" religion as a bulwark for its republicanism, was another of his wonderful but implausible dreams. He did it mostly, it is to be assumed, for his own consolation; his testament to himself that—in spite of his awful failure on emancipation, and his looming failure to provide for his family's future—he was a man of the best intentions in the world. He could read through his Gospel and say to himself, "This is the way it might be; this is the way it ought to be."

Jefferson had of course noted that a belief in immortality was a prime part of the Christian creed, but he himself wavered from time to time on the question of life after death. He believed that there was no empirical evidence for it; yet as a man leaning toward pragmatic solutions of social problems, he recognized (as he wrote to a friend in 1814) that "the prospects of a future state of retribution for the evil as well as the good done while here," as preached by most organized religions, had value as a booster of "the moral sense," urging people to be and do good. Moreover, as old age advanced unswervingly, he developed an almost passionate desire to believe that somehow there might be, after all, a sweet by-and-by. He had lost his wife, five of his six legitimate and several of his illegitimate children, and very many of his good friends by the time he was eighty, and the theme "we'll meet again" held tremendous appeal.

Still, as an enemy of superstition he struggled to arrive at some rational idea of how human personality might survive death and dissolution. He and John Adams debated at length the existence of the soul as a spiritual entity that could be separated from the body, with Jefferson sticking stubbornly to the materialistic side of the argument. "To talk of *immaterial* existences," he told Adams in 1820, "is to talk of *nothings*. To say that the human soul, angels, god, are immaterial is to say they are *nothings.*"

For a while it seemed that the speculations of Jefferson's famous and much admired friend Joseph Priestley might be of help on this difficult question. Priestley, a freethinking English clergyman who had immigrated to America, and was also an innovative scientist—he had, among other accomplishments, isolated oxygen as a separate element, although he failed to understand its function in combustion—believed that mind (or soul) and body were inseparable; but he persuaded himself that God could, and probably did, "reanimate" the body after death, and with it the soul, making an afterlife possible. But Jefferson had seen too many human bodies ravaged by fatal disease to find this credible, and in any case it was a supernatural explanation, clearly incompatible with his belief in "the laws of Nature and of Nature's God." In the end he was left, once again in his life, with an irreducible contradiction.

He continued to write letters to friends like Adams, speaking fondly, just a year before his death, of "when we meet again, at another place, and at no distant period," but these were more expressions of hope than of conviction. In a less sentimental mood he often assumed a more agnostic posture, telling Adams that when he encountered "a proposition beyond finite comprehension, I abandon it as a weight which human strength cannot lift, and I think ignorance, in these cases, is truly the softest pillow on which I can lay my head."

With all the misgivings of old age, however, Jefferson never seems to have lost his inexhaustible curiosity and his love of scientific inquiry. He stuck to his belief in the moral sense as the innate, nonrational root of moral judgments, and was pleased to find that the thinkers of the time whom he regarded as the most brilliant agreed. These, not surprisingly in view of his continuing admiration for French culture, were the members of a turn-of-the-century group who called their approach to knowledge *"idéologie,"* and who were almost counterparts in philosophy to the flaming politicians who brought on the French Revolution. The most eminent of this group was Antoine Destutt de Tracy, whom Jefferson enormously admired and some of whose works he helped to have published in America in the years following his retirement from the presidency in 1809. (Incidentally, Lafayette's son, George Washington Lafayette, was married to Tracy's daughter, which naturally facilitated the friendship between Tracy and Jefferson.)

The French ideologists, although they traced their ideas back to Locke and Hume, were more rigorous in defining their methodology. They were militant empiricists: all true human knowledge, they believed, was ultimately dependent on sense perceptions; and metaphysical speculation—for instance about the nature of God or about the creation and destiny of the universe—was literally nonsense. Philosophy for them was properly a branch of natural science. Sometimes they even referred to it as zoology, that is, the study of animals—and particularly of that animal called man, and more particularly of what Jefferson called "the thinking faculty of man." Above all they insisted on relentless observation of verifiable facts, and they believed that their method of investigation was applicable not only to what today we would call psychology, but to such subjects as political economy and sociology as well.

With his intellectual French connections, Jefferson eagerly kept up with new "ideological" developments in areas that especially interested him. He was fascinated by the work of the young French physiologist M. J. P. Flourens, who demonstrated by vivisection that consciousness was impossible without a physical brain. In 1825 Jefferson excitedly reported to Adams that with the removal of the cerebrum, "the animal loses all its senses of hearing, seeing, feeling, smelling, tasting, is totally deprived of will, intelligence, memory, perception, etc." It struck him as a stunning refutation of the centuries-old belief that mind and body were two different and separable things, and seemed to hang a big question mark over religious assurances about spiritual life after death.

Thomas Jefferson was characteristically wary of all "systems," whether philosophical, religious, or whatever, but his ultimate stand on the process by which human knowledge is acquired was essentially that of the French ideologists. He heartily endorsed their empirical, positivist approach and their scorn for theological mysteries, miracles, and revelations. Their focus on the senses as the source of knowledge became a kind of axiom for him: "When once we quit the basis of sensation," he told John Adams in 1820, in a letter attempting to explain his philosophical position, "all is in the wind." Yet he was well aware that they were discussing possibly the most baffling of all psychological problems: the mystery of human consciousness—which, as a perusal of almost any few weeks' issues of the *New York Times Book Review* will show, remains as mysterious as ever today.

Admitting his bafflement to his old friend, he put it in terms that are significant in relation to the question of whether, in his own view, he was more a man of reason or a man of feeling. "I was obliged," he says, "to recur ultimately to my habitual anodyne, 'I feel, therefore I exist.'" It was, of course, a revision of Descartes' famous "I think, therefore I am" ("*Je pense, donc j'existe*"). He had picked it up years earlier from Destutt de Tracy, who insisted that Descartes ought to have said, "*Je sens, donc j'existe.*" Jefferson agreed, and never forgot it.

14

"The Tender Breasts of Ladies": A Retrospective

———•◆•———

Penning an avuncular letter to his teenaged nephew Peter Carr in 1783, Thomas Jefferson offered this advice about women: "You will find that on rendering yourself agreeable to that sex will depend a great part of the happiness of your life: and the way to do it is to practice to every one all those civilities which a favourite one might require."

While the prescribed behavior might evoke an image of a too polished and often insincere ladies' man, the theory behind it, bluntly translated, is straightforward enough: pleasing women, and receiving pleasure from them in return, is one of the essentials of a good life.

Jefferson's own life amply displays this principle: he practiced what he preached. He intensely admired female beauty, whether embodied in the emergent charm of a teenaged Virginia debutante, the flourishing maturity of his wife Martha and his English inamorata Maria Cosway, or—we may presume—the somewhat exotic allure of the adolescent and ripening Sally Hemings, and he took great pains to render himself agreeable to such "favourites."

In general, moreover, he appears always to have been an object of fond attention from most of the discriminating women who knew him. It has become something of a historical cliché to say (as does the distinguished biographer Dumas Malone) that he was not really handsome; but the 1789 bust of Jefferson by the observant French sculptor Houdon, as well as the most accomplished portraits such as Charles Willson Peale's (1791), certainly question this. It is well attested that his tall, lean but muscular figure and his habitually erect yet relaxed bearing created a striking presence. Still, it was probably his courtesy, his courtly wit, and his easy erudition that captivated the ladies even more than his looks. Margaret Bayard Smith, a sophisticated young Washington hostess, said of her first meeting with him in 1801, "I know not how it was, but there was something in his manner, his countenance and voice that at once unlocked my heart."

Given his favorable disposition toward female company and his apparent availability as an attractive widower for the many prime years following the death of his young wife in 1782, when he was thirty-nine, it is a surprising historical fact that he never married again. His alleged vow to Martha that he never would do so of course offers something of an explanation, but not enough to prevent claims on the part of many biographers that somehow his amatory impulses went into permanent hibernation after his fling with Maria Cosway in 1786–1787. The alternative (though until lately hotly disputed) view is that his sexual needs thenceforth were well taken care of by Sally Hemings.

In any event, his criteria for a suitable life companion were undoubtedly difficult to satisfy, for his tastes were nothing if not sophisticated. As well as being available, she needed to be beautiful, good-natured, a lively and witty conversationalist, well educated in literature and the arts and to some extent in history and philosophy, musically accomplished, a gracious hostess, and thoroughly competent in the many domestic skills necessary for the management of a large household. It is likely that Martha Jefferson went a long way toward answering this description—but she was sadly lacking in an additional attribute that Jefferson must have found all the more admirable after her early death so devastated his happiness: physical strength and endurance, especially when it came to childbearing.

He was to meet and know many decidedly attractive and interesting women after the loss of his wife, both in France and in America, but those who fit his ideal paradigm were apparently few or none. For one thing, he seemed to be especially attracted to married women, a preference that was itself a deterrent to troublesome involvement. For a while, evidently, he felt that Maria Cosway was the one he had been waiting for, but the enchantment did not last very long, as we have seen.

What about Sally? Aside from the evidence that she was very beautiful and the fact that he took very good care of her as long as he lived, and saw to it that her children escaped from slavery, we know little about her character or his feelings for her. She must have been, however, smart and knowledgeable in practical matters: he made her a top house servant at Monticello, and except when his daughter Patsy was in residence there she probably fulfilled some of the duties that Martha had performed so well. He could not have married her, of course, as long as she was a slave; but he must have loved her within some definition of that term, for he was a man who, as his marriage revealed, believed that sex and love went together.

Yet with all Jefferson's respect and admiration for accomplished women, he was paramountly what nowadays would be called (at least by feminists) a male chauvinist (although he would have been astounded to be called a pig). He profoundly believed that women had been created by Providence to serve men as their mates: to love, cherish, and obey them; to bear and nurture their children; to make them comfortable and keep the home fires burning. There was a single word that for Jefferson comprehended nearly all female virtues and obligations: "domestic."

It is true that during his five years in Paris he was exposed to females who vigorously challenged that assumption, and with his typical penchant for ambivalence—sometimes about his most considered beliefs—he found himself strongly impressed by several of them. Such intellectuals as Madame Helvétius and the Comtesse d'Houdetot, who had been favorites of Benjamin Franklin, and Lafayette's vivacious relative Madame de Tessé, won Jefferson's approval, as did John Adams's bright and lively wife Abigail, and he became friendly with them on a plane that he usually reserved for distinguished male associates. He was not ready, however, to let them sway him from his determined conviction that even ladies of their mental caliber ought to have nothing to do with public affairs and politics. "The tender breasts of ladies," he wrote in 1788 to Angelica Church, Alexander Hamilton's sister-in-law, "were not formed for political convulsions, and the French ladies miscalculate much their own happiness when they wander from the field of their influence into that of politicks." The erotic tinge of his diction here colors almost all of his correspondence with the ravishing Angelica, a close friend of Maria Cosway's who had visited Paris earlier that year and spent a good deal of time in Jefferson's company; but he was nonetheless serious about his admonition. To Anne Bingham, an elegant Philadelphia beauty, he wrote less dashingly about the same time:

The gay and thoughtless Paris is now become a furnace of Politics . . . Men, women, children talk nothing else . . . But our good American ladies, I trust, have been too wise to

Angelica Schuyler Church, a portrait by John Trumbull.

wrinkle their foreheads with politics. They are contented to soothe and calm the minds of their husbands returning ruffled from political debate. They have the good sense to value domestic happiness above all other . . .

It seems ironic, with Jefferson's love for scientific knowledge, that his idea of the origin of the world and its people remained conventionally unadvanced. In spite of his hostility to organized religion, he was a creationist of a conservative stripe, believing not simply that the universe came from the hand of an almighty God, but that it had been made at some distant time and in one sweeping, omnipotent act: all the multifarious forms of life, including human beings, firmly fixed in their nature and attributes from the beginning. It is a curious fact of cultural history that he was almost an exact contemporary of the most outstanding proponent of a theory of evolution before Darwin: Jean Baptiste de Lamarck, who was born just a year after Jefferson and survived him by only three years. Moreover, Lamarck was already a nationally recognized naturalist in France by the time Jefferson arrived in Paris in 1784. Yet it appears that the two men never met, though they were on the scene at the same time and had scientific acquaintances like Georges Buffon in common.

The essence of Lamarck's theory was that acquired characteristics (like the long necks of the giraffes in one of his well-known examples, which he thought they got by assiduous stretching for high branches) could be inherited, and that by this process all the animal species were, over an enormous period of time, gradually evolved and differentiated. While Darwin effectively scotched the principle of acquired characteristics as an evolutionary mechanism, the point is that Lamarck's theory supposed a world not of static biological categories, but of flux and unpredictable potential. If Jefferson had adopted it, his rigid view of male/female differences and consequent social roles might well have been benignly modulated—to say nothing of his view of inherent differences between black and white.

Among the women who suffered from or at least were somewhat stifled by Jefferson's inflexibility on this subject were his two daughters, Patsy and Polly—and very likely Sally and her daughter Harriet as well. A man who held education to be of fundamental importance for civilization, he watched over his daughters' tutoring and schooling with a hawk's eye, and in their early years designed their course of study himself. To Patsy, who was only eleven at the time, he sent this message in 1783—the first of many much like it that were to follow:

> I expect that you will write to me by every post. Inform me what books you read, what tunes you learn, and inclose me your best copy of every lesson in drawing . . . Take care that you never spell a word wrong . . . I have placed my happiness on seeing you good and accomplished, and no distress which

this world can now bring on me could equal that of your disappointing my hopes. If you love me then, strive to be good under every situation.

He seemed to take it for granted that both of the girls would eventually become Virginia plantation wives (which in fact they did), and his ideal model for them must surely have been his own late wife—with perhaps a more elaborate formal education than she ever had been given. He continually stressed to them the need to be clean and well dressed, especially to the critical satisfaction of any observing male. He informed Patsy:

Nothing is so disgusting to our sex as a want of cleanliness and delicacy in yours. I hope therefore the moment you rise from your bed, your first work will be to dress yourself in such a stile as that you may be seen by any gentleman without his being able to discover a pin amiss, or by any other circumstance of neatness wanting.

And just before her marriage to Thomas Mann Randolph in 1790, he wrote her a letter with this helpful reminder: "The happiness of your life depends now on the continuing to please a single person. To this all other subjects must be secondary; even your love to me . . . "

Jefferson's conception of the correct balance between men and women, and how disastrous it could be when the balance was upset so that the woman got the upper hand, is wonderfully epitomized in the capsule history of the French Revolution that he inserted in his autobiography, written a few years before his death in 1826. Louis XVI, he said, "had he been left to himself" would have acquiesced in a constitutional monarchy for France, and all the bloodshed could have been avoided.

Marie-Antoinette, *by Élisabeth Vigée-Lebrun, a close friend.*

But he had a Queen of absolute sway over his weak mind and timid virtue . . . This angel . . . was proud, disdainful of restraint, indignant at all obstacles to her will, eager in the pursuit of pleasure, and firm enough to hold to her desires, or perish in the wreck. Her inordinate gambling and dissipations . . . had been a sensible item in the exhaustion of the treasury . . . her inflexible perverseness, and dauntless spirit, led herself to the Guillotine, drew the King on with her, and plunged the world into crimes and calamities which will forever stain the pages of modern history. I have ever believed, that had there been no Queen, there would have been no revolution.

This pithy account of the influence of Marie-Antoinette might serve as the starting point for a whole shelf of revisionist works of history. But if it sheds a flickering and dubious light on the ill-fated queen, it at least gives more than a hint of Thomas Jefferson's view of the right and proper role of women in the world. It was a view that many women today would hate—but it colored all of his dealings with the "opposite" sex.

15

Two Cheers for Thomas Jefferson

———•◆•———

The introduction to this book raised two basic questions about Thomas Jefferson: first, is he really an inscrutable "sphinx," or can he be understood when looked at closely in the light of his personal circumstances; and second (as a touchstone question, so to speak), does he deserve to be on Mount Rushmore? It is to be hoped that the first question has now been answered. Let's consider the second.

Except for potboiler "lives" of Jefferson, almost entirely derivative from earlier works, the tendency of late has been to produce revisionist studies, in an effort to reassess "the Jefferson legacy." The focus has been on what he has left us, in his basic ideas, that retains its validity when applied to American society and government as we head into the twenty-first century. Along with that, new interpretations of his character have been offered to explain his legacy and its lacks.

An inevitable theme in such studies is the extent to which Jefferson's vision of the future of the country has turned out to have been mistaken. The Civil War, for instance, drastically shifted the balance of states' rights vs. the power of the federal government, and the explosive expansion of the country in population and manufacturing ultimately killed Jefferson's dream of a society consisting largely of thousands of small independent farmers. Jumping ahead to the present, we find in such welfare and entitlement programs as Social Security and Medicare—to say nothing of enormous bureaucracies like the IRS, the FBI, and the numerous regulatory agencies—an involvement of government in the personal lives of citizens that would have been nearly unimaginable to Jefferson, and shocking if imagined. Add to these the extension of voting rights to include not only black Americans, but women, and millions of legal immigrants, and we have a national scene that could have given him a monumental migraine headache appropriate to the size of his image on Mount Rushmore.

One way of approaching the subject is to consider the epitaph Jefferson himself composed for his tombstone, giving the short and simple list of accomplishments by which, he said, "I wish most to be remembered":

HERE WAS BURIED

THOMAS JEFFERSON

AUTHOR OF THE DECLARATION OF AMERICAN INDEPENDENCE

OF THE STATUTE OF VIRGINIA FOR RELIGIOUS FREEDOM

& FATHER OF THE UNIVERSITY OF VIRGINIA

Many people have been surprised that he made no reference to his two terms as president, or to an act of such enormous consequence to the development of the country as the Louisiana Purchase. But the three things he did list sum up, in their implications, the very essence of Thomas Jefferson's beliefs about the necessary principles needed to build and sustain a democratic republic founded on natural law and natural human rights.

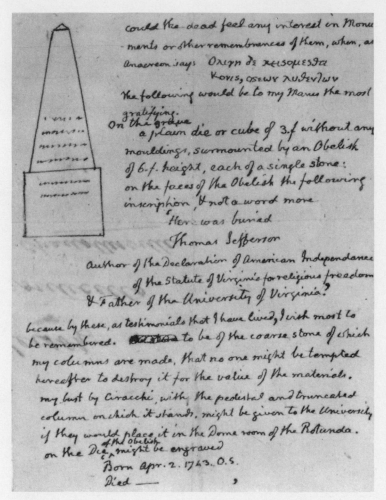

Jefferson's self-written epitaph and sketch for the design of his tombstone.

Almost everybody knows that the Declaration of Independence asserts it as a self-evident truth that "all men are created equal, that they are endowed by their Creator with certain unalienable Rights ...," and although this has been a source of inspiration to millions of people, it also has been troublesome because, as anyone over the age of six is aware, it is much more self-evident that some are born rich, smart, and beautiful (for instance), and many others poor, dull, and plain. No doubt thousands of history teachers have explained to hundreds of thousands of students that Jefferson was talking about equality of opportunity and equality before the law rather than circumstances of birth, but it would have helped if he had put the proposition more clearly to begin with.

An odd but important fact is that, in what he called his "original Rough draft," he did put it more clearly. "We hold these truths to be sacred & undeniable," he wrote, "that all men are created equal and independent; that from that equal creation they derive certain inherent & inalienable rights ... " "Created equal and independent" is better than the flat "created equal," because it focuses the meaning Jefferson intended for "equal": it implies *social* equality, with nobody naturally entitled to lord it over anyone else. Moreover, the original "from that equal creation they derive ... inherent & inalienable rights" also clarifies the import of "all men are created equal"—that is, that all are *equally entitled* (regardless of innate disparities) to "life, liberty, and the pursuit of happiness," *because* these rights are derived from the equal creation. The equal creation and the entitlement to the inalienable rights are inextricably linked: one is essentially the meaning of the other. It is not known whether Jefferson made the changes on his own (although they appear to be in his handwriting), or whether they resulted from consultations with his committee members Benjamin Franklin and John Adams. Either way, they are a demonstration that editing does not always guarantee improvement.

Having established—at least rhetorically—the basic equality of human beings, Jefferson goes on to proclaim the fundamental creed of democracy: "That, to secure these rights, governments are

A Declaration by the Representatives of the UNITED STATES OF AMERICA, in General Congress assembled

When in the course of human events it becomes necessary for one people to dissolve the political bands which have connected them with another, and to assume among the powers of the earth the separate and equal station to which the laws of nature & of nature's god entitle them; a decent respect to the opinions of mankind requires that they should declare the causes which impel them to the separation.

We hold these truths to be self-evident; That all men are created equal; that they are endowed by their creator with inherent & inalienable rights, that among these are life, liberty, & the pursuit of happiness; that to secure these rights, governments are instituted among men, deriving their just powers from the consent of the governed; that whenever any form of government becomes destructive of these ends, it is the right of the people to alter or to abolish it, & to institute new government, laying it's foundation on such principles & organising it's powers in such form, as to them shall seem most likely to effect their safety & happiness.

The opening words of the Declaration of Independence as Jefferson wrote them in his "original Rough draft." The second paragraph starts with phrases that have become world-famous—but with very interesting alterations.

instituted among men, deriving their just powers from the consent of the governed." Then, getting around to the subject at hand—the dissolving of the political connection between the United States and Great Britain—he declares the revolutionary "right of the people to alter or abolish" any government that becomes "destructive of these ends" of securing their inalienable rights.

Jefferson has lately been accused, in a book by Conor Cruise O'Brien (*The Long Affair*, 1996) about Jefferson and the French

Revolution, of being romantically obsessed with the very notion of revolution, to the point where he is better qualified as a hero to the right-wing paramilitary groups in America today who declare their hatred of the federal government, and are prepared to express it with guns and bombing, than he is as an icon of American democracy. They are fond of quoting—even on their T-shirts—Jefferson's famous remark occasioned by the feeble and short-lived Shays' Rebellion in Massachusetts in 1786–1787: "The tree of liberty must be refreshed from time to time with the blood of patriots and tyrants. It is its natural manure."

But this is an example of how Jefferson's recurrent penchant for rhetorical bravado, in the name of popular resistance to governmental excess, could lead to misunderstanding of his basic faith in democratic republicanism. He surely would have been appalled if Shays' Rebellion had ballooned into civil war, and it was a cardinal principle with him that under a properly operating representative democracy, founded on the equal civil rights of all citizens and responsive to the will of the majority, there would be little or no force necessary to guarantee a peaceful and happy society.

This is not to deny that Jefferson was forever suspicious of the tendency for power to feed upon itself and corruptly violate its responsibility. His whole career as secretary of state and vice president was a struggle to prevent the American ideals expressed in the Declaration of Independence from being subverted by an opposing force, represented by Federalist leaders like Alexander Hamilton and (to some extent) John Adams, which encouraged the idea that common people were not to be trusted: that what they needed was a strong ruling class, consisting of the wealthy and cultivated, to run the country and tell them how to behave. Jefferson's lifelong opposition to any such unbalanced "consolidation" of governmental power against the ultimate control of the people has been misinterpreted by some historians as resting on a fundamental "hostility to government," a "conviction that government is at best a necessary evil." But, as the Declaration of Independence makes abundantly clear, Jefferson understood very well that the "inalienable rights" it proclaims are not self-protecting. Indeed, it is the primary obligation of government to "secure" these rights, and to exercise its power toward the "safety & happiness" of its citizens.

Jefferson's listing of the Statute of Virginia for Religious Freedom as one of his major accomplishments has usually not been well understood. Its history goes back to 1779, when he introduced a "Bill for Establishing Religious Freedom" in the Virginia legislature. It was, for its time, extremely radical: it not only proposed sweeping away the traditional state support for the Anglican church, but ordered that

> no man shall be compelled to frequent or support any religious worship, place, or ministry whatsoever . . . nor shall otherwise suffer, on account of his religious opinions or belief; but that all men shall be free to profess, and by argument to maintain, their opinions in matters of religion . . .

This was too much for such stubborn conservatives as Patrick Henry, and the bill was shelved. The effort to pass it, however, had a result that was to prove extremely significant for the political history of the United States: it brought together Thomas Jefferson and young James Madison (eight years his junior) in what turned out to be a lifetime collaboration and close friendship.

After Jefferson went off on his mission to France in 1784, Madison took up the fight. With Henry pushing for renewed tax support of Virginia's Christian churches, Madison published, anonymously, a "Remonstrance Against Religious Assessments,"

An ACT *for establishing* Religious Freedom, *passed in the assembly of Virginia in the beginning of the year* 1786.

Well aware that Almighty God hath created the mind free ; that all attempts to influence it by temporal punishments or burthens, or by civil incapacitations, tend only to beget habits of hypocrify and meannefs, and are a departure from the plan of the Holy Author of our religion, who, being Lord both of body and mind, yet chofe not to propagate it by coercions on either, as was in his Almighty power to do ; that the impious prefumption of legiflators and rulers civil, as well as ecclefiaftical who, being themfelves but fallible and uninfpired men, have affumed dominion over the faith of others, fetting up their own opinions and modes of thinking as the only true and infallible, and as fuch endeavouring to impofe them on others, hath eftablished and maintained falfe religions over the greateft part of the world, and through all time : That to compel a man to furnish contributions of money for the propagation of opinions which he disbelieves, is finful and tyrannical ; that even the forcing him to fupport this or that teacher of his own religious perfuafion, is depriving him of the comfortable liberty of giving his contributions to the particular paftor whofe

Preamble of the Statute of Virginia for Religious Freedom

which argued specifically that such government "establishment" of religion violated an inalienable right because "the opinions of men, depending only on the evidence contemplated by their own minds, cannot follow the dictates of other men." It was circulated in the form of a petition and quickly gathered thousands of signatures. The time seemed ripe for a renewed trial of Jefferson's Bill for Establishing Religious Freedom, with its demolition of government-supported religion, plus total freedom of thought and expression on "matters of religion." A last-minute effort by the opposition to confine the benefits of the law to Christians, instead of protecting (as Jefferson put it) "the Infidel of every denomination," failed. Early in 1786, Madison was able to send his friend in Paris the news that through their collaboration, the most sweeping guarantee of freedom of conscience in the history of the Western world had become a statute of Virginia. He felt that its provisions, he wrote Jefferson, "have in this country extinguished forever the ambitious hope of making laws for the human mind." Fervently sharing this sentiment, Jefferson saw to it that the new statute was translated into French and Italian, widely published, and "inserted in the new [French] Encyclopedie." He reported "infinite approbation in Europe."

It is clear from the words of both Jefferson and Madison that to them the prohibition of government support for religious activities—which was what was meant by the word "establishment" in the eighteenth century—was simply one aspect of the protection of complete freedom of thought and expression in general. From their point of view, it was too bad that Jefferson did not get back from France in time to take part in the contentious discussions in Congress about the contents of the Bill of Rights—the first ten amendments to the new Constitution of the United States. Madison, hoping to make the emphasis on freedom of thought utterly clear, proposed an additional amendment to that effect, separating it from the amendment prohibiting church "establishment," but it got lost in the shuffle. In the end a compromise wording was agreed upon, and the result was what is today the well-known First Amendment: "Congress shall make no law respecting an establishment of religion, or prohibiting the free exercise thereof; or abridging the freedom of speech, or of the press; or the right of the people peaceably to assemble, and to petition the government for a redress of grievances."

Unfortunately, the first clause of the amendment was a masterpiece of ambiguity, and has become more so as the word "establishment" has, for many people, lost its reference—certainly intended by the Founders—to government sponsorship or support of any religious activities. And what about "respecting"? Does it mean "honoring" or does it mean "imposing"? The ambiguity has given rise to many minor events that surely would have disturbed Jefferson and Madison had they lived to see them: for instance, the interpolation in 1954 of "under God" into the national oath of allegiance.

Nevertheless, the First Amendment can be said to be the rightful descendant of Thomas Jefferson's Statute of Virginia for Religious Freedom, and effectively a "wall of separation between church and state," as Jefferson put it. To him it was crucial as a defense of democracy against despotism. For notwithstanding his recognition of the need for religious toleration in such a society, he never abandoned his intense suspicion of organized churches. "In every country and in every age," he wrote to a friend in 1814, "the priest has been hostile to liberty. He is always in alliance with the despot, abetting his abuses in return for protection to his own . . ." Jefferson's antagonism was founded on his lifelong conviction that "revealed" religion (for example, fundamentalist insistence that the Bible is "the Word of God"), which he saw as superstition by definition, was naturally incompatible with democracy. If you think you know for sure what the divine will is, by means of some privileged connection with God such as claimed by ayatollahs and popes, you need pay no attention to the will of the majority. Indeed, you may feel that it is a moral imperative to try to impose your "knowledge" of the divine will on other people.

Such absolutism about moral or ethical ideas was alien to

Jefferson's way of thinking and, he believed, to a civilized, democratic society. "The error seems not sufficiently eradicated," he wrote in a memorable passage on this subject in *Notes on Virginia*,

> that the operations of the mind, as well as acts of the body, are subject to the coercion of the laws. The legitimate powers of government extend to such acts only as are injurious to others . . . But it does me no injury for my neighbor to say there are twenty gods, or no God. It neither picks my pocket nor breaks my leg . . . Subject opinion to coercion, whom will you make your inquisitors? Fallible men, men governed by bad passions, by private as well as public reasons. And why subject it to coercion? To produce uniformity . . . Is uniformity obtainable? Millions of innocent men, women, and children, since the introduction of Christianity, have been burnt, tortured, fined, imprisoned; yet we have not advanced one inch towards uniformity.

This was the intellectual background for Jefferson's inclusion of the Statute of Virginia for Religious Freedom as one of the three most important accomplishments of his life.

The third accomplishment, the founding of the University of Virginia, doesn't call for much explanation. Jefferson was a book lover and lover of knowledge for himself all his life, and after he had developed his political and philosophical ideas it was axiomatic with him that a democratic republic would thrive or perish according to the knowledge or ignorance of its citizens. They might have the best moral impulses in the world, but without reliable information to guide their choices, they could never build and maintain a safe and happy society.

So it is not surprising that the last great enterprise of Jefferson's career was to plan and bring to reality a public university that he hoped would be among the best that America had to offer. He got state approval for it from the General Assembly of Virginia in 1819, but of course that was only the beginning of the long and hard process of acquiring the necessary funds, making architectural designs, overseeing the construction of buildings, working out a suitable curriculum, stocking the library, and hiring a good faculty.

Jefferson was nearing eighty when all this started, and he was harassed by family problems and worries about the future of the nation, but he set to it with enthusiasm. It hardly needs saying that a chief delight for him was making the architectural plans for what he liked to call his "academical village"—that is, the college campus. Although those plans encountered considerable negative criticism at the time, their ultimate accolade was to come over a century and a half later, when in 1976 the American Institute of Architects voted his design "the proudest achievement of American architecture in the past 200 years." Once the actual construction got under way, it was Jefferson's particular pleasure, on a clear blue-sky day, to take his telescope to a good vantage point on the edge of Monticello and peer down at the workmen who were bringing his dream into three-dimensional existence in Charlottesville.

Signing up a good faculty turned out to be more difficult than Jefferson had anticipated. Somewhat in contradiction to his bias in favor of all things American, he decided that the best professors would be found in Europe. An emissary sent to England and Scotland to recruit appropriate candidates discovered that not many distinguished scholars were eager to head for the semi-frontier of the United States to teach at a neonatal university that had, obviously, no reputation whatsoever. The emissary, Francis Gilmer, a bright young lawyer who had tentatively accepted the position of professor of law at the university, eventually rounded up five academicians who were willing to take the chance; but he put something of a damper on his success by telling Jefferson that having been unable to find scholars whom he "should choose to be associated with," he himself had decided not to accept an appointment.

In spite of this and many other obstacles, the University of Virginia opened for business on March 7, 1825. There were five faculty members on hand, and thirty or forty students, with more straggling in as the weeks went by. One problem that Jefferson had not foreseen—and one not unknown to this day at many American colleges—was that most of the students were found to be, as he phrased it, "wretchedly prepared": it drew his attention to the fact that elementary and secondary school education in Virginia was also in great need of improvement.

Then there was the matter of student discipline. Perhaps dreaming back to the idyllic days when he and John Page, under the charismatic spell of William Small, had been intoxicated with the sheer thrill of learning, Jefferson insisted that the Virginia curriculum should be almost entirely elective, with each student allowed to pursue his interests wherever they led. Unhappily, they now and then led to intoxication with wine and whiskey rather

The University of Virginia, 1824, *engraving by Henry Schenck Tanner.*

than books; and friction with several of the professors, one week in the fall of 1825, grew into a minor riot, with drunken and masked students throwing bottles through the windows of professorial apartments and so on. There ensued an assembly of all the students before the university's governing board, with a much disturbed Jefferson heading the painful proceedings. Disciplinary rules were tightened, and three students were expelled—one of them, to Jefferson's mortification, a great-grandnephew of his. After that things settled down considerably, and Jefferson had the comfort, about nine months later, of going to his grave with the knowledge that his vision of a great Virginia university had at least survived its troublesome birth.

Do Thomas Jefferson's character and his achievements qualify him as a great American icon, worthy of having his features colossally carved into the (more or less) eternal granite of Mount Rushmore, along with George Washington, Abraham Lincoln, and Theodore Roosevelt?

The answer, I believe, is a qualified but unhesitating yes. He did embody, outstandingly and consistently, very much of what we mean when we think of the word "American" as something to be proud of and thankful for. He did, in his two terms as president, set the country on the course that has made it the greatest representative democracy in this troubled world, potentially the best hope of mankind for a good, free, and happy life.

His worst failures, from today's perspective, were his steady relegation of women to a subordinate role in human society and his inability to cope with the core contradiction of his life—his deeply rooted prejudice against blacks plus his conviction that the two races "cannot live in the same government." This was a besmirchment of his own great testimony to freedom and human rights, the Declaration of Independence, with which it cannot be reconciled.

Garry Wills, who has made the most penetrating study of that document (*Inventing America*, 1978), has argued that, since Jefferson accorded to blacks equal endowment with the moral qualities determined by the innate "moral sense" common to all human beings, he did not regard them as essentially inferior. But this is a perpetuation of the myth, unfortunately encouraged by Jefferson himself, that mental and emotional qualities can be absolutely distinguished, instead of being, usually, inextricably intertwined. To declare that all men are equally entitled to life, liberty, and the pursuit of happiness, and then to compromise it by adding, in effect (with regard to blacks), "but in your case, because of your mental inferiority, you can only enjoy your entitlement in Africa or the West Indies, so pack up and get out of here as soon as possible," is an obvious travesty.

It also is an amazing disregard, for a man as perceptive as Thomas Jefferson, of what may be called the crossover factor. At the very least, as he well knew, some blacks were intellectually far superior to some whites, so that categorical discrimination on the basis of color was intrinsically unjust. That he paid no attention to this factor is an indication of how predominantly emotional his racial prejudice was.

And in the last analysis, Jefferson's tenacious adherence to the moral-sense theory of psychology must be judged as scientifically rather dubious. The basic distinction between value judgments and mere cognitive perceptions is valid and important as long as it is not viewed as absolute, but to postulate the moral sense as a uniquely human and altruistic faculty may seem to a modern observer insufficiently empirical. Is there really a "moral instinct" in man that is clearly distinguishable in character from, say, the compelling instinct of a cat to pursue a mouse, or a big fish to gobble a little one—or, on the other hand, of a mother lion to nourish and protect her cubs? And is there really a sharp line to be drawn between a person's moral (or immoral) impulses and his preferences in matters of aesthetics or gastronomy, or is it all finally a question of taste? It all seems either more complicated—or simpler—than Jefferson supposed.

In any event, Jefferson's belief that the moral sense was essentially appetitive rather than rational must have given, for him, an added ring to the old Roman proverb, *"De gustibus non est disputandum"*—"There's no disputing about tastes." Certainly he seldom felt any need or inclination to dispute his own personal tastes when it came to food and wine, to say nothing of his very private preferences with regard to sex and religion. He was a man, if there ever was one, who took to heart the famous advice of Polonius in *Hamlet*: "This above all: to thine own self be true, and it must follow as the night the day, thou canst not then be false to any man." There is relevance in this to the discoveries, stressed in recent biographies, that despite his didactic moralizing to his daughters and their cousins about honesty, he could occasionally be remarkably devious in situations, political or personal, where he felt that absolute honesty would be detrimental to some worthy ulterior purpose.

A curious example of this occurred when it came to choosing appropriate books for the curriculum at the University of Virginia. Jefferson had long held a violently ambivalent opinion of David Hume's *History of England*, which he considered unsurpassed in excellence of style, but often very wrong in its political judgments, tending toward derogation of "republicanism" (by which he meant democracy). Jefferson had discovered a book that, he thought, "performed a good operation" on Hume. An English historian, John Baxter, had condensed Hume's history, simultaneously revising many passages by "republicanizing" them (as Jefferson put it), yet otherwise using Hume's "own words." While Jefferson agreed that a better way to deal with Hume would be to publish an edition with corrective comments in notes, he felt that this would be unwieldy, and that Baxter's tour de force, all things considered, would save the students trouble and get them headed in the right direction

"Devious" is not quite the right word to describe Jefferson's long and steady concealment of his sexual relationship with Sally Hemings. It was a liaison that would, if openly acknowledged, have severely damaged his political viability and caused havoc in his social and family life. It seems altogether likely that keeping it secret was part of his bargain with Sally when he promised her that he would free any children she might have by him. Since the DNA investigation, there has been a great flurry of agitated discussion among Jefferson "experts" as to whether the findings diminish his moral stature as a Founding Father—should he be "banished from the pantheon," as one participant put it at a conference held at Monticello in March 1999?

But the moral status of the relationship, secrecy and all, looks respectable when fairly considered. There was no adultery involved, and there seems good reason to think that Sally viewed her treatment by her master (and mate) as highly satisfactory. Marriage was out of the question, of course, nor could he treat her children, in front of other people, as he would have had they been free, white, and legitimate. But they and their mother were provided with good shelter, excellent food, and a comfortable life, very much like specially favored family servants (which in fact they were), and the children were well trained in marketable skills by which they would be able to support themselves when they became free. Did Jefferson and Sally Hemings love each other? It's hard to believe that they did not. A point that seems to have been generally unnoticed is that, by all the evidence, they were sexually true to each other for some thirty years, despite long stretches of unavoidable separation.

In any case—and above all, at least from Thomas Jefferson's point of view—he had given the children a bequest beyond price: the assurance, by reason of their light skin, that they would be able to pass out of slavery into the world of white America. His "failure" to keep in touch (as far as we know) with the two older ones, Beverly and Harriet, after they left Monticello, has recently been cited against him. But to have done so might quite likely have jeopardized their chances of success in making the adventurous transition.

With all of Jefferson's insistence that his own moral sense must be the guide for his personal behavior—certainly, for instance, the criterion by which he judged his liaison with Sally—he did recognize, nonetheless, that in a democratic polity there must be plenty of room for discussion and dispute about particular "tastes" as to their tendency to be conducive to or detrimental to the general welfare of society—the commonweal, to use the old, evocative word. This is the point, of course, of submitting questions truly relevant to the commonweal to public opinion, and assuming, as Jefferson did, that most people, reasonably well informed, will usually make the right choices—if not directly, then through their elected representatives.

In the last fortnight of his life—eighty-three years old, painfully ill with prostate cancer, and knowing that the end was very near— Jefferson thought back on his long and active public career, and especially to its stellar moment: the writing of the Declaration of Independence. It was already late June 1826, and he was sharply aware that the fiftieth anniversary of that unforgettable time was only a few days away. On June 24 he penned a reply to an invitation to attend a Fourth of July celebration in Washington along with other surviving signers of the great document.

I should, indeed, with peculiar delight [he wrote], have met and exchanged there, congratulations personally, with the small band, the remnant of that host of worthies, who joined with us, on that day, in the bold and doubtful election we were to make for our country, between submission or the sword; and to have enjoyed with them the consolatory fact that our fellow citizens, after half a century of experience and prosperity, continue to approve the choice we made. May it be to the world . . . the Signal of arousing men to burst the chains, under which Monkish ignorance and superstition had persuaded them to bind themselves, and to assume the blessings and security of self government . . . All eyes are opened, or opening to the rights of man. The general spread of the light of science has already laid open to every view the palpable truth that the mass of mankind has not been born, with saddles on their backs, nor a favored few booted and spurred, ready to ride them. These are grounds of hope for others. For ourselves let the annual return of this day forever refresh our recollections of these rights, and an undiminished devotion to them.

This was Thomas Jefferson's last message to the people of America, just ten days before his propitiously timed death on the Fourth itself. It fittingly touched on the keynotes of his ideological credo—self-government, with equal entitlement for all to the "inalienable rights" of life, liberty, and the pursuit of happiness.

Yet, as has been seen, his own devotion to this credo was seriously flawed; and in the end it may well be that he merits the most unstinting celebration for his lifelong allegiance to complete freedom of thought and expression. Writing to his friend Benjamin Rush in 1800, shortly before he became president, he cited certain clerical "schemes" to breach the religion clause of the First

Amendment and secure the "establishment" of some form of Christianity as the official religion of the United States. He would oppose them with all his power, he said, "for I have sworn upon the altar of God, eternal hostility against every form of tyranny over the mind of man."

For that he deserves, at least, two rousing cheers.

16

Postscript:
History, Fiction, and
Probability

————◆————

Jane Austen, in her novel *Northanger Abbey*, depicts two of her characters discussing history. "I often think it odd," says one, "that it should be so dull, for a great deal of it must be invention." Dr. Johnson, mulling over the same phenomenon, announced his conclusion to Boswell: "All history, so far as it is not supported by contemporary evidence, is romance."

Serious historians, by and large, have tried to steer clear of invention and romance: they are after what really happened. Their chief reliance has been on Dr. Johnson's "contemporary evidence"—usually in the form of documents such as letters, diaries, journals, newspapers, and public records. Two troublesome problems commonly arise: the documentary evidence is often regrettably skimpy; and what there is has to be evaluated and interpreted to make coherent sense out of it. Thus even the most austere historian must sometimes resort to "probably," "very likely," or even "possibly" and "conceivably." Circumstantial as well as direct evidence must be considered, and little by little the narrative may edge toward the realm of historical fiction, especially when the author has a desire to make his account as lively and colorful as possible.

Some historical novelists have boldly challenged the categorical distinction itself, arguing that their works represent the past as validly as the soberest academic tome, and far more entertainingly. A few years ago, for example, the well-known Gore Vidal wrote a bestselling novel called *Burr*, which he coolly claimed was "history and not invention," but which included long segments of a document called "Memoirs of Aaron Burr," supposedly dictated by Burr to his secretary. The unwary reader gets no hint of the fact that no such historical document exists, the "Memoirs" having been composed by Mr. Gore Vidal. Professor George Dangerfield, sourly reviewing the novel for the *New York Times*, declared that there is no respectable place for historical fiction unless "the characters are all imaginary," as in Thackeray's *Vanity Fair*. Dumas Malone, angry because *Burr* represents Jefferson as devious, shrewd but shallow, and always a ruthless opportunist, joined in: "The book is a mishmash of fiction and fact that leaves one in horrid confusion . . . It is a pernicious book; it undercuts the tremendous efforts of scholars to get as near the truth as you can get." And yet it must be conceded that any intelligent reader would get from this well-written novel a rather complete and fairly accurate idea of Aaron Burr's career, as well as a striking and historically sound picture of New York City in the 1830s, and that among the many thousands who bought it, probably very few had ever read or were ever going to read an actual biography of Burr. Clearly, to make a balanced judgment of such a book's historical value is not a simple matter.

Jefferson's private life, not surprisingly, has attracted the attention of several novelists and scriptwriters, and it is interesting to look at what they have done with this rather elusive subject. Most recently, the widely admired filmmakers Merchant and Ivory produced *Jefferson in Paris*, starring Nick Nolte, which opened in the spring of 1995. It is a very lavish movie, with enormous attention to historical accuracy in terms of costume, décor, the general ambiance of Paris during the first events of the French Revolution, and so on. The French characters, for instance, speak French—not English with a French accent, as in most American films set in France: English subtitles convey what is being said to the 99 percent of the audience whose knowledge of French is inadequate to the situation. This certainly heightens the verisimilitude, though it may strike some movie-watchers as irritatingly pedantic.

The main storyline, of course, revolving around Jefferson, Maria Cosway, Patsy Jefferson, and Sally Hemings, doesn't have to deal with the language problem, except for decisions about what sort of accent to give each of them. It is an odd but unavoidable fact that nobody really knows what an upper-class Virginia accent of the late eighteenth century actually sounded like. The cultural background of the colony was overwhelmingly British, and many of the men Jefferson associated with were English-born, so it is altogether likely that despite his deep American roots he spoke with what today would be heard as some sort of English accent. But actor Nick Nolte, whose usual roles have been anything but effete, would have sounded very strange affecting even a suggestion of Oxford speech, and Merchant and Ivory wisely chose to let him talk organically grown American.

Greta Scacchi, the actress playing Maria Cosway, has a mixed Italian and English background, just as Cosway did, so there was no problem with her accent. With Sally Hemings, however, the question was how far to go in portraying her as a plantation slave with distinctly "Negro" speech mannerisms. It's arguable that the producers went too far, forgetting that the historical Sally Hemings had grown up from birth in the atmosphere of a genteel and aristocratic Virginia household, where most of the language she heard as a child was decidedly cultivated, however Southern.

A much more critical distinction was over what skin color would be appropriate for the actress playing Sally Hemings. For dramatic effect it was no doubt essential that she should contrast sharply with Maria Cosway and appear unequivocally "black," yet the real-life Sally, a quadroon, was described as "mighty near white." Thandie Newton, the Sally of *Jefferson in Paris*, is extremely pretty and charming, but certainly does not match that description—and this is a significant departure from historical probability. Jefferson, with his intense distaste for miscegenation and its consequences, would have been most unlikely to allow himself a sexual relationship with a dark-skinned slave girl no matter how beautiful and winsome. With contraception presumably out of the question he had to assume that any such relationship would result in children, and only a conviction that they would be practically white could, in all probability, have reinforced his desire sufficiently to overcome his inhibition.

Merchant-Ivory's casting choices along this line reach their nadir, unfortunately, in the opening scene of their film, which shows Sally's son Madison Hemings explaining the family history to an inquiring reporter in 1873. Since there is solid historical evidence that his siblings Beverly, Harriet, and Eston were all white enough to pass for white, to have the part of Madison played by James Earl Jones as a man obviously black—and incidentally, one so untutored that he seldom makes a verb agree with its subject, as in "we was the only ones"—seems absurd, and gets the film off to an unpromising start with respect to historicity.

Jefferson in Paris oddly makes both too much and too little of Thomas Jefferson's romantic infatuation with Maria Cosway. The chronology of the affair is loosely represented: it is made to drag on over a period of nearly three years, whereas in reality it was essentially over in less than a year and a half. This matters little in itself, but it is done in order to have Maria play a part in encouraging Patsy Jefferson to become a nun—for which there is no historical support. The difficult problem of making something cinematic out of the famous Head vs. Heart letter from Thomas Jefferson to Maria is solved by turning its content into a picnic word game played by them and a group of sophisticated young nobles—a clever solution, except that it fails to show Jefferson's overheated fervor for Maria, or to advance the plot in any other way. The sexual tension between the couple is in fact portrayed as remarkably slack: there is a good deal of coquettish palaver, but only one kiss to stand for passion. What would seem like a good chance for an excitingly jealous confrontation between Maria and Sally (after all, the two relationships with Jefferson did overlap each other historically) is forgone, and even the physicality of his seduction of Sally (or hers of him) is merely hinted at.

The unhappy result, overall, is that although the claim of the film's scriptwriter, Ruth Prawer Jhabvala, to have told a story that is "completely true" historically is not justified, the timidity of the production is such that (as the reviewer for *The New Yorker* observed), a "rich and engaging subject" has, somehow, been turned into "a dull film." As a wry postscript it might be noted that Nick Nolte, though he gives a sensible performance, was ten years too old for the part—in his mid-fifties when the film was made, while Jefferson was forty-one when he arrived in France and forty-six when he left. On the other hand, Nolte was still young enough to express (after reading several standard biographies of Jefferson) amused contempt for the prevailing denial of the Jefferson-Hemings liaison: "The historians like to think, " he told an interviewer, "that after Jefferson's wife died, his dick fell off! They do!"

Timidity is not a fault that can be charged against the novel *Sally Hemings*, by Barbara Chase-Riboud, originally published in 1979, with a revised version in 1994. Determined to make Sally—about whom, historically, so very little is positively known—into an epic and tragic figure who would be "the emblematic incarnation of the forbidden, the outcast," and the "rejection" of the "national identity" epitomized by Thomas Jefferson, the author endows her heroine with very explicit characteristics that include dazzling beauty (eyes of "deep amber yellow . . . fringed with thick black lashes and with heavy eyebrows . . . cheekbones abnormally high . . . eyes wide-spaced . . . "), an exquisitely sensitive intellect, and a writing style, revealed in voluminous (and entirely invented) diary entries, as lavishly expressive as that of Chase-Riboud herself. She is so stunningly attractive that the white census clerk who comes, in the opening chapter, to check out the residents of the cottage taken near Charlottesville by Madison, Eston, and Sally after Thomas Jefferson's death, falls in love with her and keeps coming back to visit her whenever he gets a chance—the first of Chase-Riboud's many imaginative contributions to history.

Sally's relationship with her master develops slowly but surely. ("Perhaps I had always known that he would claim me," she tells her diary; "I knew as sure as death that I belonged to Thomas Jefferson.") She waits anxiously, losing a lot of sleep, for the great moment; and on the night before his departure to Amsterdam to meet John Adams it finally comes, in a style worthy of a ladylike but heavy-breathing romance: "I bent forward and pressed a kiss on the trembling hands that encompassed mine, and the contact of my lips with his flesh was so violent that I lost all memory of what came afterward. I felt around me an exploding flower . . ." and so on to a big-bang conclusion, if you can endure this kind of prose long enough.

But to track all of Chase-Riboud's nervy and often egregious fictive inventions through her plump novel, sorting them out from the actual historical facts with which they are mixed like too many potatoes in a meat stew, would take a great deal of time and surely leave most readers more confused about American history than they were to begin with. One of the curious facts about the work is that it barely mentions Maria Cosway, as if the author didn't wish to allow that much competition with her gorgeous heroine. Perhaps the most significant thing to be learned from a book like this is that often the quality of the writing is something of an index to the reliability of the "historical" information that is conveyed.

Jefferson, a novel by Max Byrd published in 1993, is a far more sophisticated work of fiction than *Sally Hemings*, and far less destructive to the actual history on which it is based. Although the mise en scène is Paris in the years just before the French Revolution, with the principal focus on Jefferson, Byrd gives the story a wider biographical scope by telling his tale largely from the point of view of William Short, Jefferson's young secretary in Paris. Short hero-worships Jefferson and is working in his spare time on a biographical memoir (actually contrived, of course, by Mr. Byrd), excerpts from which interrupt the flow of the immediate narrative from time to time. Moreover, Short himself becomes one of the most interesting characters in the novel, falling desperately in love with the beautiful Rosalie, the young wife of the Duc de La Rochefoucauld. This is in accordance with well-documented history, but for some reason—perhaps to make Short's adulterous passion seems less shameful—Byrd has persuaded himself that Rosalie's husband was around sixty-five, when in fact he was, like Jefferson, in his mid-forties.

There are some scenes in which Short cannot serve as the center of vision for the simple reason that he isn't there. Byrd succeeds very well at picturing the Parisian hoi-polloi of the period: the crowded streets and alleys teeming with peddlers, beggars, prostitutes, ragged political protesters, strolling minstrels, and con artists of every description; but to avoid showing all this just as seen by a passing member of the upper classes—Jefferson riding by in his carriage, for instance—he makes good use of James Hemings. James, who is being paid wages by Jefferson and has a certain amount of time off from his work as a pastry cook at the Hôtel de Langeac, is keenly aware that in Paris he is on the verge of escaping from slavery, and indulges himself freely at various bars and whorehouses. These episodes are related from James's point of view, which gives them a vivid immediacy.

A lot of attention is paid to Maria Cosway, usually with Short on hand as commentator. He sees her as beautiful but essentially shallow as well as nonsensual: "What a man wanted, Maria might not willingly surrender." Yet earlier Jefferson takes Maria to a deluxe and very private dinner in a suburban rendezvous with Short nowhere around—the point of view is Maria's—and the excursion ends with the infatuated couple heading upstairs, presumably to make love (or at least give it a try). The reader never finds out for sure, which is in keeping with Byrd's apparent determination to stay as close as he can to what he calls "generally agreed-upon facts," with only the elasticity of probability to facilitate fictional speculation.

With so much specificity lavished on other characters, the reader waits expectantly to see what this author will do about Sally Hemings. The answer is: almost nothing at all. She is slightly more visible than she is in Dumas Malone's volume on Jefferson in France (where she is mentioned only once and is called "Sally Heming"); but Byrd is as skeptical as Malone ever was when it comes to the Jefferson-Sally story, hewing stoutly to the line that nothing sexual took place between them.

This leads to some strange assertions. Jefferson says to Short, in anticipation of the arrival in Paris of Polly and Sally, "I haven't seen Sally Hemings since the day she was born"—a very odd remark, since historically, of course, Sally had been a member of the household at Monticello from her infancy, and reportedly was even at Martha Jefferson's bedside when she died in 1782. The next thing we hear is "Sally Hemings had grown to be five feet six inches tall, straight as a stick. She wore a faded calico dress . . ." In spite of (according to the book jacket) five years of research on his subject, Byrd seems to have let his preconception about Sally blur his attention to such clues as Abigail Adams's overestimate of her age—"15 or 16," in all probability bespeaking womanly phenomena such as menstruation and well-developed breasts—and the bill sent by Abigail to Jefferson for new clothes for both Sally and Polly before they left London for Paris.

This dismissal of Sally Hemings is the more striking since Byrd displays an open mind with regard to the possibility of sexual activity between Jefferson and Maria Cosway, and constantly depicts William Short as a highly sexed young man who visits a Parisian brothel (colorfully rendered), and who enjoys from the lovely Rosalie de La Rochefoucauld a delicately described act of fellatio at a romantic secret rendezvous.

Sally Hemings is thus the be-all and end-all of Barbara Chase-Riboud's fictional treatment of Jefferson's life, and practically a zero in Max Byrd's—a good demonstration of the fact that in this artistic realm as in academic historiography, radically different interpretations of the same basic material are quite possible.

These novels also stand almost as exemplars of two extremes in the writing of historical fiction—on the one hand the extravagantly imaginative, which recklessly fabricates characters and incidents with little or no regard for reliable historical sources, in the interest of a sensational story, and on the other the highly responsible, which introduces no principal characters not found in real life, sticks essentially to actions that are supported by historical evidence, and holds steadfastly to the criterion of probability for whatever novelistic inventions are added—dialogue, minor incidents, "extra" characters, details of dress and demeanor, and so on—to bring the story to life.

One interesting aspect of this subject is the difference in impact between a novel and a play or film. The theatrical experience is frankly make-believe, and hardly anybody in the audience is likely to suppose that what is being seen is actual history—though admittedly some recent television "docudramas" have done their best to conflate the illusion and the reality. But everyone knows that those are actors up there, not the real people they are playing, and there seems to be a corresponding leeway extended to the playwright when it comes to representing the historical truth. The artistic medium used by the historical novelist, on the other hand, is basically the same as that of the biographer or historian: a book. With this fundamental similarity, it is sometimes easy for the novel to masquerade as history, and especially so if the author has done a reasonable amount of homework on his subject, so that his narrative can give the effect of probability even when large chunks of it are entirely made up.

It is here that the vulnerability of history itself plays in the novelist's favor: sophisticated readers are aware that many established historical "truths" are themselves only probabilities. Did Edwin Stanton really say, at the moment of Lincoln's death, "Now he belongs to the ages"—or, as another person present reported, "Now he belongs to the angels"? We tend to be rather naive about Dr. Johnson's criterion, contemporary evidence; documents seem to pick up an aura of truth as they grow older. We know that today's newspaper is speckled with lies and errors; that last week's newsmagazine, while possibly a little more reliable, is still an incomplete and unbalanced summary; that even our own diaries and letters fail to tell what really happened last weekend. But let the newspaper be dated a hundred years ago, the news summary be from a *Harper's Weekly* for 1857, or the diaries and letters be found among the relics of our great-grandfather, and we treat them with great respect: these, we think, are the real clues to the past.

And in truth, they are nearly all we have, such documents. The past is never fully recoverable, and any history will indeed be fiction to some extent. Still, a line between history and historical fiction can be meaningfully drawn, as well as a line between respectable historical fiction and romantic fustian; and documentation, carefully judged and interpreted, remains the essential criterion.

Yet over both enterprises, the scholarly and the fictive, the beacon of that mysterious essence *probability*, which governs so many of our judgments of actions both past and future, swings with an illuminating beam that can be disregarded only with peril.

NOTES

—————— •◆• ——————

The following notes give sources for quotations and statements of fact in this book, and in some instances also augment the text with further information or comments that I think clarify or illustrate certain points. The notes are not numbered by chapters; instead, each note is keyed numerically to the page of the text to which it applies, and is headed by a phrase or word from the relevant text passage.

A few sources are cited so frequently that short titles, or initials, or names of authors are used to identify them. For example, *The Papers of Thomas Jefferson*, an ongoing multivolume work published by the Princeton University Press (1950—), which will eventually include all of his extant and available correspondence, is referred to as *Papers*. Since the letters are arranged in chronological order, all that is needed to find a given letter is its date, plus the name of the correspondent and the number of the volume containing it—for example, a letter to or from James Madison on March 12, 1787, will be cited as "12 March 1787, *Papers*, 11." Other "short" references are "Malone" for *Jefferson and His Time* (6 vols., Little, Brown, 1948–1981), by Dumas Malone; "Brodie" for *Thomas Jefferson: An Intimate History* (Bantam paperback edition, 1975), by Fawn M. Brodie; "K&P" for *The Life and Selected Writings of Thomas Jefferson* (Random House, Modern Library, 1944) edited by Adrienne Koch and William Peden, which contains Jefferson's *Autobiography*, and his *Notes on Virginia*, plus selected public papers and letters; and "L&B" for *The Writings of Thomas Jefferson* (20 vols., Washington, D.C., 1903), edited by Andrew A. Lipscomb and Albert E. Bergh. For other works, full titles and authors' names are given on first citation, and authors' last names and a partial title only for subsequent citations.

CHAPTER 1: "THE VAUNTED SCENE OF EUROPE"

Page

1 **Lafayette** Of the many biographies of the famous Frenchman, a lively and fairly recent one is *Lafayette, Hero of Two Worlds*, by Olivier Bernier (1983). For the

ambiance of Paris during the early phases of the French Revolution, *Citizens*, by Simon Schama (1989) is superb.

3 *Les Liaisons dangereuses* Claude Manceron, in *Their Gracious Pleasures*, vol. 3 of his *Age of the French Revolution* (1976), gives an interesting account of the effect of the novel, and a biographical sketch of Choderlos de Laclos, the author.

5 **"domestic bonds . . . done away"** To Eliza Trist, 18 Aug. 1785, *Papers*, 8.

6 **"the strongest of all the human passions"** To John Bannister, Jr., 15 Oct. 1785, *Papers*, 8.

8 **"wrapturously"** Abigail Adams to Royal Tyler, 4 Jan. 1785, *Adams Family Correspondence*, ed. Lyman H. Butterfield (1963), vol. 6, 48.

8 **"I felt my delicacy wounded"** Abigail to her sister Mary Cranch, 20 Feb. 1785, *Adams Family Correspondence*, vol. 6, 67. (This shocked reaction, as Abigail admits later in the same letter, wore off with repeated visits to the ballet, so that "I see them now with pleasure.")

8 **a long stay in Russia** John Quincy Adams, at the age of fourteen, went to St. Petersburg in 1781 as an assistant to Francis Dana, an American diplomat.

9 **"one of the choice ones of the earth"** Abigail to Mary Cranch, 8 May 1785, *Adams Family Correspondence*, vol. 6, 119.

10 **inferior in size, strength, and vigor to those of Europe** In addition to his stalwart defense of the qualities of the American Indian in part 6 of *Notes on Virginia*, Jefferson tells a supporting anecdote in some biographical notes on Benjamin Franklin that he sent to an American journalist in 1818. Franklin was at a dinner party given by the Abbé Raynal, a colleague of Buffon's, in Paris, where some of the guests were French and some American. The abbé "got on his favorite theory of the degeneracy of animals, and even of man, in America." At that point, as Jefferson tells the story, Franklin spoke up: "We are here one half Americans and one half French, and it happens that the Americans have placed themselves on one side of the table, and our French friends on the other. Let both parties rise, and we will see on which side nature has degenerated." Franklin had noticed, of course, that all of the Americans present (except himself) were unusually tall and the French "remarkably diminutive, and the Abbé himself particularly, was a mere shrimp." When they all stood up, the argument was ludicrously over. K&P, 179.

12 **"rich . . . carnivorous animals"** To Abigail Adams, 21 June 1785, *Papers*, 8.

CHAPTER 2: SURGES OF YOUTH

Page

13 **unexpectedly died** Peter Jefferson was only forty-nine when he died. It is not known what killed him, but it seems likely that it was one of the bacterial or viral diseases for which, at the time, no effective medicine existed.

13 **exceedingly studious** Dumas Malone gives a good account of TJ's early education, basing much of it on the earliest "professional" biography, Henry S. Randall's three-volume *The Life of Thomas Jefferson* (1858).

14 **his sister Martha** This name echoed through Jefferson's family history: his wife and his eldest daughter were also Marthas.

14 **College of William and Mary** This was the second (after Harvard) oldest institution of higher learning in America, founded in 1693 and named after the then reigning monarchs of England. It was still very small—about a hundred students—when Jefferson went there in 1760.

15 **His principal college instructor** Jefferson was well aware of William Small's extraordinary quality. Remembering him sixty years later in his autobiography, he described it as "my great good fortune, and what probably fixed the destinies of my life" to have been his student in mathematics, philosophy, and "belles lettres," K&P, 4. Significantly, Small was the only faculty member at that time who was not a clergyman; he was also a bachelor and only about ten years Jefferson's senior, so that the two almost inevitably became close companions.

16 **when he specifically censured it** Jefferson associated prostitution with, among other things, disease. See his letter of 15 Oct. 1785 to young John Bannister, *Papers*, 8.

17 **a series of intimate letters** Jefferson's youthful letters to John Page are shown in sequence by their dates in 1763 and 1764; in *Papers*, 1.

17 **"not without charm and cleverness"** Malone, vol. 1, 81.

19 **under the aegis of George Wythe** It was William Small who introduced TJ to Wythe, "my faithful and beloved mentor in youth, and my most affectionate friend through life," as Jefferson put it in his autobiography, K&P, 5. Wythe was also a regular at Governor Fauquier's intimate dinners, where (TJ wrote reminiscently many years later) "I have heard more good sense, more rational and philosophical . . . conversation than in all my life besides." Letter to L. H. Girardin, 15 Jan. 1815, quoted by Brodie, 58.

20 **"recommended them to their practice"** Letter to William Fleming, 20 March 1764, *Papers*, 1.

21 **Ah, Joanna, puellarum optima!** Jefferson's description of the proposed "small Gothic temple" and the Latin epitaph were written in his account book for the year 1771, when he was planning Monticello. *Jefferson's Memorandum Books: Accounts. With Legal Records and Miscellany, 1767–1826*, eds. James A. Bear, Jr., and Lucia C. Stanton (1997), 247.

22 **"New York . . . depravities of human nature"** To William Short, 1823, quoted in *The Jefferson Encyclopedia*, ed. John P. Foley (1967).

22 **a man named James Burnside** Jefferson's summary of this case is in *Jefferson's Memorandum Books*, 8.

25 **"all the oblivion of which it is susceptible"** Quoted by Brodie, 493.

25 **"You will perceive . . . I acknolege [sic] its incorrectness"** Brodie quotes this from the original, which is in the Huntington Library in Pasadena, California. Brodie, 501.

26 **"As a gentleman"** Malone, vol. 1, 448.

27 **in a letter to Henry Lee** The entire letter is reproduced by Brodie, 79, 80. It is, however, a copy made by Lee (now in the Library of Congress), rather than Walker's lost original, so some of its incoherence may be Lee's.

CHAPTER 3: "UNCHEQUERED HAPPINESS"

Page

29 **"unchequered happiness"** *Autobiography*, K&P, 53.

29 **"then twenty-three years old"** Ibid., 5,6.

29 **"the cherished companion of my life"** Ibid., 53.

30 **"great industry . . . most agreeable companion"** Ibid., 6

32 **"for parlour for kitchen and hall"** Letter to James Ogilvie, 10 Feb. 1771, *Papers*, 1.

33 **One story told fondly** This incident is told one way or another in nearly every Jefferson biography, starting with Randall in his 1858 opus, *The Life of Thomas Jefferson*.

34 **"the deepest snow we have ever seen"** *Thomas Jefferson's Garden Book, 1766–1824*, ed. Edwin M. Betts (1944), 33.

34 **"the horrible dreariness"** Randall, *Life of Thomas Jefferson*, vol. 1, 64.

36 **"Nothing can preserve affections"** Letter to Polly Jefferson, 7 Jan. 1798, quoted by Jack McLaughlin in *Jefferson and Monticello: The Biography of a Builder* (1988), 193.

37 **Dumas Malone remarks** Malone, vol. 1, 397.

37 **"sensible & accomplished Lady"** quoted by Malone, vol. 1, 296.

38 **pork eaten at the master's dwelling** McLaughlin, *Jefferson and Monticello*, 182.

38 **brewing of . . . "small beer"** Ibid., 180.

38 **Soap . . . was made** Ibid., 180.

38 **candles . . . were molded** Ibid., 182.

40 **"with a cookery book in her hand"** "Memoirs of a Monticello Slave," in *Jefferson at Monticello*, ed. James A. Bear, Jr. (1967), 3.

40 **Philip Mazzei** Malone, vol. 1, 164–165.

40 **Friedrich von Riedesel**, Ibid., 294–295.

41 **may have miscarried at least once** Brodie, 150.

41 **saucy remarks in letters** John Adams, 26 May 1777, *Papers*, 2; Edmund

Pendleton, 24 May 1776, *Papers*, 2; John Page, 9 Dec. 1780, *Papers*, 4; Pendleton, 10 Aug. 1776, *Papers*, 1.

43 **seven pairs of women's gloves** Malone, vol. 1, 229.

44 **"the unvarnished truth"** Ibid., 341

44 **the famous cavalryman Banastre Tarleton** Fawn Brodie unearthed the entertaining fact that after his war service in America, Tarleton took up with a noted English court beauty, Perdita Robinson, who was a friend of Maria Cosway, the object of Jefferson's affection in Paris in 1786; and that all four of them happened to be there in September of that year. Later, Perdita wrote a book with the broad-gauge title *The Progress of Female Virtue and Female Dissipation*, which Maria illustrated with etchings. Brodie, 257, 709.

45 **"perpetual decrepitude"** 28 Oct. 1781, *Papers*, 6.

46 **"Let me describe to you a man . . . so many minutes"** Marquis de Chastellux, *Travels in North America in the Years 1780, 1781 and 1782*, trans. Howard C. Rice (1963), vol. 2, 40.

48 **"Mrs. Jefferson has added another daughter"** Letter to James Monroe, 20 May 1782, *Papers*, 6.

48 **As she recalled it** Brodie, 210. Patsy Jefferson's account of her mother's death and her father's reaction was first published in one of the earliest biographies, *The Life of Thomas Jefferson*, by George Tucker (1837).

49 **Edmund Bacon . . . gave this hearsay account** Hamilton W. Pierson, *Jefferson at Monticello: The Private Life of Thomas Jefferson* (1862), 106, 107.

50 **"the only Monticello she knew"** McLaughlin, *Jefferson and Monticello*, 202.

50 **"Time wastes too fast . . . shortly to make"** The original lines copied (with a few minor changes) by the Jeffersons are to be found at the end of Chapter IX of Book IX—the concluding book—of Laurence Sterne's *The Life and Opinions of Tristram Shandy*, originally published in 1767, and of course reprinted in many subsequent editions.

52 **"that stupor of mind . . . loss occasioned it"** 26 Nov. 1782, *Papers*, 6.

53 **"Of all machines ours is the most complicated"** 31 Aug. 1783, *Papers*, 6.

53 **"the best poets and prosewriters . . . graver sciences"** Letter to François de Barbé-Marbois, 5 Dec. 1783, *Papers*, 6.

53 **a series of admonitory letters** For TJ's 1783 correspondence with Patsy, see *The Family Letters of Thomas Jefferson*, eds. Edwin M. Betts and James A. Bear (1966), 19–26.

54 **"the fate of millions . . . the tongue of one man"** This was part of a commentary Jefferson wrote in France in 1786 for an entry on "États-Unis d'Amerique," prepared for a French encyclopedia by the historian J. N. Demeunier. *Papers*, 10, 58.

CHAPTER 4: MY HEAD, MY HEART, AND . . .

Page

59 **"more wretched, more accursed"** To Eliza Trist, 18 Aug. 1785, *Papers*, 8.

60 **"And this is the truest wisdom"** To Abigail Adams, 9 Aug. 1786, *Papers*, 10.

60 **What about her?** For a brief account of Maria Cosway's life, see Charles B. van Pelt, "Thomas Jefferson and Maria Cosway," *American Heritage*, August 1971.

61 **"the most pregnant passages"** To the Marquis de Chastellux, Oct. 1786, *Papers*, 10, 498.

62 **"With her how I stray'd"** For Jefferson's little anthology of English verse, see L&B, vol. 18, 426–443.

62 **Out for a walk along the Seine with Maria** The facts about Jefferson's wrist injury have been obscured by his own reluctance to talk about it. He wrote to an American friend, "How the right hand became disabled . . . was by one of those follies from which good cannot come, but ill may." (To William Stephens Smith, 22 Oct 1786, *Papers*, 10). Some of the usual assumptions about it may have been wrong. Jack McLaughlin, author of *Jefferson and Monticello*, found at the Library of Congress a letter to Jefferson in 1807 from a William Goldsmith that said: "when your Excellency had the misfortune to hurt his Arm by a fall from his horse, while living at Chaillot [the Paris gate near Jefferson's mansion on the Champs-Élysées], the writer was honored to write dictated by your Excellency himself." McLaughlin, *Jefferson and Monticello*, 419. Besides casting doubt on the standard "out for a walk" version, this suggests the possibility that some examples of Jefferson's "left-handed writing" (perhaps including the famous "Head vs. Heart" letter to Maria Cosway) may in fact have been put on paper by Goldsmith.

64 **the longest . . . personal letter** To Maria Cosway, 12 Oct. 1786, *Papers*, 10. The entire letter is also reproduced as appendix 2 of Brodie.

65 **"let the gloomy Monk"** (same letter) *Papers*, 10, 450.

65 **"When nature assigned us"** Ibid.

66 **"when I look back"** Ibid., 452.

66 **"were it only for that"** Ibid.

66 **Maria's answer to "My Head and My Heart"** 30 Oct. 1786, *Papers*, 10.

66 **"Your letter,"** she wrote in the most lucid passage Ibid.

67 **"I am determined when you come next"** 29 Nov 1786, *Papers*, 10.

67 **Maria . . . long epistle on New Year's Day** 1 Jan 1787, *Papers*, 11.

68 **recently it has been argued** See Schama's discussion of the Assembly of Notables in *Citizens*, 237–246.

68 **"the number of puns and bon mots it has generated"** 22 Feb 1787, *Papers*, 11.

69 the length did not improve its quality 15 Feb 1787, *Papers*, 11.

CHAPTER 5: SUNNY INTERLUDE

Page

70 forty-plus pages of meticulous notes 1787, *Papers*, 11, 415–463.

70 "inclined to think that your voyage" Patsy to TJ, 8 March 1787, *Papers*, 11.

71 "to see what I have never seen before" 11 April 1787, *Papers*, 11.

71 "I find here several interesting articles" 4 April 1787, *Papers*, 11.

71 Heading his list . . . the olive April 1787, *Papers*, 11.

72 "absolutely the same as ours" 4 May 1787, *Papers*, 11.

72 But Jefferson's particular passion 1787, *Papers*, 11, 415–463.

73 "I am now in the land of corn" 27 March 1787, *Papers*, 11.

74 "I was alone thro the whole" 19 June 1787, *Papers*, 11.

74 "I have derived as much satisfaction" 15 March 1787, *Papers*, 11.

75 "A traveller, sais I" 5 April 1787, *Papers*, 11.

76 "Here I am, Madam," 20 March 1787, *Papers*, 11.

76 Michael Angelo Slodtz Little known today, Slodtz was highly respected in eighteenth-century France—partly because he had been a prominent teacher of the famous Jean-Antoine Houdon.

76 "it carries the perfection of the chisel" 29 March 1787, *Papers*, 11. Note the plump little cupid, who seems well aware of what's going on.

77 "the most celebrated actress" 29 March 1787, *Papers*, 11.

78 "You know what have been my fears" 28 March 1787, *Papers*, 11.

78 "I have already begun to study more" 9 April 1787, *Papers*, 11.

78 "There was a gentleman, a few days ago" Ibid.

78 "I wish with all my soul" 3 May 1787, *Papers*, 11.

79 "I dismounted my carriage from its wheels" 21 May 1787, *Papers*, 11.

80 "a specimen of . . . the very best Bordeaux" 26 May 1787, *Papers*, 11.

CHAPTER 6: END OF AN AFFAIR

Page

81 "Come then, my dear Madam" 1 July 1787, *Papers*, 11.

81 "Do you deserve a long letter" 9 July 1787, *Papers*, 11.

82 "I am almost the same way with her" 6 July 1787, *Papers*, 11.

82 "Her temper, her disposition" 10 July 1787, *Papers*, 11.

82 "In my life I never saw a more charming Child" 10 July 1787, *Papers*, 11.

82 "bursting into tears" 6 July 1787, *Papers*, 11.

83 "Mrs. Cosway desires me" 10 July 1787, *Papers*, 11.

83 "My love to Mrs. Cosway" 16 July 1787, *Papers*, 11.

84 "only by scraps" 24 April 1788, *Papers*, 12.

84 "she has happened to be from home" 13 Nov. 1787, *Papers*, 12.

85 "confus'd and distracted" 10 Dec. 1787, *Papers*, 12.

85 "I cannot breakfast with you" 7 Dec. 1787, *Papers* 12.

CHAPTER 7: A BIG SURPRISE: SALLY HEMINGS

Page

86 "about 15 or 16" 27 June 1787, *Papers*, 11.

87 "The Girl who is with her . . . is quite a child" Ibid.

89 "facts, little facts" To James Currie, 27 Sept. 1785, *Papers*, 8.

90 "Dashing Sally" Brodie, 477.

91 The piece resulting from this Madison Hemings's memoir, originally published in the *Pike County Republican* in 1873, was not publicly available again until Fawn Brodie reprinted it as an appendix to her *Thomas Jefferson: An Intimate History* a hundred years later. Brodie, 637–644.

CHAPTER 8: EROS ON THE CHAMPS-ÉLYSÉES

Page

97 whether Sally and her master had a long-term love affair Although some diehard disbelievers still dispute the truth of the liaison, by January 2000 even the conservative Thomas Jefferson Memorial Foundation at Monticello had accepted it as historically valid.

98 "the seducer of a young, innocent, attractive colored girl, hardly out of puberty" John C. Miller, *The Wolf by the Ears: Thomas Jefferson and Slavery* (1977), 164.

99 "Mons. Le Général Jefferson" See photographic reproduction of the bill in *Papers*, 13, opposite page 17.

100 "Your long silence is impardonable" 6 March 1788, *Papers*, 12.

100 "I should have been dead five or six thousand years" 24 April 1788, *Papers*, 13.

102 a continuation of Sterne upon noses" Ibid.

103 "not find one word to write *but on Noses*?" 29 April 1788, *Papers*, 13.

104 "no romantic adventure with anybody else" Malone, vol. 2, 81.

105 Short was totally lovestruck For an account of his love affair with Rosalie, see Marie Kimball, *Jefferson: The Scene of Europe* (1950).

106 conventional expressions of affection For example, Jefferson wrote to Maria on July 27, 1788, with many flattering phrases, but on the same day he wrote

an equally flattering letter to Angelica Schuyler Church (whose daughter, Kitty, was in Paris at the convent school with Patsy and Polly). 27 July 1788, *Papers*, 13.

106 "lay my soul in her lap" 24 Aug. 1788, *Papers*, 13.

107 "a mere Oran-ootan, it has been a severe trial" 14 Jan. 1789, *Papers*, 14.

107 "over those of his own species" K&P, 256.

110 not going around in rags The costuming of Patsy and Sally is summarized by Brodie, 309, 310.

111 "think of claiming freedom" Letter to Paul Bentalou, 25 Aug. 1786, *Papers* 10.

CHAPTER 9: RETURN OF THE NATIVES

113 "establishment of a good constitution" 18 Sept. 1789, *Papers*, 15.

115 "some blubbering and crying—others laughing" Quoted by Brodie from the early Jefferson biography by George Tucker, *The Life of Thomas Jefferson*. Brodie, 321.

115 "young gentleman . . . honorable mind" *Autobiography*, K&P, 112.

116 "even temper of both Mr. Randolph and yourself" 4 April 1790, *Papers*, 16.

118 "the best man on the farm" *Thomas Jefferson's Farm Book*, ed. Edwin M. Betts (1953), 46.

120 "don't know what became of her" Pierson, *Jefferson at Monticello*, 102.

121 "one foot in the grave" 7 Aug. 1825, L&B, vol. 16, 119.

CHAPTER 10: ON THE BRIDGE OF THE SHIP OF STATE

Page

124 "Let those flatter who fear" 1774, *Papers*, 1, 134, 135.

125 "The sacred rights of mankind" *The Papers of Alexander Hamilton* (Columbia University Press), ed. Harold C. Syrett (1961–87), vol. 1, 122.

125 "I consider civil liberty" Ibid., 165.

126 "a man whose history" K&P, 521.

126 "the promoter of national disunion" 29 Sept. 1792, *Gazette of the United States*, under pseudonym "Catullus," in *Alexander Hamilton and Thomas Jefferson*, ed. Frederick C. Prescott (1934), 134, 135.

128 the best in the world K&P, 126.

128 "the poison" of democracy *Papers of Alexander Hamilton*, vol. 26, 309.

129 "The greatest man that ever lived . . . Julius Caesar" K&P, 609. Richard Brookhiser, in his lively biography *Alexander Hamilton, American* (1999), raises some doubts about the veracity of Jefferson's anecdote.

129 **forceful acquisition of additional territory** In 1803, for an interesting instance, before the Louisiana Purchase, Hamilton urged (in a newspaper piece written under the name "Pericles") that the United States should *declare war* on France and force it to hand over the territory at a bargain price. Prescott, 177.

130 **"a second Buonaparty"** Quoted by Adrienne Koch in her *Power, Morals, and the Founding Fathers* (Cornell University Press, 1961), 75.

131 **"A national debt . . . a national blessing"** Ibid., 55, 56; see also John Steele Gordon, *Hamilton's Blessing* (1997).

131 **"We are ruined"** 17 April 1791, *Papers*, 20.

133 *"that the earth belongs in usufruct to the living"* *Papers*, 6 Sept. 1789, 15.

133 **"every constitution . . . at the end of 19 years"** Ibid.

134 **"The right to utilize"** *American Heritage Dictionary*.

135 **"half the earth desolated . . . Adam and Eve"** 3 Jan. 1793, K&P, 522.

137 **countered if not destroyed** Unhappily for Jefferson, the War of 1812 very quickly brought about a resurgence of the national debt.

CHAPTER 11: SLAVE MASTER—AND RACIST

Page

141 **"the loudest *yelps*"** *Boswell's Life of Johnson*, ed. G. B. Hill (1950), vol. 3, 201. Boswell refers the quote to Johnson's pamphlet, *Taxation No Tyranny* (1775).

141 **"under the law of nature"** *The Writings of Thomas Jefferson*, ed. Paul L. Ford (1892–99), vol. 1, 380.

143 **those who . . . labored for his happiness** In a letter to Angelica Church, Jefferson spoke of his obligation to watch over "the happiness of those who labor for mine." 27 Nov. 1793, *Papers*, 27.

143 **Lucia Stanton . . . recent monograph** *Slavery at Monticello*, published by The Thomas Jefferson Memorial Foundation, 1996.

143 **"a dozen little boys"** Letter to J. B. Demeunier, 29 April 1795, K&P, 533.

144 **"severely flogged"** *Thomas Jefferson's Farm Book*, 35.

145 **"put out of the way by death"** Ibid., 19.

145 **"husbands and wives abroad"** *Thomas Jefferson's Garden Book*, 510.

147 **"never . . . received a blow from any one"** *Thomas Jefferson's Farm Book*, 22.

148 **"The whole commerce between master and slave"** K&P, 278.

149 **"The first difference which strikes us . . . out with the first dawn of the morning"** Ibid., 256, 257.

149 **"They are at least as brave . . . dull, tasteless, and anomalous"** Ibid., 257.

150 **"Whether further observation will or will not verify . . . gratitude, and unshaken fidelity"** Ibid., 260, 261.

150 **"The opinion that they are inferior . . . body and mind"** Ibid., 261.

151 "The improvement of the blacks . . . condition in life" Ibid., 259.

151 "cannot live in the same government" Ibid., 51.

152 "brought up, at the public expense" Ibid., 255

152 "beyond the reach of mixture" Ibid., 255.

153 "The amalgamation of whites with blacks" *Writings of Thomas Jefferson*, Ford, vol. 9, 478–479.

153 "the extermination of one or the other race" K&P, 256.

154 "murderers of our own children" To St. George Tucker, 28 Aug. 1797, L&B, vol. 9, 418.

157 "most fortunate those who can do it first" 26 Dec. 1820, *Writings of Thomas Jefferson*, L&B, vol. 10, 15.

157 "the knell of the Union" To John Holmes, 22 April 1820, *Writings of Thomas Jefferson*, L&B, vol. 10, 157.

157 "we have the wolf by the ear . . . let him go" L&B, vol. 10, 158. This famous metaphor is often quoted as "the wolf by the ears," but it appears that Jefferson wrote "by the ear"—which sounds even more dangerous.

157 "a solace which few laborers of England possess" To Thomas Cooper, 10 Sept. 1814, L&B, vol. 14, 183.

159 "My doubts were the result of personal observation . . . with the other colors of the human family" Letter to Henri Gregoire, 25 Feb. 1809, K&P, 595.

160 "incapable as children of taking care of themselves" To Edward Coles, 25 Aug. 1814, L&B, vol. 9, 478–479.

CHAPTER 12: BLINKERED HISTORIANS

Page

161 **Brodie** Author of *Thomas Jefferson: An Intimate History* (1974). Long a distinguished professor of history at the University of California, Los Angeles, Fawn M. Brodie had previously published well-received biographies of Sir Richard Burton (the spectacular explorer-scholar who provided Victorian England with a shockingly unexpurgated translation of *The Arabian Nights*); Thaddeus Stevens (the fiercely anti-Confederate congressman and nemesis of President Andrew Johnson); and Joseph Smith (founder of the Mormon religion and active proponent of polygamy). Her biography of Jefferson, however, with its innovative emphasis on Sally Hemings, was such a jolt to some well-known Southern historians that they not only denounced her, but treated her in print like an amateur upstart nobody had ever heard of—frequently referring to her as "Mrs. Brodie" (never "Dr. Brodie" or "Professor Brodie"), as if she might have done her research between making the beds and preparing hors d'oeuvres for a ladies' luncheon.

But Brodie had written the most original Jefferson biography of the century.

She, more than anyone else, cleared away the cloud of ignorance, obfuscation, and denial that had enveloped the story of Jefferson's long liaison with Sally Hemings, bringing into the light the convincing evidence that supported its validity. Although it took nearly a quarter of a century of debate, plus the hugely reinforcing impact of Annette Gordon-Reed's *Thomas Jefferson and Sally Hemings: An American Controversy* (1997) and, finally, the DNA results in 1998 to vindicate Brodie in the eyes of most of the academic community, the fact is that she already had presented all the basic points of evidence needed to justify belief in the liaison. But beyond that, Brodie's biography is a complete study of Jefferson's career in all its aspects, thoroughly researched, well written, and meticulously documented. It deserves to be considered as one of the very best single-volume biographies of Jefferson ever written.

Fawn Brodie died of cancer in 1981, at the age of sixty-six.

164 **"immaculate a man as God ever created"** Brodie, 672. (Brodie reprints in full, as part of her Appendix III, the letter from the historian Henry S. Randall to historian James Parton, in which Randall recounts a conversation he had with Jefferson's grandson, Thomas Jefferson Randolph, sometime in the 1850s. This letter is the principal source of what Brodie calls "the family denial" that Jefferson had fathered Sally's children. Brodie, 669–674.

164 **"There was a better excuse for it"** Ibid., 670.

164 **"not the shadow of suspicion"** Ibid., 671.

165 **"tears coursing down his cheeks"** Ibid., 672.

166 **"a tawdry and unverifiable story"** Quoted by Scot A. French and Edward L. Ayers, in "The Strange Career of Thomas Jefferson," *Jeffersonian Legacies*, ed. Peter S. Onuf (1993), 437.

166 **television series was eventually dropped** But CBS screened a similar project, purportedly based on Fawn Brodie's biography, in February 2000.

166 **"has ever declared his belief"** Merrill D. Peterson, *The Jefferson Image in the American Mind* (1960), 186.

167 **"a latter-day abolitionist"** *Jeffersonian Legacies*, 461.

167 **"published for a propagandist purpose"** *Journal of Southern History* 41, no. 4 (November 1975): 526.

167 **"a well known peculiarity of the colored race"** Ibid., 527.

168 **"this fastidious gentleman . . . vulgar liaison"** Malone, vol. 4, 214.

168 **"massive self-deception or outright lying"** Joseph J. Ellis, *American Sphinx: The Character of Thomas Jefferson* (1997), 21.

169 **as if they were equally convincing** Ibid., 304. This is like putting a lion on one end of a seesaw and a squirrel on the other and declaring them to be in balance.

169 **likelihood of the liaison . . . "remote"** Ibid., 305.

169 "for most of his adult life . . . more sentimental regions" Ibid., 305, 306.

169 "His most sensual statements . . . beautiful women" Ibid., 306.

170 "world of his bedchamber" Ibid., 97.

170 "the most unscrupulous scandalmonger of the day" Miller, *Wolf by the Ears*, 153.

171 **Michael Durey's study** Michael Durey's *"With the Hammer of Truth": James Thomson Callender and America's Early National Heroes* (1990), an original and well-documented biography, has been paid too little attention. In my brief account of Jefferson's relationship with Callender, I rely chiefly on Durey.

173 "Her name is SALLY" *Richmond Recorder*, 1 Sept. 1802. Callender's famous report has been quoted in many Jefferson biographies; it is given a fuller transcription as appendix B of *Sally Hemings and Thomas Jefferson*, eds. Jan Ellen Lewis and Peter S. Onuf (1999), a collection of recent essays.

175 "later been found to be true" Durey, *"With the Hammer of Truth,"* 160.

175 "that Being who sees himself our motives" Jefferson to Abigail Adams, 22 July, 1804; quoted by Durey, *"With the Hammer of Truth,"* 112.

175 "sufficient data and adequate criteria" Malone, vol. 1, 267

176 "bewildering confusion of principles" Merrill D. Peterson, *Thomas Jefferson and the New Nation* (1970), 262.

176 "miscegenous relationship . . . revolted his whole being" Ibid., 707.

176 "utter defiance . . . loathing of racial mixture" Miller, *Wolf by the Ears*, 176.

177 "a third cross clears the blood" Letter to Francis C. Gray, 4 March 1815, Brodie, 586, 587. (Jefferson's genetic "chart" is reproduced here.)

179 "the love of one's family only" To Polly Jefferson Eppes, 26 Oct. 1801; "nothing but love and delight" To Martha Jefferson Randolph, 23 Nov. 1807. Both cited by Jan Lewis, "Blessings of Domestic Society," in *Jeffersonian Legacies*, 110.

179 "bordered on the excessive" Malone, vol. 4, 214.

179 "The first time . . . 'how much I love you all'" To Polly Jefferson, 26 June 1791, Lewis, "Blessings of Domestic Society," 111, 112.

CHAPTER 13: THE HEART OF THE MATTER

Page

181 "one was the master, the other the servant" Peterson, *Jefferson and the New Nation*, 349.

181 "proud of its monarch and happy in its rule" *Papers*, 10, 453, footnote.

181 "sentiment over reason" Malone, vol. 2, 77.

182 "giving life to all nature!" *Papers*, 10, 448.

184 "really indescribable" K&P, 197.

184 "The moon was in full splendor" To John Adams, 11 June 1812. *The Adams-Jefferson Letters*, ed. Lester J. Cappon (1987), 307.

185 "You will mix with us by marriage" Anthony F. Wallace, *Jefferson and the Indians: The Tragic Fate of the First Americans* (1999), 317.

186 "driven beyond the Mississippi" Ibid.

186 "How he loved this bird!" Margaret Bayard Smith, *The First Forty Years of Washington Society* (1906), quoted by McLaughlin, *Jefferson and Monticello*, 325.

186 "the negroes' dogs must all be killed" To Edmund Bacon, 26 Dec. 1808, *Thomas Jefferson's Garden Book*, 383.

187 "How long shall we weep on Lena" *Jefferson's Literary Commonplace Book*, ed. Douglas L. Wilson (1990), 150.

188 "book and bowl . . . far into the night" Chastellux, *Travels in North America*, vol. 2, 392. Jefferson never lost his admiration for "Ossian," even after he learned that by and large the poems were contrived by James Macpherson. Writing to his daughter Polly in 1799, he told her that her recent letter to him was "as Ossian says, or would say, like the light beam of the moon on the desolate heath." 7 Feb. 1799, *Family Letters of Thomas Jefferson*, 173.

190 "I would tear it out of my book" Laurence Sterne, *The Life and Opinions of Tristram Shandy, Gentleman* (1759–1767), Book I, Chapter XXV; last sentence in the chapter. (There are so many editions of *Tristram Shandy* that instead of referring a quote to a page number, I refer it to the relevant book and chapter.)

191 "rumple the one,—you rumple the other" Ibid., Book III, opening sentence of Chapter IV.

191 "a certain mien and motion of the body" Ibid., Book VI, Chapter V.

193 "to be sure, Mr. Shandy" Ibid., Book IX, Chapter XI.

193 "and that's enough for us" Ibid., Book IV, Chapter XVII.

194 "And whereabouts, dear Sir, quoth Mrs. Wadman" Ibid., Book IX, Chapter XXVI.

195 "as brisk and lively a French girl" Laurence Sterne, *A Sentimental Journey Through France and Italy* (1768), closing episode.

195 "'Tis a pretty picture!" Sterne, *Tristram Shandy*, Book IX, Chapter VI.

198 "indulgences of Epicurus ensure" Letter to William Short, 31 Oct. 1819, K&P, 695.

198 "eating the means to obtain it" Ibid., 696.

198 **Lord Bolingbroke** Henry St. John (later to become Lord Viscount Bolingbroke) was born in England in 1678, attended Eton and Oxford, and by his early twenties had achieved a reputation for rather wild and profligate behavior. Apparently intrigued by political intrigue, he plunged into it in 1701, and soon became a leading Tory statesman under Queen Anne, appointed successively secretary of war and secretary of state. Hobnobbing with such intellectual Tory pro-

pagandists as Jonathan Swift, and himself an extraordinarily eloquent orator, he was by 1712 (when he became Lord Bolingbroke) one of the most famous politicians in the nation. With the death of Queen Anne in 1714, however, and the arrival of the Hanoverian George I as King of England and the resulting Whig administration, Bolingbroke was not only dismissed from office but impeached for alleged treason. He quickly took refuge in France, and got involved in the schemes of other Tory exiles (the "Jacobites") who hatched an unsuccessful foray in 1715 to put James Stuart (the "Old Pretender") on the English throne. Belatedly pardoned by George I in 1723, he returned to England and busied himself with frequent and often influential political pamphleteering for another decade. Finally tired of all that, he retreated to his estate in France, where he wrote many philosophical essays as well as a book with the interesting title *The True Use of Retirement.* Despite his long identification with conservative politics, Bolingbroke was decidedly liberal in many of his views and has sometimes been called "the Tory democrat." He died in 1751 at the age of seventy-three.

198 **"a blunderbuss against religion and morality"** *Boswell's Life of Johnson,* vol. 1, 268.

199 **"an aggregate of miracles"** *Literary Commonplace Book,* 134.

200 **"particular qualities or characters"** David Hume, *A Treatise of Human Nature* (1740), quoted by Garry Wills in *Inventing America* (1978), 197. Wills demonstrates convincingly that Hume based his moral-sense philosophy essentially on the work of his older friend Francis Hutcheson, and acknowledged it.

200 **"to serve and obey them"** Hume, *Treatise of Human Nature,* 415.

201 **"led astray by artificial rules"** To Peter Carr, 10 Aug. 1787, K&P, 430.

201 **"to succor their distresses"** To Thomas Law, 13 June 1814, K&P, 638.

201 **"some impulsive feeling"** Ibid., 640.

202 **"ever been taught by man"** To Dr. Benjamin Rush, 21 April 1803, K&P, 570.

202 **"never claimed any other"** Ibid., 567.

207 **"retribution for the evil as well as the good"** To Thomas Law, 13 June 1813, K&P, 639.

208 **"to say they are *nothings"*** To John Adams, 15 Aug. 1820. K&P, 701.

208 **"ignorance . . . softest pillow"** To John Adams, 14 March 1820, L&B, vol. 15, 239.

210 **"deprived of will . . . perception"** To John Adams, 8 Jan. 1825, K&P, 716.

Oddly, Jefferson closes this letter with the remark, "But all this, you and I shall know better when we meet again, in another place, and at no distant period." He was aware, of course, that Adams firmly believed in life after death, and perhaps wanted to soften the impact of Flourens's discovery about the cerebrum with this conventional *au revoir.*

210 **"all is in the wind"** To John Adams, 15 Aug. 1820, K&P, 701.

210 **"I feel, therefore I exist"** Ibid., 700.

CHAPTER 14: "THE TENDER BREASTS OF LADIES": A RETROSPECTIVE

Page

211 **an avuncular letter** To Peter Carr, 11 Dec. 1783, *Papers*, 6.

212 **not really handsome** Malone, vol. 1, 48.

212 **"unlocked my heart"** Smith, *First Forty Years of Washington Society*, 6.

214 **"tender breasts of ladies"** To Angelica Church, 21 Sept. 1788, *Papers*, 13.

215 **"domestic happiness above all other"** To Anne Bingham, 11 May 1788, *Papers*, 13.

215 **Jean Baptiste de Lamarck** See the study by Richard W. Burkhart (1977).

217 **"be good under every situation"** To Patsy, 22 Dec. 1783, *Papers*, 6.

217 **"Nothing is so disgusting"** Ibid.

217 **"even your love to me"** To Patsy, 4 April 1790, *Papers*, 16.

218 **Élisabeth Vigée-Lebrun** Simon Schama, in *Citizens*, gives a lavishly illustrated account of this briliant young painter's success in pre-revolutionary Paris.

219 **"no Queen . . . no revolution"** *Autobiography*, K&P, 104, 105.

CHAPTER 15: TWO CHEERS FOR THOMAS JEFFERSON

Page

225 **"the blood of patriots and tyrants"** To William Stephens Smith (son-in-law of John Adams), 13 Nov. 1787, *Papers*, 12.

225 **to guarantee a peaceful and happy society** See, for example, Jefferson's letter to Edward Carrington, 16 Jan. 1787, K&P, 411.

226 **"their opinions in matters of religion"** K&P, 313.

227 **"cannot follow the dictates of other men"** James Madison, *A Remonstrance Against Religious Assessments* (1785). *The Papers of James Madison*, eds. Robert A. Rutland and William M. E. Rachal, vol. 8, 299.

228 **"laws for the human mind"** Madison to Jefferson, 22 Jan. 1786, *Papers*, 9.

229 **"wall of separation between church and state"** Letter to the Danbury Baptist Association, 1 Jan. 1802, L&B, vol. 16, 281–82.

229 **"the priest has been hostile to liberty"** Letter to Horatio Gates Spafford, 17 May, 1814, L&B, vol. 14, 119.

230 **"The error seems not sufficiently eradicated . . ."** K&P, 175, 176.

231 **"proudest achievement of American architecture"** Quote verified by a phone call to the American Institute of Architects, Washington, D.C.

235 **more complicated—or simpler—than Jefferson supposed** He himself made a supposedly sharp distinction between taste and the moral sense in terms of what each was concerned with: beauty (for taste) and behavior (for the moral sense). See his letter of 13 June 1814 to Thomas Law, K&P, 637.

235 **choosing appropriate books . . . University of Virginia** There is a good account of this episode in Leonard W. Levy's *Jefferson and Civil Liberties: The Darker Side* (1963); TJ's own version of it is summarized in a letter to a prospective student, 25 Oct. 1825, K&P, 723–726.

238 **"an undiminished devotion to them"** 24 June 1826, K&P, 729, 730.

239 **"every form of tyranny over the mind of man"** To Benjamin Rush, 23 Sept. 1800, K&P, 558.

ACKNOWLEDGMENTS

————— • ◆ • —————

I want to thank the following people for help and encouragement on the book: Lucia (Cinder) Stanton, the Senior Research Historian at Monticello (who quite probably knows more about Thomas Jefferson than anyone else in the world); Annette Gordon-Reed, for many hours of talk about Jefferson, and especially for enabling me to see him from a black perspective; Hugh Van Dusen and Sally Kim, my superb editors at HarperCollins; Laurie Platt Winfrey, for expert assistance on illustrations; Doris Kearns Goodwin, Stephen Ambrose, and Geoffrey Ward, for reading and reacting wonderfully to the manuscript; Virginia Peckham, for patiently offering corrective suggestions as the project evolved through several stages; Marc Parent, for following up a couple of elusive leads in France on my behalf; Rick Hertzberg, of The New Yorker, for urging me not to quit when, a few years ago, a long article about Jefferson and Sally was bought by the magazine but cancelled by the then editor-in-chief at the last moment; and my sons Mark and Kim, plus my friends of auld lang syne, Jack and Stella Suberman, all of whom undoubtedly often wished that I would get the thing done and talk about something else for a change.

INDEX

———— • ◆ • ————

Page numbers in *italics* refer to illustrations.

271

Index

Short, William (*cont.*)
   Jefferson's correspondence with,
      73–74, 76, 77–79, 123, 135,
      197–98, 203
   as Jefferson's secretary, 70, 77–79,
      110, 113
   love affair of, 104–5, 113, 198,
      246, 248
   portrait of, *105*
Skelton, Bathurst, 29, 30, 31
Skelton, Jack, 30, 35
Skelton, Martha Wayles, *see* Jefferson,
   Martha Wayles
Skelton, Reuben, 31
Skipwith, Robert, 51
slavery:
   abolition of, 148, 154, 156–57,
      159–60, 167
   diffusion of, 156–57
   fear and guilt about, 151, 154
   Jefferson's views on, xi–xii, 36,
      53–54, 141–60, 161, 233–34
   at Monticello, 114–15, 142–48,
      158, 162–63, 182
   sexual relations and, 16–17, 31,
      86–87, 158–59, 169–70, 176
   in Virginia, 154–56, 159–60, 168
slaves:
   emancipation of, 110–12, 118–23,
      141–42, 143, 146, 147–48,
      151–52, 154, 158, 159–60,
      162–63, 177–78, 213
   families of, 145–48, 157
   flogging of, 144
   Jefferson as owner of, xi–xii, 32,
      36, 90, 92, 98, 110–12, 114–15,
      118–23, 141–60, 161, 162–63
   legal definition of, 176–77
   mixed ancestry of, 163, 175–78,
      243

   rebellions of, 138, 150, 152,
      153–57
   run-away, 145
   sale of, 123, 144–45, 147–48, 156
   surplus, 156
   see also individual slaves
Slodtz, Michael Angelo, 76, 77
Small, William, 15, 16, 188, 200, 232,
   253*n*
Smith, Margaret Bayard, 186, 212
Smith, Robert, 25
Smith, William Stephens, 256
soap, 38
soul, 207–8, 210
Spain, 137
Stanton, Edwin, 249
Stanton, Lucia, 143, 146, 163–64
states' rights, 128, 156, 220–21
Statute of Virginia for Religious
   Freedom, 221, 226–30, *227*
Sterne, Laurence, 50–51, 64, 74,
   102–4, 188–96, *189*, 255*n*,
   264*n*
Stiles, Ezra, 55
Stoics, 197, 201–2
Stuart, Gilbert, *88*
sublime, 183–84
"Summary View of the Rights of
   British America, A" (Jefferson),
   124–25
Swift, Jonathan, 13, 186, 264*n*–65*n*

Tanner, Henry Schenck, *232*
Tarleton, Banastre, 44–45, 255*n*
taxation, 128, 141, 226
tenant farmers, 159–60
Ten Commandments, 199, 204
Terror, the, 113
Tessé, Madame de, 75–76, 214
Thackeray, William Makepeace, 241

ILLUSTRATION CREDITS

———•◆•———

Illustration Credits